NORTH CASCADES
NATIONAL PARK REGION

SECOND EDITION

100 Hikes in™ Washington's
NORTH CASCADES
NATIONAL PARK REGION

SECOND EDITION

Ira Spring
& Harvey Manning

THE
MOUNTAINEERS

Published by
The Mountaineers
1001 SW Klickitat Way, Suite 201
Seattle, Washington 98134

First edition 1987; second edition: first printing 1994, second printing 1996, third printing 1997

Published simultaneously in Great Britain by Cordee, 3a DeMontfort Street, Leicester, England, LE1 7HD

Manufactured in the United States of America

Edited by Dana Lee Fos
Maps by Helen Sherman
Photographs by Bob and Ira Spring except as noted
Book design by Marge Mueller
Typesetting and layout by The Mountaineers Books

Cover photograph: Winchester Mountain trail, Mt. Shuksan in distance. Mt. Baker Wilderness. Photo © Bob & Ira Spring.
Frontispiece: Larch trees ringing Sunrise Lake, Hike 54

Library of Congress Cataloging in Publication Data
Spring, Ira.
    100 hikes in Washington's North Cascades National Park Region / by Ira Spring and Harvey Manning. —2nd ed.
        p.   cm.
    Includes index.
    ISBN 0-89886-401-1
    1. Hiking—Washington (State)—North Cascades National Park Region—Guidebooks. 2. North Cascades National Park Region (Wash.)—Guidebooks. I. Manning, Harvey. II. Title. III. Title: One hundred hikes in Washington's North Cascades National Park Region.
GV199.42.W22N677   1994
796.5'1'0979773—dc20   94-18161
                                              CIP

CONTENTS

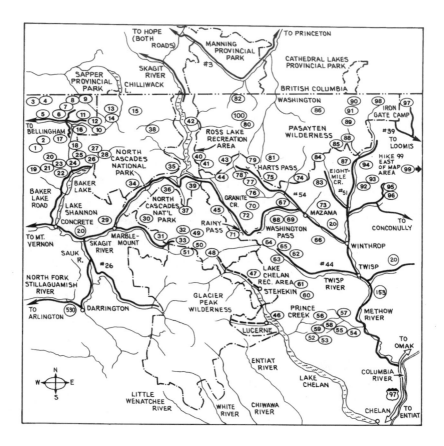

Map Legend

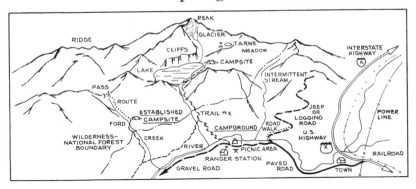

9

Clouds and peaks from Sahale Arm, Hike 33

FOREWORD:
SAVING OUR TRAILS

In 1946 the U.S. Forest Service inventory showed 144,000 miles of trails in the national forests of the United States. By 1980 the total had been reduced to 101,000 miles—a loss of 30 percent. The Forest Service would like us to believe this was purely a bookkeeping loss, that the old inventory included stock driveways and wagon roads which weren't real trails anyhow; subtracting these and adding new-built trails, the reduction was a mere 2 percent.

In other parts of the nation the explanation may or may not be true. Here in the Northwest, there is no covering up the barefaced fact that the loss of Forest Service trails to logging roads in the State of Washington has been at the very least 30 percent. (The loss on state and private lands during this period was close to 100 percent.)

Hikers, mainly living in wooden houses and reading and writing books made of paper from wood pulp, freely concede that many of the trails obliterated in the years immediately following World War II were in areas better suited to tree-farming, car-camping, and road-touring than to hiking. However, in recent years miles and miles of roads have been built through forests whose timber value was meager but whose value for trail recreation and other roadless-area resources was immense.

The juggernaut rumbles on. The damage of the past decade and a half in the Cascade Range of Washington has been staggering; that planned for the next 15 years would be a catastrophe. In the preferred management alternatives published by the Forest Service, the following miles of trail are jeopardized by new road construction.

Trails in Jeopardy

Okanogan National Forest: 381 miles, or 62 percent, of its non-wilderness trails

Wenatchee National Forest: 966 miles, or 78 percent, of its non-wilderness trails

Mt. Baker–Snoqualmie National Forest: 484 miles, or 48 percent, of its non-wilderness trails

Gifford Pinchot National Forest: 544 miles, or 78 percent, of its non-wilderness trails

Total: 2375 miles in jeopardy

Forest Service explainers claim those figures lie, that many of the miles will be on temporary logging roads which afterward will revert to trails, that on some steep hillsides no road at all will be built, the logging done by helicopters. Perhaps so, if hikers and environmental groups watch the logging plans like hawks.

The explainers further declare that many miles of the "jeopardy" trails are perfectly safe except for a very few feet of their length where they are crossed by roads. Using this defense, Okanogan and Wenatchee National Forests promise that not more than 2 percent of their trails will be lost to roads. This figure fails to acknowledge that, though a hiker can be happy enough on a trail that starts out in or through a clearcut, a road crossing makes it useless to him or her; road-broken trails are not maintained for hikers, but for motorcyclists.

Preservation Goals for the 1990s and Beyond

In the 1960s The Mountaineers began publishing trail guides as another means of working "to preserve the natural beauty of Northwest America," through putting more feet on certain trails, in certain wildlands. We suffered no delusion that large numbers of boots improve trails or enhance wildness. However, we had learned to our rue that "you use it or lose it," that threatened areas could be saved only if they were more widely known and treasured. We were criticized in certain quarters for contributing to the deterioration of wilderness by publicizing it, and confessed the fault, but could only respond, "Which would you prefer? A hundred boots in a virgin forest? Or that many snarling wheels in a clearcut?"

As the numbers of wilderness lovers have grown so large as to endanger the qualities they love, the rules of "walking light" and "camping no trace" must be the more faithfully observed. Yet the ultimate menace to natural beauty is not hikers, no matter how destructive their boots may be, nor even how polluting their millions of *Giardia* cysts, but doomsday, arriving on two or three or four or six or eight wheels, or on tractor treads, or on whirling wings—the total conquest of the land and water and sky by machinery.

Victories Past

Conceived in campfire conversations of the 1880s, Olympic National Park was established in 1938, the grandest accomplishment of our most conservation-minded president, Franklin D. Roosevelt. (Confined to a wheelchair and never himself able to know the trails with his own feet, FDR nevertheless saw the fallacy in the sneering definition of wilderness areas as "preserves for the aristocracy of the physically fit"; he knew the value of dreams that never could be personally attained.)

A renewal of the campaigns after World War II brought—regionally, in 1960—the Glacier Peak Wilderness and—nationally, in 1964—the Wilderness Act, whereby existing and future wildernesses were placed beyond the fickleness of bureaucracies, guarded by Congress and the president against thoughtless tampering.

Nineteen-sixty-eight was the year of the North Cascades Act, achieving another vision of the nineteenth century, the North Cascades National Park, plus the Lake Chelan and Ross Lake National Recreation Areas, Pasayten Wilderness, and additions to the Glacier Peak Wilderness.

In 1976 the legions of citizens laboring at the grass roots, aided by the matching dedication of certain of their congresspersons and senators, obtained the Alpine Lakes Wilderness.

In 1984 the same alliance, working at the top and at the bottom and all through the middle, all across the state, won the Washington Wilderness Act, encompassing more than one million acres, including, in the purview of this volume, three new wildernesses—Lake Chelan–Sawtooth, Mt. Baker, and Noisy-Diobsud; additions to the Pasayten Wilderness; and a Mt. Baker National Recreation Area and a North Cascades Scenic Highway Corridor.

Is, therefore, the job done? Absolutely not.

Goals Ahead

Had hikers been content with the victory of 1938 there never would have been those of 1960, 1968, 1976, and 1984. The United States as a whole has a step or two yet to go before attaining that condition of flawless perfection where it fits seamlessly into the final mosaic of the Infinite Plan, and the same is true of the National Wilderness Preservation System. In the trail descriptions of this book, we have expressed some of the more prominent discontents with the 1984 Act.

Among the omissions are the Alma-Copper and Hidden Lake areas, adjacent to the North Cascades National Park; Beaver Meadows, Tiffany Mountain, and Chopaka Mountain, near the Okanogan; and the Golden Horn area near the North Cascades Highway.

There also are faults of omission from the newly created wildernesses: from the Noisy-Diobsud Wilderness, the lower reaches of its two namesake creeks, the upper Baker River, and Rocky and Thunder Creeks; from the Mt. Baker Wilderness, Damfino Creek, Church Mountain, Warm Creek, and Shuksan Lake; from the Lake Chelan–Sawtooth Wilderness, Foggy Dew, Safety Harbor, and Eagle Creeks on the south and Cedar Creek on the north.

The existing Pasayten Wilderness still does not enclose the upper Methow River, lower Lost River, South Twentymile Peak, and the Chewuch River at Thirtymile Campground.

The North Cascades Scenic Highway gives only modest protection; at that, it leaves out upper Canyon Creek, upper East Creek, and Driveway Butte.

As for the Mt. Baker National Recreation Area, it was specifically designed to permit snowmobiles to go to the very summit.

The preceding is only a very partial list of the remaining tasks. A very notable—and notorious—remaining problem is the management of the Lake Chelan National Recreation Area and its failure, to date, to give the Stehekin valley the care expected by the 1968 North Cascades Act.

It needs to be kept uppermost in mind that designation as "wilderness" or "national park" or "national recreation area" is a means, not the end. The goals ahead are not words on a document or lines on a map but the protection of the land these symbols may signify. Any other symbols that do the job are satisfactory. The protection is the thing.

In contrast to the immediate past, the preservationist agenda of the immediate future (that is, the coming several years) focuses less on redrawing maps than employing any practical method to preserve roadless areas from further invasion by machinery. In fact, we are now at a stage where the saving of trails, important though that is, has a lower priority than the saving of fisheries and wildlife resources, scientific values, gene pools, and another contribution of wildland too long neglected—the provision of dependable and pure water for domestic and agricultural needs.

What in the World Happened to Us?: A Tale of Two Trails

"Mirror mirror on the wall, who is fairest of them all?" As the saying goes, beauty is in the eye of the beholder. Most hikers would be hard-pressed to know which are the fairest, the three Oval Lakes (Hike 61) or the five lakes on the Cooney Lake (Hike 55). However, the Oval Lakes are trampled by several thousand feet every year, whereas the lakes on the Golden Lakes Loop see maybe a couple hundred.

The difference is easy to explain. The Oval Lakes trail is in wilderness and thus free of motors, but the Forest Service actually promotes motorcycles on all but a small section of the Golden Lakes Loop trail. In a backward way, this is a blessing. Few motorcycles use the trail because it is too short, not worth trailering a machine to the trailhead for an hour's ride; those riders who do come seldom leave their machines to walk the few hundred feet to the lakeshores. So, a hiker

brave enough to take the trail has a better chance of solitude on the lovely Golden Lakes Loop than at the wilderness-protected Oval Lakes. The bottom line, however, is that with the overuse of wilderness and the resulting restrictions on hiking wilderness trails, motorized use of non-wilderness trails such as the Golden Lakes Loop is unacceptable. (Motorcyclists who seek the scenery enjoyed by hikers can leave their machines and walk. Most are healthy young males, quite capable of doing so.)

The wheel is more than the symbol. It is the fact. The National Wilderness Act so recognizes by banning "mechanized travel," including but not limited

Cooney Lake: Motorcycles allowed and therefore nobody comes, Hike 55

to motorized travel; bicycles—"mountain bikes"—are excluded too, for the simple reason that in appropriate terrain they readily can go 5–10 miles per hour, an "unnatural" speed always incompatible with the "natural" 1–3 miles per hour of the traveler on foot.

Outside the boundaries of dedicated wilderness, some trails can be amicably shared by bicycles and pedestrians, both capable of being quiet and minimally destructive and disruptive of the backcountry scene. Attach a motor to the wheels, however, and the route no longer deserves to be called a "trail"—it becomes a road.

In the past quarter-century, conservationists have been busy saving Washington trails by creating a new national park and a bouquet of new wildernesses. Meanwhile, the Forest Service, without filing environmental impact statements, has been assiduously converting true trails (that is, paths suitable for speeds of perhaps up to 5 or so miles per hour, the pace of a horse) to motorcycle roads (that is, "trails" built to let off-road vehicles—the ORVs—do 15–30 miles per hour).

In this quarter-century the concerted efforts of tens of thousands of conservationists protected large expanses of wildland from invasion by machines—but during the same period a comparative handful of ORVers have taken away more miles of trails, converted them to *de facto* roads, than the conservationists have saved. (In backroom lobbying they got a private "boodle," a fund from the state gas tax specifically allotted to converting foot trails to motorcycle roads.) As the score stands, only 45 percent of Washington trails are machine-free by being in national parks and wildernesses; of the other 55 percent, half are open to motorcycles and thus not truly trails at all.

When automobiles arrived in the United States, the citizenry and government were quick to see they should not be permitted on sidewalks. The Forest Service is slower to recognize that whenever there are more than a few scattered travelers of either kind the difference in speed and purpose between motorized wheels and muscle-powered feet is irreconcilable.

Thinking to serve the laudable purpose of supplying "a wide spectrum of recreational opportunities," the Forest Service initially tolerated ORVs, then began

Oval Lake: Motorcycles banned and therefore crowded by hikers and horses, Hike 61

encouraging them, widening and straightening and smoothing "multiple-use trails" to permit higher speeds, thus increasing the number of motors and discouraging hikers, in the end creating "single-purpose ORV trails"—specifically, narrow roads.

Federal funds were employed for the conversion until that source dried up; since 1979 the Forest Service has relied heavily on the "boodle" money allocated by the State of Washington Interagency Committee for Outdoor Recreation (IAC). The Forest Service could not engage in such large-scale, long-term conversion of trails to roads if hikers were given the respect (by the Forest Service *and* the IAC) their numbers—overwhelming compared to the motorcyclists—deserve.

Hikers spoke up for the Washington Wilderness Act of 1984. By the many thousands they wrote letters to congresspersons and senators. The pen is mightier than the wheel, and it must be taken up again, by those same tens of thousands, to write letters to congresspersons and senators, with copies to the Regional Forester, Region 6, USFS, 319 SW Pine Street, P.O. Box 3623, Portland, Oregon 97208, asking the following:

1. Trails should be considered a valuable resource, treated as a separate category in all USFS plans.
2. All trail users should be notified of public meetings concerning any USFS plan affecting trails; public meetings should be held in metropolitan areas as well as in small, remote communities near the trails.
3. To eliminate the conflict between hikers and ORVs, the concept of multiple-use must be dropped and separate ORV trails built out of sound and sight of hikers and horse-riders.

INTRODUCTION

Broad, smooth, well-marked, heavily traveled, ranger-patrolled paths safe and simple for little kids and elderly folks with no mountain training or equipment, or even for monomaniacs dashing from Canada to Mexico. Mean and cruel and mysterious routes through evil brush, over fierce rivers, up shifty screes and moraines to treacherous glaciers and appalling cliffs where none but the skilled and doughty should dare, or perhaps the deranged. Flower strolls for an afternoon, or heroic adventures for a week.

A storm side (the west) where precipitation is heavy, winter long, snows deep, glaciers large, peaks sharply sculptured, vegetation lush, and high-country hiking doesn't get comfortably underway until late July. A lee side, a rainshadow side (the east) where clouds are mostly empties, summer is long, vegetation sparse, ridges round and gentle, and meadows melt free of the white by late June.

Places as thronged as a city park on Labor Day, places as lonesome as the South Pole that Scott knew. Scenes that remind of the High Sierra, scenes that remind of Alaska.

In summary, to generalize about the North Cascades: To generalize about the North Cascades is foolish.

Rules, Regulations, and Permits

Except for blocks of state (Department of Natural Resources) land around Chopaka Mountain, scattered enclaves of private lands mostly dating from mining and homestead days, and such miscellaneous bits as the Seattle City Light holdings on the Skagit River, the entirety of the northernmost section of the North Cascades is federally administered. The U.S. Forest Service is the principal trustee, responsibility shared by Mt. Baker–Snoqualmie, Wenatchee, and Okanogan National Forests. Since 1968 the National Park Service has been on the scene in the North Cascades National Park and the accompanying Ross Lake and Lake Chelan National Recreation Areas, essentially parts of the park but permitting some activities banned within the park proper.

Most of the national forest lands are under "multiple-use" administration, with roads, with logging, mining, and other economic exploitation, and with motorcycles allowed on (too) many trails. Some areas, however, have statutory protection within the National Wilderness Preservation System, where the Wilderness Act of 1964 guarantees that "the earth and its community of life are untrammeled by man, where man himself is a visitor who does not remain." The Glacier Peak Wilderness was established in 1960 and the Pasayten Wilderness in 1968. The Washington Wilderness Act of 1984 made additions to these two wildernesses and in the far north of the North Cascades established these new ones: Mt. Baker, Noisy-Diobsud, and Lake Chelan–Sawtooth. Within these, motorized travel is banned, as is any mechanized travel, such as "mountain bikes." Horse travel is carefully regu-

17

lated, and though wilderness permits are not currently required for hiking, hikers are subject to restrictions on party size and camping, and must acquaint themselves with the travel regulations before setting out.

The North Cascades National Park, established in 1968, was set aside, to use the words of the National Park Act of 1916, "to conserve the scenery and the natural and historic objects and the wildlife...." Each visitor therefore must enjoy the park "in such manner and by such means as will leave it unimpaired for the enjoyment of future generations." Most of the park is further covered by the Wilderness Act, giving a still higher degree of protection.

To help attain these goals, the Park Service requires each trail user to have a backcountry permit that must be shown on request to a backcountry ranger. Permits may be obtained by mail from the Park Service or in person from ranger stations on the major entry roads.

Maps

The sketch maps in this book are intended to give only a general idea of the terrain and trails. Once out of the city and off the highways, the navigation demands precision.

In the 1980s the Forest Service renumbered its roads. A veteran traveler relying on a faithful file of well-worn Forest Service maps had best never leave civilization without a full tank of gas, survival rations, and instructions to family or friends on when to call out the Logging Road Search and Rescue Team. If maps are older than 10 years, a party would do better to obtain the current National Forest recreational maps, which are cumbersome for the trail but essential to get about on the renumbered roads.

The new U.S. Forest Service system of road numbers gives main roads two numerals. For example, the Goat Creek road is No. 52 and is shown on the Forest Service maps as 52 and described in this guidebook as road No. 52. The secondary roads have the first two numbers of the main road plus two additional numbers. For example, from road 52 the secondary road toward Goat Peak is 5225, and it is shown on Forest Service maps as 5225 . Three additional numbers are added for a spur road. The Goat Peak trailhead road becomes 5225200, shown as 200 on Forest Service maps, as 200 on Forest Service signs, and as road No. (5225)200 in this guidebook.

The best maps in the history of the world are the topographic sheets produced by the U.S. Geological Survey (USGS). However, research on trails was poorly done and many trails described in this book were left out. Revision is so occasional that information on roads and trails is always largely obsolete. Essential as they are for off-trail, cross-country explorers, in this book we have recommended them only on Mount Bonaparte where there is no alternative. The USGS maps for the 100 hikes are listed in the Appendix.

Among the merits of the USGS is that it sells the data "separations" (from which its sheets are published) on a non-profit, cost-only, public-service basis. This has enabled commercial publishers to buy the separations and issue maps designed specifically for hikers. In the Green Trails series, which covers virtually all hiking areas in the Cascades and Olympics, obsolete information (trails that no longer exist) is edited out and surviving trails delineated by a green-ink overlay. Updated versions are issued every two years. Each hike description in this book lists the most useful topographic map, usually the Green Trails modification of the base map produced by the USGS. The Green Trails and USGS sheets are sold at mountain equipment and map shops, which also carry the quite accurate and up-to-date National Forest recreation maps. These also may be obtained for a small fee at ranger stations or by writing the following forest supervisors:

Mt. Baker–Snoqualmie National
   Forest
21905 64th Avenue W
Mountlake Terrace,
   Washington 98043 (206) 775-9702

Okanogan National Forest
P.O. Box 950
Okanogan, Washington 98840
(509) 422-2704

Current Information

Neither maps nor guidebooks can keep up with changes by nature and humans. When current information about trails is sought, the hiker should visit or telephone the Forest Service/Park Service ranger station listed in the text. Following are the addresses and phone numbers:

Mount Baker Ranger Station
Sedro Woolley, Washington 98284
(360) 856-5700

Park Service–Forest Service
   Information Center
Chelan, Washington 98816
(509) 682-2549
   Or contact the Marblemount
   Office

Tonasket Ranger Station
Tonasket, Washington 98855
(509) 486-2186

North Cascades National Park,
   Marblemount Ranger Station
Marblemount, Washington 98284
(360) 873-4500

Glacier Public Service Center
Glacier, Washington 98244
   (360) 599-2714

Methow Valley Ranger District
Twisp, Washington 98856
(509) 997-2131

Information Summaries

Information summaries for trips generally contain the following information.

"Round trip xx miles" and "Elevation gain xxxx feet" tell a person if the trip fits his/her energy and ambition.

"Hiking time x hours" must be used with a personal conversion factor. The figures here are based on doing about 2 miles an hour and an elevation gain of about 1000 feet an hour, about "average" on good trail with a moderate pack. If, instead, the hike is described as "Allow x days," the length is greater than the ordinary person will want for a single day.

"Hikable month through month" primarily has to do with how much snow falls in winter and how long it mucks up the trail in spring-summer and when it goes at it again in the fall. Estimates are based on experience over the years and total ignorance of what the sky has in mind for the future. By "hikable" is meant, of course, what can be done encumbering the feet no more complexly than with boots.

"One day or backpack," or "One day," or "Backpack" introduces personal judgments. Often the information summary will say "One day" and then the details will note the possibility of camping, which in the opinion of the authors is not, for the trip in hand, a good idea. No water after June? Meadowlands too fragile for prone bodies en masse? Obviously, camping is always theoretically possible by carrying water, eating cold food, and lying on naked rock. But we say "Backpack" only when the site is desirable or the trip length requires more than a day.

Clothing and Equipment

Many trails described in this book can be walked easily and safely, at least along the lower portions, by any person capable of getting out of a car and onto their feet, and without any special equipment whatsoever.

To such people we can only say, "Welcome to walking—but beware!" Northwest mountain weather, especially on the ocean side of the ranges, is notoriously undependable. Cloudless morning skies can be followed by afternoon deluges of rain or fierce squalls of snow. Even without a storm a person can get mighty chilly on high ridges when—as often happens— a cold wind blows under a bright sun and pure blue sky.

No one should set out on a Cascade trail, unless for a brief stroll, lacking warm long pants, wool (or the equivalent) shirt or sweater, and a windproof and rain-repellent parka, coat, or poncho. (All these in the rucksack, if not on the body during the hot hours.) And on the feet— sturdy shoes or boots plus wool socks and an extra pair of socks in the rucksack.

As for that rucksack, it should also contain the Ten Essentials, found to be so by generations of members of The Mountaineers, often from sad experience:

1. Extra clothing—more than needed in good weather.
2. Extra food—enough so something is left over at the end of the trip.
3. Sunglasses—necessary for most alpine travel and on snow.
4. Knife—for first aid and emergency firebuilding (making kindling).
5. Firestarter—a candle or chemical fuel for starting a fire with wet wood.
6. First aid kit.
7. Matches—in a waterproof container.
8. Flashlight—with extra bulb and batteries.
9. Map—be sure it's the right one for the trip.
10. Compass—be sure to know the declination, east or west.

Camping and Fires

Indiscriminate camping blights alpine meadows. A single small party may trample grass, flowers, and heather so badly they don't recover from the shock for several years. If the same spot is used several or more times a summer, year after year, the greenery vanishes, replaced by bare dirt. The respectful traveler always aims to camp in the woods or in rocky morainal areas. These alternatives lacking, it is better to use a meadow site already bare—in technical terminology, "hardened"—rather than extend the destruction into virginal places nearby.

Particularly to be avoided are camps on soft meadows on the banks of streams and lakes (hard rock or bare dirt or gravel sites may be quite all right). Delightful and scenic as waterside meadows are, their use may endanger the water purity as well as the health of delicate plants. Further, no matter how "hard" the site may be, a camp on a viewpoint makes the beauty unavailable to other hikers who simply want to come and look, or eat lunch, and then go camp in the woods.

Carry a collapsible water container to minimize the trips to the water supply that beat down a path. (As a bonus, the container lets you camp high on a dry ridge, where the solitude and the views are.)

Carry a lightweight pair of camp shoes, less destructive to plants and soils than trail boots.

As the age of laissez-faire camping yields to the era of thoughtful management, different policies are being adopted in different places. For example, high-use spots may be designated "Day Use Only," forbidding camps. In others there is a blanket rule against camps within

Campsite on Mount Baker's Ptarmigan Ridge, Hike 18

100–200 feet of the water. However, in certain areas the rangers have inventoried existing camps, found 95 percent are within 100 feet of the water, and decided it is better to keep existing sites, where the vegetation long since has been gone, than to establish new "barrens" elsewhere. The rule in such places is "use established sites"; wilderness rangers on their rounds dis-establish those sites judged unacceptable.

Few shelter cabins remain—most shown on maps are not there anymore—so always carry a tent or tarp. Never ditch the sleeping area unless and until essential to avoid being flooded out—and afterward be sure to fill the ditches, carefully replacing any sod that may have been dug up.

Always carry a sleeping pad of some sort to keep your bag dry and your bones comfortable. Do not revert to the ancient bough bed of the frontier past.

The wood fire also is nearly obsolete in the high country. At best, dry firewood is hard to find at popular camps. What's left, the picturesque silver snags and logs, is part of the scenery, too valuable to be wasted cooking a pot of soup. It should be (but isn't quite, what with the survival of little hatchets and little folks who love to wield them) needless to say that green, living wood must never be cut; it doesn't burn anyway.

For reasons of both convenience and conservation, the highland hiker should carry a lightweight stove for cooking (or should not cook—though the food is cold, the inner man is hot) and depend on clothing and shelter (and sunset strolls) for evening warmth. The pleasures of a roaring blaze on a cold mountain night are indisputable, but a single party on a single night may use up ingredients of the scenery that were long decades in growing, dying, and silvering.

At remote backcountry camps, and in forests, fires perhaps may still be built with a clear conscience. Again, one should minimize impact by using only established fire pits and using only dead and down wood. When finished, be certain the fire is absolutely out—drown the coals and stir them with a stick and then drown the ashes until the smoking and steaming have stopped completely and a finger stuck in the slurry feels no heat. Embers can smoulder underground in dry duff for days, spreading gradually and burning out a wide pit—or kindling trees and starting a forest fire.

If you decide to build a fire, do not make a new fire ring—use an existing one. In popular areas patrolled by rangers, its existence means this is an approved, "established," or "designated" campsite. If a fire ring has been heaped over with rocks, it means the site has been dis-established.

Litter and Garbage and Sanitation

The rule among considerate hikers is: If you can carry it in full, you can carry it out empty. Thanks to a steady improvement in manners over recent decades, American trails are cleaner than they have been since Columbus landed.

On a day hike, take back to the road (and garbage can) every last orange peel and gum wrapper.

On an overnight or longer hike, burn all paper (if a fire is built) but carry back all unburnables, including cans, metal foil, plastic, glass, and papers that won't burn. Do not bury garbage. If fresh, animals will dig it up and scatter the remnants. Burning before burying is no answer either. Tin cans take as long as 40 years to disintegrate completely; aluminum and glass last for centuries. Further, digging pits to bury junk disturbs the ground cover, and iron eventually leaches from buried cans and "rusts" springs and creeks.

Do not leave leftover food for the next travelers; they will have their own supplies and won't be tempted by "gifts" spoiled by time or chewed by animals.

Do not cache plastic tarps. Weathering quickly ruins the fabric, little creatures nibble, and the result is a useless, miserable mess.

Keep the water pure. Do not wash dishes in streams or lakes, loosing food particles and detergent. Haul buckets of water off to the woods or rocks, and wash and rinse there. Eliminate body wastes at least 200 feet from watercourses: first, dig a shallow hole in the "biological disposer layer"; then, if not using leaves, pack out your toilet paper—do not burn it. Where privies are provided, use them.

Water

No open water ever, nowadays, can be considered certainly safe for human consumption. Any reference in this book to "drinking water" is not a guarantee.

In the late 1970s a great epidemic of giardiasis began, caused by a vicious little parasite that spends part of its life cycle swimming free in water, part in the intestinal tract of beavers and other wildlife, dogs, and people. Actually, the "epidemic" was solely in the press; *Giardia* were first identified in the eighteenthth century and are present in the public water systems of many cities of the world and many towns in the United States—including some in the foothills of the Cascades. Long before the "outbreak" of "beaver fever" there was the well-known malady, the "Boy Scout trots." This is not to make light of the disease; though most humans feel no ill effects (but become carriers), others have serious symptoms, which include devastating diarrhea; the treatment is nearly as unpleasant. The reason giardiasis has become "epidemic" is that there are more people in the backcountry. More people drinking water contaminated by animals. More people contaminating the water.

Whenever in doubt, boil the water 20 minutes. Keep in mind that *Giardia* can survive in water at or near freezing for weeks or months—a snow pond is not necessarily safe. Boiling is 100 percent effective against not only *Giardia* but also the myriad other filthy little blighters that may upset your digestion or, as with some forms of hepatitis, destroy your liver.

If you cannot boil, use one of the several iodine treatments (chlorine compounds have been found untrustworthy in wildland circumstances), such as Potable Aqua or the more complicated method that employs iodine crystals. Rumor to the contrary, iodine treatments pose no threat to the health.

Be wary of filters. The technology is advancing and several products claim to provide some protection, but others are of dubious value, if any, and a person must ask if he or she wishes to trust their liver to an advertised guarantee.

Party Size

One management technique to minimize impact in popular areas is to limit the number of people in any one group to a dozen or fewer. Hikers with very large families (or outing groups from clubs or wherever) should check the rules when planning a trip.

Pets

The handwriting is on the wall for dogs. Pets always have been forbidden on national park trails and now some parts of wildernesses are being closed to them as well. How fast the ban spreads will depend on the owners' sensitivity, training, acceptance of responsibility, and courtesy.

Where pets are permitted, even a well-behaved dog can ruin someone else's trip. Some dogs noisily defend an ill-defined territory for their master, "guard" him or her on the trail, snitch enemy bacon, and are quite likely to defecate on the flat bit of ground the next hiker will want to sleep on.

The family that wants to go where the crowds are must leave its best friend home. Do not depend on friendly tolerance of wilderness neighbors. Some people are so harassed at home by loose dogs that a hound in the wilderness has the same effect on them as a motorcycle.

Horses

As the backcountry population has grown, encounters between hikers and horse-riders have increased. Even though hikers are distressed by campsites that look like barnyards, the animals and their riders generally are good wilderness neighbors.

Most horse-riders do their best to be so on the trail and know how to go about it. The typical hiker, though, is ignorant of the difficulties inherent in maneuvering a huge mass of flesh (containing a very small brain) along narrow paths on steep mountains.

The first rule is, the horse has the right of way. For his/her own safety as well as that of the rider, the hiker must get off the trail, preferably on the downhill side, giving the heavy animal and its rider the inside of the tread. If necessary—as, say, on a steep hillside—retreat some distance to a safe passing point.

The second rule is, when you see the horse approaching, do not keep silent or stand still in a mistaken attempt to avoid frightening the beast. Continue normal motions and speak to it, so the creature will recognize you as just another human and not think you a silent and doubtless dangerous monster.

Finally, if you have a dog along, get a tight grip on its throat to stop the nipping and yapping, which may endanger the rider and, in the case of a surly horse, the dog as well.

Theft

Equipment has become so fancy and expensive, so much worth stealing, and hikers so numerous, their valuables so tempting, that theft is a growing problem. The professionals who do most of the stealing mainly concentrate on cars. Authorities have the following recommendations.

Do not make crime profitable. If the pros break into a hundred cars and get nothing but moldy boots and tattered T shirts, they'll give up. On an extended car trip, store extra equipment at a nearby motel.

Be suspicious of anyone waiting at a trailhead. One of the tricks of the trade is to sit there with a pack as if waiting for a ride, watching new arrivals unpack—and hide their valuables—and maybe even striking up a conversation to determine how long the marks will be away.

The ultimate solution, of course, is for hikers to become as poor as they were in the olden days. No criminal would consider trailheads profitable if the loot consisted solely of shabby khaki war surplus.

Safety Considerations

The reason the Ten Essentials are advised is that hiking in the backcountry entails unavoidable risks that every hiker must know about and respect. The fact that a trail is described in this book is not a representation that it will be safe for you. Trails vary greatly in difficulty and in the degree of conditioning and agility one needs to enjoy them safely. On some hikes routes may have changed or conditions may have deteriorated since the descriptions were written. Also, trail conditions can change even from day to day, owing to weather and other factors. A trail that is safe on a dry day or for a highly conditioned, agile, properly equipped hiker may be completely unsafe for someone else or unsafe under adverse weather conditions. You can minimize your risks on the trail by being knowledgeable, prepared, and alert.

These warnings are not intended to scare you off the trails. Hundreds of thousands of people have safe and enjoyable hikes every year. However, an element of the beauty, freedom, and excitement of the wilderness is the presence of risks that do not confront us at home.

To help hikers have a safe and enjoyable trail experience by matching the trip to experience and physical condition, the Forest Service has begun signing trails as follows:

Requires limited skill and has little physical challenge. Tread is smooth, level, and wide, with generous clearing of trees, limbs, and other vegetation above and on each side of the trail to permit easy passage. Elevation gain or loss is minimal. Streams are most often crossed with bridges.

Requires a moderate skill level and provides a moderate physical challenge. Tread surface contains roots and embedded rocks. Clearing trees, limbs, and other vegetation above and to each side of the trail results in occasional contact by users. Elevation gain or loss is moderate. Streams are most often crossed by fords.

Requires a high degree of skill and provides a lot of physical challenge. Tread is seldom graded except on steep slopes for safety and prevention of soil erosion. Minimal clearing of trees, limbs, and other vegetation results in hampering the progress of the user. Elevation gain or loss is usually severe. Streams are crossed by fording and are sometimes difficult.

This rating system is good for comparing one trail to another. The actual difficulty encountered by a hiker, however, will vary with the time of year, weather conditions, and the individual's physical ability.

Volunteers for Outdoor Washington

For 10,000 years or so the only trails in the North Cascades were those beaten out by the feet of deer, elk, bear, coyotes, marmots, and the folks who had trekked on over from Asia. For some 50 years, starting in the late nineteenth century, the "dirty miners in search of shining gold" built and maintained hundreds of miles of trails, often wide and solid enough for packtrains. During the same period many a valley had a trapline, a trapper, and a trapper's trail, and many a ridge had a sheepherder's driveway. For 30-odd years, roughly from World War I to World War II, U.S. Forest Service rangers built trails to serve fire lookouts atop peaks and to give firefighting crews quick walking to blazes. In the late 1930s the trail system attained its maximum mileage and excellence.

Then the rangers began taking to airplanes and parachutes and the prospectors to helicopters, and the trail system began to deteriorate. Eventually the Forest Service expanded the concept of multiple-use to encompass spending money on trails where recreation was the main or only use, instead of a subsidiary one as was formerly the case. Just about that time the United States fell on hard times and the funds for Forest Service—and Park Service—trails were largely diverted to maintaining troops in foreign nations.

Hikers long took for granted that Uncle Sam would look after Forest Service trails, but Uncle can't even take care of the homeless, let alone 12,000 miles of trail. If you want good trails, you have to do it yourself. With a little effort, a surprising amount can be accomplished. When walking a trail, remove fallen rocks, limbs, and litter. Such solo efforts are helpful; for major projects such as restoring tread and replacing waterbars, a coordinated effort is needed. Volunteers for Outdoor Washington (VOW) is part of the national trend toward construction and maintenance of trails by unpaid volunteers. The principle is simple: If each hiker spends several days a year working on a crew, trails can continue to be easily walked that otherwise would be abandoned by the government for lack of money. So, would you rather devote some days to whacking at slide alder with an ax or cutting through windfall with a saw, or would you rather devote tortured hours to hauling your pack through brush and crawling over logs?

For information on how your organization, or you as an individual, can join the VOW effort, contact Volunteers for Outdoor Washington, 4516 University Way NE, Seattle, Washington 98105, or phone (206) 545-4868.

Protect This Land, Your Land

The Cascade country is large and rugged and wild—but it is also, and particularly in the scenic climaxes favored by hikers, a fragile country. If humans are to blend into the ecosystem, rather than dominate and destroy, they must walk lightly, respectfully, always striving to make their passage through the wilderness invisible.

The public servants entrusted with administration of the region have a complex and difficult job, and they desperately need the cooperation of every wildland traveler. Here, the authors would like to express appreciation to these dedicated men and women for their advice on what trips to include in this book and for their detailed review of the text and maps. Thanks are due the supervisors of the Mt. Baker–Snoqualmie and Okanogan National Forests and the superintendent of the North Cascades National Park and their district rangers and other staff members.

On behalf of the U.S. Forest Service, National Park Service, and The Mountaineers, we invite Americans—and all citizens of Earth—to come and see and live in some of the world's finest wildlands and to vow henceforth to share in the task of preserving the trails and ridges, lakes and rivers, forests and flower gardens for future generations, our children and grandchildren, who will need the wilderness experience at least as much as we do, and probably more.

A Note About Safety

Safety is an important concern in all outdoor activities. No guidebook can alert you to every hazard or anticipate the limitations of every reader. Therefore, the descriptions of roads, trails, routes, and natural features in this book are not representations that a particular place or excursion will be safe for your party. When you follow any of the routes described in this book, you assume responsibility for your own safety. Under normal conditions, such excursions require the usual attention to traffic, road and trail conditions, weather, terrain, the capabilities of your party, and other factors. Keeping informed on current conditions and exercising common sense are the keys to a safe, enjoyable outing.

The Mountaineers

HELIOTROPE RIDGE

Round trip 6½ miles
Hiking time 5 hours
High point 5600 feet
Elevation gain 2000 feet
Hikable August through
September

One day or backpack; *no fires*
Map: Green Trails No. 13 Mt.
Baker
Current information: Ask at
Glacier Public Service Center
about trail No. 677

A splendid forest walk leading to a ramble-and-scramble on flowery moraines below (and above) the ice chaos of the rampaging Coleman Glacier. See the mountain climbers—by the hundreds on many summer weekends, because this is the most popular route to the summit of Mt. Baker. They're a harmless and unobtrusive lot, boisterous in camp but sacking out early, rising somber and quiet in the middle of the night, and spending all day on the glaciers, out of sight and sound. Along the trail, hikers can be hugely entertained by the bizarre and colorful displays of tents and axes and ropes and helmets and hardware.

Drive Highway 542 to the town of Glacier and 1 mile beyond to Glacier Creek road No. 39. Turn right some 8 miles to a parking lot at the sign "Heliotrope Ridge Trail," elevation 3650 feet.

Hike 2 miles, traversing and switchbacking through tree shadows, over cold little creeks, to the site of historic Kulshan Cabin, 4700 feet, near but still below timberline.

The fun country is above. From the cabin site the trail climbs, crossing several streams which on a hot day may be gushers from melting snowfields. The way passes below steep flower-covered meadows, groves of alpine trees, over a rocky moraine whistling with marmots to another moraine with a large glacier-scoured rock on the brink of

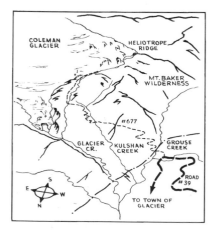

a gravel precipice, about 5600 feet. Look down to the blue-white jumble of the Coleman Glacier and up to the gleaming summit of ice-capped Mt. Baker. Follow the moraine upward—stopping well short of the living glacier. Good camps below the trail in the timber.

Because of the enormous snowfall on Mt. Baker, and because this is the north side of the mountain, hikers who come earlier than August are liable to be surrounded by snow—and potential danger—above treeline. The crevasses, of course, are always there, visible or invisible.

Coleman Glacier from trail's end

2 SKYLINE DIVIDE

Round trip to Knoll 6215 6 miles
Hiking time 4 hours
High point 6650 feet
Elevation gain 2200 feet
Hikable August through
September

One day or backpack; *no fires*
Map: Green Trails No. 13 Mt.
Baker
Current information: Ask at
Glacier Public Service Center
about trail No. 678

A large, green meadow. An enormous white volcano—pound for pound, the iciest in the Cascades. Views of forests and glaciers, rivers and mountains, sunsets and sunrises.

Drive Highway 542 to 1 mile beyond the town of Glacier. Turn right on Glacier Creek road No. 39, and in a hundred yards turn sharply left on Deadhorse road No. 37. Follow the south side of the Nooksack River some 4 level and pleasant miles. The road then climbs abruptly. At 7.5 miles pause to view a lovely waterfall splashing down a rock cleft, coming from the country where you're going. At 13 miles is the parking lot and trailhead, elevation 4300 feet. Find the trail at the upper end of the lot.

The trail, moderate to steep, climbs 1500 feet in 2 miles through silver firs and subalpine glades to an immense ridge-top meadow at 5800 feet and the beginning of wide views. South are the sprawling glaciers of the north wall of Mt. Baker. North, beyond forests of the Nooksack Valley, are the greenery of Church Mountain and the rock towers of the Border Peaks and, across the border, the Cheam (Lucky Four) Range. On a clear day saltwater can be seen, and the Vancouver Island Mountains, and the British Columbia Coast Range. Eastward is Mt. Shuksan and a gentler companion, little Table Mountain, above Heather Meadows.

The broadest views are atop the 6215-foot knoll to the south; from the meadow, follow the trail ¾ mile along the ridge and take the sidepath up the knoll. Sprawl and enjoy. (*Note to photographers:* The

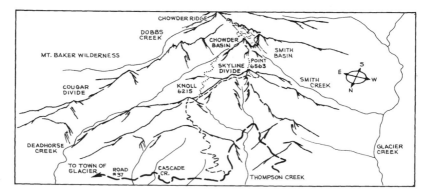

Flower-covered Skyline Divide and Mount Baker

best pictures of Baker from here generally are taken before 10:00 A.M. and after 4:00 P.M.)

Beyond the knoll the trail follows the ridge another ½ mile to a saddle at 6000 feet and then splits. The left contours a scant mile to a dead end in Chowder Basin, headwaters of Deadhorse Creek, and campsites with all-summer water. The right climbs a step in Skyline Divide to 6500 feet and proceeds along the tundra crest 2 miles to a 6300-foot saddle (and, perhaps, a snowmelt pool) at the foot of the abrupt upward leap to Chowder Ridge, whose summit is accessible on a track suitable for goats, climbers, and life-weary hikers.

In early summer, water is available for camping all along Skyline Divide, but later a party often must look for springs in Chowder and Smith Basins or snowfield dribbles on the ridge.

In benign weather the supreme overnight experience is atop the 6500-foot tundra, watching the Whulge (the name given by the original residents to "the saltwater we know") turn gold in the setting sun and the lights of farms and cities wink on, then awaking at dawn to watch Baker turn shocking pink. However, though the tundra is tough enough to withstand sun and frost and storm, it cannot take human abuse. Do not build fires; if chilly, crawl in your sleeping bag. Do not sack out on soft turf; lay your sleeping pad and bag on a hard rock or bare dirt.

3 CANYON RIDGE—POINT 5658

Round trip to ridge crest 6 miles
Hiking time 3 hours
High point 5400 feet
Elevation gain 1200 feet
Round trip to Point 5658 6 miles
Hiking time 4 hours
High point 5658 feet
Elevation gain 1300 feet

Hikable August through September
One day
Map: Green Trails No. 13 Mt. Baker
Current information: Ask at
Glacier Public Service Center
about trail Nos. 625, 688,
and 689

In an area offering so many spectacular viewpoints, why bother hiking to those that rate no better than merely excellent? For one reason, people. On a day when they're swarming all over the spectacular, a hiker on the Canyon Ridge trail may have the excellent all to himself/herself. Also, scenery isn't everything. (In the fog it's nothing.) The forest here is lovely, the flowers bloom by the million, and the heather-and-huckleberry meadows are large and lonesome. Try these trails in early August for the climax of the flower show, or in September when the frost has turned the mountain ash leaves to the color of gold and the blueberry leaves to the color of wine. A party with two cars can do a very difficult one-way trip of 8 miles. The description here is round trips to two of the more excellent views: south to the snowy summits of Church Mountain and the network of logging roads in Canyon Creek valley, and north to Canadian mountains and the network of Canadian logging roads.

Drive Highway 542 beyond the Glacier Public Service Center 1.8 miles. Turn left on Canyon Creek road No. 31 and drive 14.6 miles from the highway to the trailhead, elevation 4277 feet.

Start on Damfino trail No. 625, climbing gently through forest. In a long ½ mile, turn left on Canyon Ridge trail No. 689. At approximately 1 mile from the road is a junction and choice. To the right are Boundary

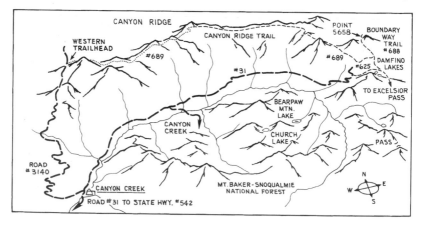

Boundary Way trail

Way trail No. 688 and Point 5658—more later. For the ridge crest continue on. At approximately 1½ miles traverse a large sidehill meadow, steep and unstable, the tread often slumped out. At a long 2 miles the trail crosses Canyon Ridge from the south side to the north and emerges from forest to mountain ash, then heather. The way climbs to a shoulder a few feet from the top of a 5400-foot knob less than 1½ miles from Canada. Excellent enough.

The trail continues on to the western trailhead on road No. 3140, but it is not maintained and is best described as a bushwhack. Hey, don't complain! Were it not for the unstable hillside on the east end and the bushwhack on the west, the trail would be open to motorcycles.

For Point 5658, back at the junction go right on Boundary Way trail No. 688, through a swampy little cleft, then up in forest to a large meadow. At about 2½ miles from the road, attain a 5050-foot ridge top and look across the broad, deep gulf of Tomyhoi Creek into Canada.

The Boundary Way trail goes right, down along the ridge, 2 miles toward—but not to—the border. Don't go. Climb left on the sidepath to the crest of the summit ridge, to an elevation about 3 feet lower than Point 5658. To gain the tippy-top one would have to creep along a knife-edge catwalk. Dogs will prefer to sit down here and chew their bones while enjoying the view north to Canada, west to flatland farm geometry, south to Church Mountain and Mt. Baker, and east to Mt. Shuksan, Tomyhoi, and the garish red masses of the Border Peaks—American Border, Larrabee, and Canadian Border.

In the beginning no mountains had names, yet the flowers then were as bright in the meadows and the views to far horizons as inspiring. After the map industry took off, almost everything got a name, needed or not. Peak 5658 was missed. So was K2 in the Karakorum. Ponder that as you gaze to panoramas of the North Cascades and whatever, if anything, they call all those mountains in Canada.

4 EXCELSIOR MOUNTAIN

Round trip (from Canyon Creek road) 6½ miles
Hiking time 4 hours
High point 5712 feet
Elevation gain 1500 feet
Hikable mid-July through September

One day or backpack; *no fires*
Map: Green Trails No. 13 Mt. Baker
Current information: Ask at Glacier Public Service Center about trail No. 625

Views from this meadow summit include Nooksack valley forests and saltwater lowlands, Mt. Baker and the Border Peaks, the southernmost portion of the British Columbia Coast Range, and more. Flowers in July, berries and colors in September. Three trails lead to the site of a long-gone lookout cabin; the easiest and most scenic is recommended here, but take your pick.

Drive Highway 542 to the Glacier Public Service Center and 1.8 miles beyond to Canyon Creek road No. 31. Turn left 14.6 miles to the parking lot in a clearcut at the start of trail No. 625; elevation 4277 feet.

Mount Baker from near top of Excelsior Mountain

Climb gently through forest ½ mile to the junction with Canyon Ridge trail No. 689. Keep right and go a bit more to 4500-foot Damfino Lakes, two small ponds surrounded by acres of super-delicious blueberries (in season). Campsites and running water near the smaller lake.

Climb another timbered mile, then go up a narrow draw and shortly enter meadows. Cross a notch, sidehill forest, then broad meadows, rising in ½ mile to 5300-foot Excelsior Pass, some 2½ miles from the road. (Pleasant camps at and near the pass when there is snowfield water—perhaps until early August.) Follow the trail another ½ mile, traversing under the peak through meadows and views, then left ¼ mile to the 5712-foot peak.

Sit and look. See the glaciers of Mt. Baker across forests of the Nooksack. See more ice on Mt. Shuksan and other peaks east. See the steep-walled Border Peaks and snowy ranges extending far north into Canada. And see green meadows everywhere.

The summit is a magnificent place to stop overnight in good weather, watching a sunset and a dawn; no water, though, except possible snowmelt.

Two alternate trails can be used to vary the descent. (They can also be used to ascend the peak but, for reasons that will be obvious, are not the best choices.)

Alternate No. 1. From Excelsior Pass, descend trail No. 670 4 miles and 3500 feet to the highway, reached 8 miles east of Glacier at a small parking area (with trail sign on opposite side of road). The trail switchbacks steeply on south-facing slopes that melt free of snow relatively early in the season; an excellent hike from the highway in May or June, turning back when snowfields halt progress. In summer this route to high country is long and hot and dry.

Alternate No. 2. From the peak traverse High Divide trail No. 630 along Excelsior Ridge 5 miles to Welcome Pass and descend steeply 2½ miles to the trailhead on an unmaintained logging road (described in Hike 6, Welcome Pass—Excelsior Ridge). Experienced off-trail roamers can extend their flower wanders west from Excelsior Pass toward Church Mountain and east from Welcome Pass to Yellow Aster Butte.

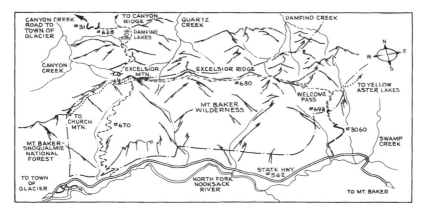

5   CHURCH MOUNTAIN

Round trip 8½ miles
Hiking time 6 hours
High point 6100 feet
Elevation gain 3800 feet
Hikable late July through
    September

One day
Map: Green Trails No. 13 Mt. Baker
Current information: Ask at
    Glacier Public Service Center
    about trail No. 671

White paintbrush on slopes of
Church Mountain

The first thrilling view of emerald meadowland gained while driving east along Mt. Baker Highway is on Church Mountain. The view is straight up, nearly a vertical mile, yet the green is so vivid and appears so close a person cannot but wish to go there. A person can readily do so but must be a sturdy person and carry much water because the climb is far longer than it looks and by midsummer is dry. However, the views back down to the valley and out to Mt. Baker and Shuksan are worth the sweat. In certain kinds of weather the problem is not heat. The viewpoint, on the east peak of Church, is a small platform atop a rocky pinnacle, just large enough to hold the lookout building that used to be here until it was abandoned because wind kept blowing the structure off its foundation.

Drive Highway 542 to the Glacier Public Service Center and 5.1

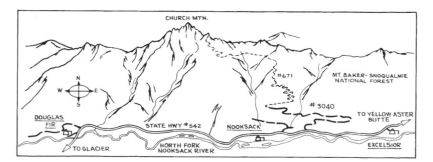

Mount Shuksan from side of Church Mountain

miles beyond. Turn left on road No. 3040, signed "Church Mountain Road." Drive 2.6 miles (sign says 4 miles) to the road-end and trailhead, elevation 2300 feet.

The trail begins on an abandoned logging road, switchbacks up a clearcut to virgin forest, and ascends relentlessly, zigging and zagging. In a bit more than 3 miles the way opens out in heather and flowers and the trail cut can be seen switchbacking up the emerald meadowland to the rocky summit. Shortly below the top is an old storage shed, now a marmot condominium. From here the path, carved from rock, passes an odd-shaped outhouse to the lookout site.

Look down to bugs creeping along the concrete ribbon beside the silver ribbon of river. Look east into the North Cascades, north to Canada, south toward Mt. Rainier. To the west are frightful cliffs of 6315-foot Church Mountain, only 200 feet higher than the lookout peak. Below are the two little Kidney Lakes, snowbound much of the year.

In March and April and May, when the color scheme on high is more white than green, the lower part of the trail offers a fine walk in wildwoods and forest flowers.

6 WELCOME PASS— EXCELSIOR RIDGE

Welcome Pass
Round trip to the pass 6 miles
Hiking time 6 hours
High point 5200 feet
Elevation gain 2400 feet

Grand Traverse Excelsior Ridge
One way from road No. 31
** 10 miles**
Hiking time 6 hours
High point 5699 feet
Elevation gain 1800 feet

Hikable July through
** September**
One day or backpack
Maps: Green Trails No. 14 Mt.
** Shuksan, No. 13 Mt. Baker**
Current information: Ask at
** Glacier Public Service Center**
** about trail No. 698**

An old-fashioned trail, and the only one left in the Mt. Baker area that starts near the valley bottom, climbs through virgin forest carpeted with woodland flowers to alpine meadows of Excelsior Ridge, rich with flowers, heather, and views. The trail is old-fashioned in another way too, having been built by old-fashioned foresters bent on getting somewhere fast, the 15–22 percent grade switchbacking sixty-seven times up a super-steep hillside. Most trails in the Mt. Baker area start high, giving easy access to striking scenery; this one therefore is pretty lonesome.

By shuttling cars some 30 miles between trailheads, a one-way traverse of Excelsior Ridge could be done, a spectacular way to spend a day or, with sidetrips, a week.

Drive Highway 542 from the Glacier Public Service Center 11.4 miles and between mileposts 45 and 46 go left on the unmarked, unmaintained Welcome Pass trailhead road. (If you reach the Highway Department barn, you have gone too far.) Drive 0.7 mile to the road-

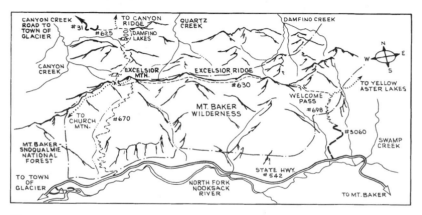

Mount Shuksan, and mountain bistort at Welcome Pass

end parking. The road to the trailhead is a fright, impossible for a low-slung car. Find trail No. 698, 100 feet from the parking spot, elevation 2450 feet.

A pleasant forest walk on a long-abandoned logging road. The first mile gains only 400 feet. Then the fun begins. The trail gains 2000 feet in the next 2 miles, going from steep to steeper. Grueling, to be sure, but brightened by forest flowers, an occasional view out to Mt. Shuksan, and bits and pieces of Mt. Baker gleaming through little openings in the trees. At 5200 feet the trail abruptly levels off and bursts into meadows of Welcome Pass with views out to Tomyhoi Peak, numerous unnamed peaks of Excelsior Ridge, and miles of meadows, both left and right.

What to do? Round-trippers content with a grand panorama go right, up a steep boot-beaten path ¾ mile to a 5743-foot high point and views of Mt. Baker, Mt. Shuksan, and endless glaciered peaks. If energy is not all spent, in another mile a 5933-foot high point overlooks the many lakes below Yellow Aster Butte.

For the grand traverse, go left on High Divide trail No. 630, do the ups and downs of Excelsior Ridge meadows, through breathtaking views, westward 5 miles (adding another 1000 feet of elevation) to Excelsior Mountain (Hike 4), and from there drop to the Canyon Creek Road. However, logic would say to start from the higher trailhead on Canyon Creek Road (Hike 4) and end at Welcome Pass, saving almost 2000 feet of elevation gain.

7 YELLOW ASTER BUTTE

Round trip 6 miles
Hiking time 8 hours
High point 6100 feet
Elevation gain 3200 feet
Hikable mid-July through
   October

One day or backpack; *no fires*
Map: Green Trails No. 14
   Mt. Shuksan
Current information: Ask at
   Glacier Public Service Center
   about trail No. 699

If views turn you on, there's plenty to exclaim about here—across the Nooksack valley to Mt. Baker and Mt. Shuksan, over the headwaters of Tomyhoi Creek to gaudy walls of the Border Peaks, and down to mile-long Tomyhoi Lake and out the valley to farms along the Fraser River. However, many a hiker never aspires for the summit, never lifts eyes from the meadows and snowy-cold lakes and ponds set in pockets scooped from the rock by the glacier that appears to have left about a half-hour ago. Try the trip in late July for the flower show, in late August for the blueberry feast, and in October for autumn colors and winter frost.

Drive Highway 542 for 12.8 miles past the Glacier Public Service Center. Just past the highway maintenance sheds is a sign, "Tomyhoi Trail 5, Twin Lakes 7." Turn left up narrow, steep, rough road No. 3065 for 2.3 miles, then left 0.2 mile to the Yellow Aster Butte trail No. 699, elevation 2960 feet. *Please note:* In the next few years the trailhead will be moved.

The old name Keep Kool Trail, of course, is intended to mock the laboring hiker as he/she sets out up a grown-over logging road of the 1940s, proceeds on a straight-up cat track of the same era (high-grading the giant Douglas firs), and continues in virgin forest on a wall-climbing prospectors' trail, gaining 1200 feet in the first mile. It is nevertheless difficult to get overheated, what with the magnificent deep forest and the creeks. After the first mile the angle relents and at 4700 feet,

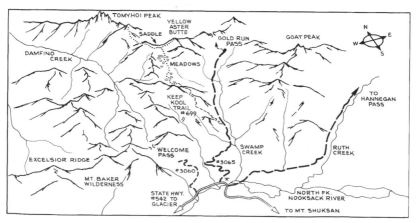

about 2 miles, the way flattens to cross a delightful meadow shelf with grand views, bubbling creeks, and superb camps. A steep tilt up through parkland leads to the first tarn at 5200 feet, followed in quick succession by more tarns at 5400 feet and the beginning of holes and rusty junk left by the prospectors lest we forget them. At 5500 feet, some 2½ miles, the route (there is now no real trail, nor is one needed) enters the glory hole—a basin with lakes and ponds and pools almost beyond counting. (More are more tucked in pockets on the ridge.)

An easy stroll leads to the summit of Yellow Aster Butte. A much longer walk climbs from lush herbaceous meadows to tundra to lichen-black felsenmeer very near the summit of 7451-foot Tomyhoi Peak, whose final hundred feet are for climbers only.

Now then: The area having been (largely) given wilderness protection in 1984, the "yellow asters" (actually golden daisies) no longer need the mass support of citizen-hikers or their boots—and certainly not their fires. The crying need is hikers who walk softly, cook on stoves or eat cold food, and scatter themselves about on the ridge and in secluded nooks. In summary, particularly tender loving care for the most beautiful spot on the entire Nooksack Crest.

Goat Mountain from Keep Kool Trail

8 GOLD RUN PASS— TOMYHOI LAKE

**Round trip to Gold Run Pass
4 miles
Hiking time 3 hours
High point 5400 feet
Elevation gain 1800 feet**

**Round trip to Tomyhoi Lake
10 miles
Hiking time 7 hours
High point 5400 feet
Elevation gain on return
1600 feet**

**Hikable July through October
One day or backpack
Map: Green Trails No. 14 Mt.
Shuksan
Current information: Ask at
Glacier Public Service Center
about trail No. 686**

Views across the Nooksack valley to Mt. Baker and Mt. Shuksan. Views over the headwaters of Tomyhoi Creek to Tomyhoi Peak and the tall, rough walls of Mt. Larrabee and American Border and Canadian Border Peaks. Views down to a mile-long lake and north into Canada. Mountain meadows along a pretty trail—but a hot and dry trail on sunny days, so start early and carry water.

Drive Highway 542 for 12.8 miles past the Glacier Public Service Center. Just past the highway maintenance sheds is a sign, "Tomyhoi Trail 5, Twin Lakes 7." Turn left on road No. 3065, increasingly narrower, steeper, and rougher. At 4.5 miles on a sharp switchback is the Tomyhoi Lake trail sign, elevation 3600 feet. Very limited parking.

The trail switchbacks steadily up, first in trees, then meadows, then trees, then meadows again. In 1½ miles the way leaves forest the last time and enters an open basin, snow-covered until

Mount Shuksan from side of Yellow Aster Butte

July. South are Baker and a shoulder of Shuksan. Above is Yellow Aster Butte. The display of wildflowers begins here with avalanche lily and spring beauty in mid-June and continues with other species through the summer. At 2 miles is Gold Run Pass, 5400 feet. No camping at the pass. Good campsites (no fires) ½ mile farther at Coyote Flats.

Further explorations are inviting. Tomyhoi Lake, 3800 feet, is 2 miles and 1600 feet below the pass. The lake is less than 2 miles from the border; Canadian logging roads can be seen. Avalanche snow floats in the waters until early summer. Good campsite; fires allowed.

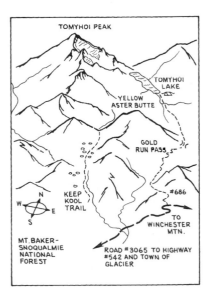

9 TWIN LAKES— WINCHESTER MOUNTAIN

**Round trip to Twin Lakes from
Tomyhoi Lake trailhead 4 miles**
Hiking time 3 hours
High point 5200 feet
Elevation gain 1600 feet
Hikable July through September

**Round trip to Winchester
Mountain from Tomyhoi Lake
trailhead 9 miles**
Hiking time 6 hours
High point 6521 feet
Elevation gain 3000 feet

**Hikable late July through
September**
**One day; *no fires on Winchester
Mountain or High and Low
Passes***
**Map: Green Trails No. 14
Mt. Shuksan**
**Current information: Ask at
Glacier Public Service Center
about trail No. 685**

An easy and popular trail through alpine meadows to two delightful alpine lakes and then to a summit view of Baker, Shuksan, Border Peaks, and Tomyhoi, plus looks far down to Tomyhoi Lake and forests of Silesia Creek. Especially beautiful in fall colors.

Drive Twin Lakes road No. 3065 (Hike 8) 4.5 miles to the Tomyhoi Lake trail sign, elevation 3600 feet. Parking is very limited.

The Twin Lakes road is not the work of the Forest Service or built to its specifications. A "mine-to-market" road, it was constructed by the county and is maintained in the upper reaches solely by prospectors, and then only when they are engaged in their sporadic activity, and then only minimally. The first 4.5 miles to the Tomyhoi Lake trailhead usually can be driven by the family car, but the final 2.5 miles to Twin Lakes, culminating in five wickedly sharp switchbacks, are something else. Some years an agile car may do ¾ mile beyond the Tomyhoi trail but the rest of the way is drivable only by a four-wheel-drive vehicle. Most hikers prefer to protect cars and nerves from damage by parking near the Tomyhoi Lake trailhead and walking to the lakes. When the miners finally sell out, the road will be abandoned, returning Twin Lakes to the realm of trail country—where they belong.

The two lakes, lovely alpine waters at an elevation of 5200 feet, often are frozen until early August, though surrounding parklands melt

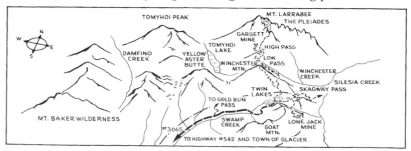

free earlier. Between the lakes is an undeveloped campsite with a classic view of Mt. Baker.

Find the Winchester Mountain trail at the road-end between the lakes. Within ¼ mile is a junction with the High Pass (Gargett Mine) trail. Take the left fork and climb a series of switchbacks westerly through heather, alpine trees, and flowers. Near the top a treacherous snowpatch, steep with no runout, often lasts until late August. It may be possible to squirm between the upper edge of the snow and the rocks. Otherwise, drop below the snow and climb to the trail on the far side. Don't try crossing the snow without an ice ax and experience in using it.

In 1½ miles the trail rounds a shoulder and levels off somewhat for the final ½ mile to the summit, a fine place to while away hours surveying horizons from saltwaterways and lowlands to the Pickets and far north into Canada.

Twin Lakes make a superb basecamp for days of roaming high gardens, prowling old mines, and grazing September blueberries. Even if the upper road must be walked, access is easy for backpacking families with short-legged members.

For one of the longer explorations of the many available, take the High Pass trail No. 676 (see earlier). A steep snowfield near the beginning may stop all but trained climbers; if not, there is no further barrier to Low Pass (about 1½ miles) and 5900-foot High Pass (2½ miles). Follow an old miners' trail high on Mt. Larrabee to a close view of the rugged Pleiades. Investigate the junkyard of the Gargett Mine. Wander meadow basins and admire scenery close and distant.

Upper Twin Lake, abandoned mining road, and Canadian peaks

10 NOOKSACK CIRQUE

Round trip to end of gravel bars
12½ miles
Hiking time 6–8 hours
High point 3100 feet
Elevation gain 600 feet
Hikable August through September
One day or backpack

Map: Green Trails No. 14 Mt.
Shuksan
Current information: Ask at
Glacier Public Service Center
about trail No. 680
Park Service backcountry use
permit required for camping

A wild, lonesome cirque, a wasteland of glacial violence, one of the most dramatic spots in the North Cascades. Icefalls, waterfalls, rockfalls, moraines, a raging river, the stark pinnacle of Nooksack Tower, and the 5000-foot northeast wall of Mt. Shuksan. But the way is only partly on trail, the rest being bushwhacking and cobble-hopping. The trip can only be recommended to rational people for late summer when Ruth Creek is low enough to wade and the Nooksack River is low enough to fully expose gravel bars.

Drive Highway 542 east from Glacier Public Service Center 13 miles. Just before the Nooksack River bridge, turn left on Nooksack River road No. 32. In 1.3 miles take the right fork, road No. 34, and go another 1 mile to the abandoned bridge over Ruth Creek. (A new trailhead is planned for 1995.) Ford the creek and walk 2 miles to the trailhead at the old road-end, elevation about 2550 feet.

The way starts on a grown-over logging road of the 1950s, descending to the right and then climbing, at about ¾ mile reaching the end of the clearcut, and enters Mount Baker Wilderness and the beginning of true trail at about 2800 feet. Constructed tread goes 1 mile through gorgeous big trees, an old-growth museum, to the end by the river. Cross a large tributary on logs (or an upstream footlog).

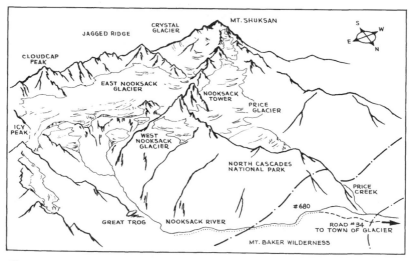

East Nooksack Glacier from Nooksack Cirque

For the next ¾ mile there are two alternate ways. Depending on how high the river is and where its channel happens to be, scenic gravel bars may be continuous. Icy Peak appears, then the cirque itself, hanging ice cliffs of the East Nooksack Glacier falling from Cloudcap (Seahpo) Peak and Jagged Ridge. If the gravel won't go, the woods will. Find the boot-beaten path across some small sloughs, the start marked by a rock cairn. At several places the woods path and the gravel bars are connected by linking paths, permitting alternation.

At the end of this ¾ mile, at about 2800 feet, the trail enters the national park and goes out on the gravel for good, a large cairn often marking the spot. The next 1 mile is on gravel bars (which may be under water) or on the riverbank terrace, partly in timber but mostly in fierce brush, particularly nasty on an enormous alluvial fan issuing from a big gulch.

At the fan-maker creek, 2950 feet, are the last of the big trees. The next ¾ mile is easy, walking mossy gravel on brushfree terraces well above high water.

At 3100 feet, about 4¼ miles from the road, the good times are over and the sensible hiker will make this the turnaround. The view of the cirque, "the deepest, darkest hole in the North Cascades," is superb. The camping (no fires allowed; bring a stove) is splendid.

Upstream from here the river gushes from a virtual tunnel through overhanging alder, no gravel bars even in the lowest water. If you insist on persisting, dive into the slide alder, watching for cut branches and blazes and cairns. After about ¾ mile you'll attain the Great Trog (a large rock with an overhang), 3600 feet, formerly the grandest storm camp in the Cascades but now full of boulders. Exploring upward from here is tough going except in spring, when the moraines and cliffs and boulders are buried under fans of avalanche snow, and then it's dangerous.

11 GOAT MOUNTAIN LOOKOUT SITE

Round trip 5 miles
Hiking time 3 hours
High point 4115 feet
Elevation gain 1500 feet
Hikable late June through October
One day; *no fires*

Map: Green Trails No. 14 Mt.
    Shuksan
Current information: Ask at
    Glacier Public Service Center
    about trail Nos. 673 and 673A

The views up and down the Nooksack River are tremendous. The looks at the ice hanging on the north face of Mt. Shuksan—the West Nooksack Glacier, the Price Glacier, and a lot of little nameless chunks—are stupendous. The viewpoint described here was the site of a fire-lookout cabin removed in the early 1960s. Sometimes the trail is hikable to the site in April and May. The trail continues 3 more miles to heather fields, blueberry patches, and camps at the 6000-foot level. The views are at least half again better.

Drive Highway 542 east from the Glacier Public Service Center 13 miles. Just before the Nooksack River bridge, go left on road No. 32. At 1.3 miles from the highway stay left and at 2.5 miles find Goat Mountain trail No. 673, elevation 2500 feet. Park either just before or after the trail sign.

Presumably the trail was built by miners with tongues hanging out to lap up the pot of gold. The steeper the trail the quicker the riches, that was the philosophy. At approximately 2 miles the trail briefly flattens, then switchbacks, and about ¼ mile beyond enters the Mount Baker Wilderness and comes to a junction. The main trail proceeds onward and upward 3 miles, as already noted. An unmarked and unmaintained trail turns off right and contours ½ mile to the rocky knoll where the lookout cabin was perched. In addition to valley and

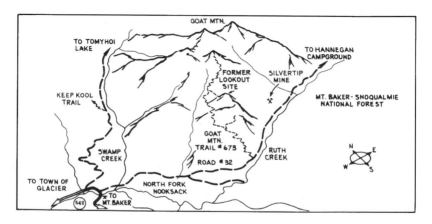

Mount Shuksan from old lookout site on Goat Mountain

glacier views, the highway to Baker Lodge can be seen, the roofs of the recreation area buildings, and all the cars going to and fro, up and down.

Most hikers are content to stop here; the views are superb, though they do get better up higher, where there also are flower fields and blueberries. Passable campsites.

Looking north from side of Hannegan Peak

NOOKSACK RIVER
Mount Baker Wilderness

12 HANNEGAN PASS AND PEAK

**Round trip to Hannegan Pass
  8 miles**
Hiking time 6 hours
High point 5066 feet
Elevation gain 2000 feet

**Round trip to Hannegan Peak
  9½ miles**
Hiking time 8 hours
High point 6186 feet
Elevation gain 3100 feet

**Hikable mid-July through
  September**
One day or backpack
**Map: Green Trails No. 14 Mt.
  Shuksan**
**Current information: Ask at
  Glacier Public Service Center
  about trail No. 674**

The classic entry to the Chilliwack and Picket section of the North Cascades National Park begins in a delightful valley dominated by the white serenity of Ruth Mountain and concludes in a relaxed wander to a meadow summit offering a panorama of the north wall of Shuksan, the Pickets, and wildness high and low.

Drive Highway 542 east from Glacier Public Service Center 13 miles to the Nooksack River bridge. Just before the bridge turn left on Nooksack River road No. 32. In 1.3 miles take the left fork, Ruth Creek road No. 32, and continue 5.4 miles to road-end at Hannegan Campground, elevation 3100 feet.

The trail enters the Mount Baker Wilderness and for the first mile ascends gently through trees and avalanche-path greenery near Ruth Creek, with looks upward to the waterfall-streaked cliffs and pocket icefields of Mt. Sefrit and Nooksack (Ruth) Ridge. At a bit more than 1 mile the snow dome of Ruth Mountain comes into sight—a startling expanse of whiteness for so small a peak. Now the path steepens, climbing above the valley floor.

Rest stops grow long, there is so much to see. At 3½ miles, 4600 feet, the trail swings to the forest edge beside a meadow-babbling creek; across the creek is a parkland of heather benches and alpine trees. Splendid campsites, the best on the route. No fires here. (*Note:* Due to bear problems camping is temporarily prohibited within 1 mile of the pass. If this is the case during your visit, proceed 1½ miles into the park to Boundary Camp, where a Park Service camping permit is required.) The final ½ mile switchbacks in forest to Hannegan Pass, 5066 feet.

Views from the pass are so restricted by trees that hikers wishing a climactic vista must take a little sidetrip. Visitors usually are drawn southward and upward on the climbers' track toward Ruth Mountain, a path to lovely meadows and broader views but before long dwindling to nothing, tempting the unwary onto steep and dangerous snow. Leave Ruth to the climbers. There's a better and safer sidetrip.

From the pass, follow the Hannegan Peak trail ¾ mile up open forest, emerging into a steep, lush meadow, break through a screen of trees to heather and flowers, and wander wide-eyed up the crest of a rounded ridge to the summit plateau of Hannegan Peak, 6186 feet. Roam the meadow flats, looking down into valley forests of Ruth and Silesia Creeks and Chilliwack River, looking out to glaciers and cliffs of Baker, Shuksan, Ruth, Triumph, Challenger, Redoubt, Slesse, and dozens of other grand peaks.

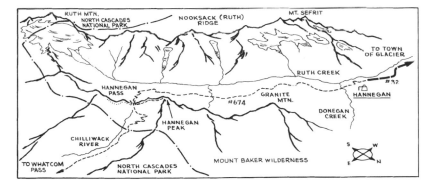

13 COPPER MOUNTAIN

**Round trip to Copper Mountain
Lookout 20 miles
Allow 2–3 days
High point 6260 feet
Elevation gain about 4500 feet in,
1100 feet out
Hikable August through September**

**Maps: Green Trails No. 14 Mt.
Shuksan, No. 15 Mt. Challenger
Current information: Ask at
Glacier Public Service Center
Park Service backcountry use
permit required for camping**

A remote meadow ridge on the west edge of the North Cascades National Park, offering a rare combination of easy-walking terrain and panoramas of rough-and-cold wilderness. Views across far-below forests of the Chilliwack River to the Picket Range—and views west to other superb peaks and valleys. However, hikers planning a visit should be aware of restrictions on use of the area. Due to a water shortage, the Park Service currently permits use of only eleven campsites on the entire 6-mile length of the ridge. Hikers who plan trips for midweek generally have no trouble obtaining a site. No fires allowed anywhere; carry a stove.

Drive to Hannegan Campground and hike 4 miles, gaining 2000 feet, to Hannegan Pass (Hike 12). Descend forest switchbacks into avalanche-swept headwaters of the Chilliwack River, then sidehill along talus and stream outwash patched with grass and flowers. Note chunks of volcanic breccia in the debris and look up to their source in colorful cliffs—remnants of ancient volcanoes.

At 1 mile and 650 feet below Hannegan Pass is a 4400-foot junction and a nice riverside campsite, Boundary Camp. The Chilliwack River trail goes right, descending. Take the Copper Mountain trail left and up, entering forest and climbing steadily, switchbacking some, crossing the upper portion of Hells Gorge (sliced in volcanic rocks), and emerging into parkland.

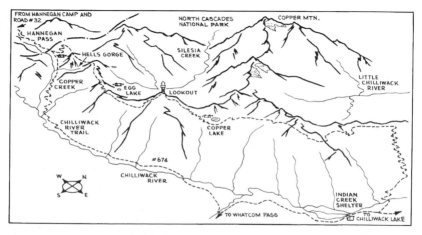

At 7 miles the trail attains the 5500-foot ridge crest between Silesia Creek and the Chilliwack River. A memorable look back to Hannegan Pass, Ruth Mountain, and Shuksan—and the beginning of miles of constant views.

The trail continues along the open crest, up a bit and down a bit, then climbs around a knob to a wide, grassy swale at 8 miles. Some 300 feet and a few minutes below the swale is little Egg Lake, 5200 feet, set in rocks and flowers. Three legal campsites are at the lake; two others are on Knob 5689 and at Silesia Camp.

The way goes up and down another knob to a broad meadow at 9 miles. Now comes the final mile, gaining 1100 feet to 6260-foot Copper Mountain Lookout, the climax. Beyond the green deeps of Silesia Creek are the Border Peaks and the incredible fang of Slesse—and far-off in haze, ice giants of the British Columbia Coast Range. Look down and down to the white thread of the Chilliwack River and beyond its forest valley to Redoubt and Bear and Indian and the magnificent Pickets. Also see Shuksan and Baker. And more peaks and streams, an infinity of wildland.

Beyond the lookout the trail descends about 1½ miles to the three campsites at 5200-foot Copper Lake (blue waters under steep cliffs), then traverses and descends about 7 more miles. Views much of the way. (The trail is in poor shape but scheduled to be rebuilt in 1998.) At 2300 feet is the Chilliwack River trail, 15 miles from Hannegan Pass. A 34-mile loop trip using this return route adds low-valley forests to the high-ridge wander.

For another exploration leave the trail before the steep descent to Copper Lake and investigate ridges and basins toward the 7142-foot summit of Copper Mountain.

Ruth Mountain, left, *and Mount Shuksan,* center, *from Copper Ridge*

14   EASY RIDGE

Round trip 27 miles
Allow 3 days
High point 6100 feet
Elevation gain 5500 feet in,
   2400 feet out
Hikable late July through
   September

Maps: Green Trails No. 14 Mt.
   Shuksan, No. 15 Mt. Challenger
Current information: Ask at
   Glacier Public Service Center
Park Service backcountry use
   permit required for camping

A not-so-easy trail to a high green ridge surrounded by rugged and icy peaks. Wander to an old lookout site amid picturesque alpine trees, fields of flowers, and small tarns, admiring the Chilliwack wilderness of the North Cascades National Park. The difficulty of the trip is compensated for by the privacy—and the views. For some unknown reason the Park Service does not admit the existence of this trail but does maintain it.

Drive to Hannegan Campground and hike 4 miles, gaining 2000 feet, to Hannegan Pass (Hike 12). Descend the Chilliwack River trail, dropping 2300 feet in 5½ miles. At 9½ miles, elevation 2800 feet, is the unmarked but easy-to-see Easy Ridge trail junction. Go right a few feet to the Chilliwack River. Except perhaps in late summer, the river is too deep, swift, and cold to ford. Some years a log can be found within ¼ mile, upstream or down. Give preference to searching upstream, since on the far side the trail parallels the river about ¼ mile before heading uphill along Easy Creek. A good plan is to camp the first night at Copper Creek Camp.

The trail was built to a Forest Service fire-lookout cabin, long since demolished. The Park Service maintains the tread for "resource protection," a college-educated term meaning the fallen trees are cut out and

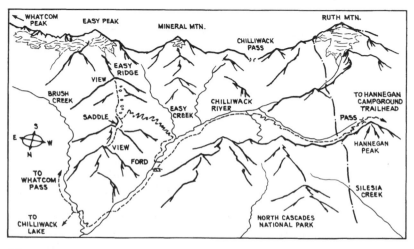

Whatcom Peak and a small tarn on side of Easy Ridge

water drained off. That's good enough, brush being no problem. The hillside forest is entirely dry so fill canteens at the bottom. Or use the old Boy Scout trick of sucking a prune pit.

The trail switchbacks steeply 2½ miles, gaining 2600 feet, to the first views at a 5200-foot saddle in Easy Ridge. From the saddle the trail continues north ½ mile to the old lookout site on a 5640-foot knoll overlooking the junction of Brush Creek and the Chilliwack River; great looks down into valleys, across to the pleasant ridge of Copper Mountain, and off to rough, white peaks. For the broadest views leave the trail at the saddle and walk the main ridge south, climbing open slopes, past a number of tarns, to a heather-covered knoll at 6100 feet. A tiny pool here, good for cold drinks while looking at Shuksan and Icy Peak west, Canadian peaks north, Redoubt northeast, Whatcom Peak close by to the east, and mountains and valleys beyond number. Wonderful camps near the small tarns. Camp only on bare ground or snow. No fires.

The route to the 6613-foot summit of Easy Peak may be blocked by a steep snow slope—do not try it without an ice ax and knowledge of self-arrest technique. The view from the top isn't much better than from the heather knoll.

NOOKSACK RIVER
North Cascades National Park

15 WHATCOM PASS

Round trip 34 miles
Allow 3–5 days
High point 5200 feet
Elevation gain 5700 feet in,
2600 feet out

Hikable late July through
September

Maps: Green Trails No. 14 Mt.
Shuksan, No. 15 Mt. Challenger
Current information: Ask at
Glacier Public Service Center
Park Service backcountry use
permit required for camping

A long hike on an old miners'
route to the Caribou goldfields in
Canada, entering the heart of the
most spectacular wilderness remaining in the contiguous forty-eight
states. Virgin forests in a U-shaped valley carved by ancient glaciers;
rushing rivers; mountain meadows; and a sidetrip to lovely Tapto Lakes,
a blend of gentle beauty and rough grandeur. Whatcom Pass is the high
point on the walk across the North Cascades National Park from the Mt.
Baker region to Ross Lake, a classic of North American wildlands.

Drive to Hannegan Campground and hike 4 miles, gaining 2000 feet,
to Hannegan Pass (Hike 12). Descend the Chilliwack River trail, which
drops rapidly at first and then gentles out in delightful forest, reaching
U.S. Cabin Camp at 10 miles.

At about 11 miles, elevation 2468 feet (2600 feet down from Hannegan
Pass), the trail crosses the Chilliwack River on a cablecar and climbs
moderately to the crossing of Brush Creek at about 12 miles. Here is a
junction.

The Chilliwack trail goes north 9 miles to the Canadian border and
about 1 mile beyond to Chilliwack Lake. The forest walk to the border
is worthy in its own right; parties visiting the region during early summer when the high country is full of snow may prefer pleasures of the
low, green world. (See note on border crossing in Hike 100, Pacific Crest
Trail.)

From the 2600-foot junction the Brush Creek trail climbs steadily,
gaining 2600 feet in the 5 miles to Whatcom Pass. At 13 miles is
Graybeal Camp (hikers and horses), at 16½ miles the two excellent
sites of Whatcom Camp (no fires), and at 17 miles 5200-foot Whatcom
Pass (no camping).

Views from the meadowy pass are superb but there is vastly more to
see. First, ramble the easy ridge south of the pass to a knoll overlooking the boggling gleam of Challenger Glacier. Tapto Lakes are next.

Mount Challenger from Whatcom Pass

alpine forest. When the hillside levels off continue left in meadows to rocky ground above the lakes. Enjoy the waters and flowers, the stupendous view of Challenger.

In addition to the on-trail camps, cross-country camping (no fires) is permitted at Tapto Lakes and on Whatcom Arm. The "across the National Park" hike from Hannegan Campground to Big Beaver Landing on Ross Lake covers 38½ up-and-down miles on easy trail beside wild rivers, through gorgeous forests, over three passes. Total elevation gain on the way is 5400 feet. To have time for sidetrips, a party should allow 7–9 days. From Whatcom Pass drop abruptly (fifty-six switchbacks!) into headwaters of Little Beaver Creek, an enchanting place where waterfalls tumble from cliffs all around. Camping here at Twin Rocks Camp, 3000 feet. At 6 miles from Whatcom Pass is Stillwell Camp and the 2400-foot junction with the Beaver Pass trail. To conclude the cross-park journey, see Hike 33, Cascade Pass—Sahale Arm.

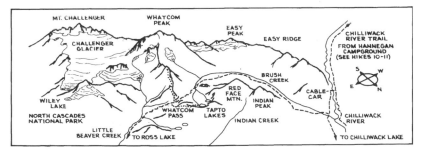

16   LAKE ANN

Round trip 8 miles
Hiking time 6–8 hours
High point (at the saddle) 4800 feet
Elevation gain about 1000 feet in,
   1000 feet out
Hikable August through September

One day or backpack; *no fires*
Map: Green Trails No. 14 Mt.
   Shuksan
Current information: Ask at
   Glacier Public Service Center
   about trail No. 600

When North Cascades climbers and hikers compare memories of favorite sitting-and-looking places, Lake Ann always gets fond mention. The Mt. Shuksan seen from here is quite different from the world-famous roadside view, yet the 4500-foot rise of glaciers and cliffs is at least as grand. And there is plenty to do. However, if taking the trip on a weekend, make it a day hike—you'll be hard-pressed to find an empty campsite.

Drive Highway 542 to the Mt. Baker ski area. Continue on paved road about 1.5 miles upward to the parking lot at Austin Pass, elevation 4700 feet. Until August, snow usually blocks the road somewhere along the way, adding ½ mile or so of walking.

The trail begins by dropping 600 feet into a delightful headwater basin of Swift Creek. Brooks meander in grass and flowers. Marmots whistle from boulder-top perches. Pleasant picnicking.

From the basin the trail descends a bit more and traverses forest, swinging around the upper drainage of Swift Creek. At 2¼ miles, after a loss of 800 feet, reach the lowest elevation (3900 feet) of the trip, an attractive camp in meadows by a rushing stream, and a junction with the Swift Creek trail. If camping beyond here, carry a stove; the era of building fires at and near the lake is long past.

Continuing left at the junction, now starts a 900-foot ascent in 1½ miles, first in heather and clumps of Christmas trees, then over a granite rockslide into forest under a cliff, to a cold and open little valley. If the way is snow-covered, as it may be until mid-August, plod onward and upward to the obvious 4800-foot saddle and another ½ mile

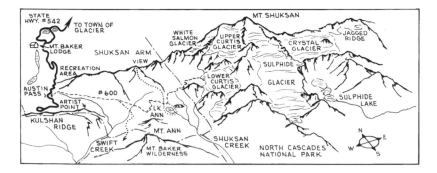

Curtis Glacier and Mount Shuksan from Lake Ann

to Lake Ann. When whiteness melts away, the waterfalls and moraines and flowers and ice-plucked buttresses of the little valley demand a slow pace.

What to do next? First off, sit and watch the living wall of Shuksan. Then, perhaps, circumnavigate the lake, noting the contact between granitic rocks and complex metamorphics. In September, blueberry upward on the ridge of Mt. Ann. If time allows, go on longer wanders.

Recommended Wander No. 1. Follow the trail from Lake Ann as it dips into the headwater basin of Shuksan Creek, then switchbacks up and up toward Shuksan. At a rocky gully a climbers' track branches steeply to the left. Just here the main trail may be non-existent for a few yards; if so, scramble across gravel to regain the tread. Continue to a promontory a stone's throw from the snout of the Lower Curtis Glacier. Look up to the mountain. Look down forests to Baker Lake. Look beyond Swift Creek to the stupendous whiteness of Mt. Baker.

Recommended Wander No. 2. From the Lake Ann saddle, climb the heathery spur to Shuksan Arm, with spectacular campsites (snowbanks for water) and views of both Baker and Shuksan.

17 CHAIN LAKES LOOP

Round trip to Iceberg Lake 5 miles
Hiking time 4 hours
High point 5200 feet
Elevation gain 100 feet in,
700 feet out
Loop trip 9 miles
Hiking time 5 hours
High point 5400 feet
Elevation gain 1600 feet

Hikable late July through October
One day; *no fires*
Map: Green Trails No. 14 Mt.
Shuksan
Current information: Ask at
Glacier Public Service Center
about trail No. 682

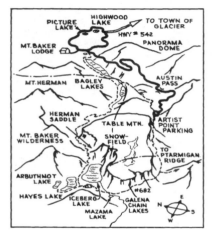

Alpine meadows loaded with blueberries (in season), a half-dozen small lakes, and at every turn of the trail a changing view, dominated by "the magnificent pair," the white volcano of Mt. Baker and the massive architecture of Mt. Shuksan. The area is a wildlife sanctuary, so deer and goat are frequently seen. All this on an easy hike circling the base of a high plateau guarded on every side by impressive lava cliffs.

Drive Highway 542 to closed-in-summer Mt. Baker Lodge (Heather Meadows Recreation Area). Continue 3 miles upward to the 5100-foot road-end at the Artist Point parking area. The winter snowpack here is often 25 feet deep on the level, with much greater depths in drifts, so the road commonly is snowbound until late August. Drive as far as possible and walk the rest of the way.

In the parking lot find the Table Mountain–Chain Lakes trailhead in the middle of the west side. In a few feet go left. Do not make the mistake of going uphill, toward Table Mountain—unless, of course, that's where you *want* to go. The Table Mountain trail climbs 500 feet through lava cliffs to grand views atop the plateau; the walk is easy to here but steep snow banks make the route so difficult that the summit traverse is not recommended.

The Chain Lakes trail traverses almost on the level a scant 1 mile around the south side of Table Mountain to a saddle between Table Mountain and Ptarmigan Ridge. At the junction here take the right fork, dropping 700 feet to the first of the four Chain Lakes, tiny Mazama Lake, reached about 1¾ miles from the road. A bit beyond is aptly named Iceberg Lake, which many years never melts out completely. Halfway around the shore on the left, a sidetrail follows the

Mount Baker reflected in Iceberg Lake

Hayes Lake shore and crosses a low rise to Arbuthnot Lake. Camp at designated sites marked by posts.

The main trail now begins a 600-foot climb to 5400-foot Herman Saddle, attained at about 3 miles. Cliffs of the narrow slot frame Baker west, Shuksan east. Spend some time sitting and looking from one to the other. Then descend amid boulders, heather, and waterfalls, dropping 1100 feet to meadow-surrounded Bagley Lakes. Pause to wander flower fields of the inlet stream. Look for skiers on the north side of Table Mountain; diehards ski the permanent snowfields all summer and fall, until winter sends them to other slopes.

Between the Bagley Lakes find a stone bridge and trail climbing to the Austin Pass Warming Hut and the Artist Point parking area, gaining 900 feet in 2 miles. If transportation can be arranged (by use of two cars or a helpful friend), this final ascent from Bagley Lakes can be eliminated.

18 PTARMIGAN RIDGE

**Round trip to Camp Kiser about
8 miles**
Hiking time 6–8 hours
High point 6200 feet
**Elevation gain 1400 feet in,
600 feet out**
**Hikable mid-August through
September**

One day or backpack; *no fires*
**Map: Green Trails No. 14 Mt.
Shuksan**
**Current information: Ask at
Glacier Public Service Center
about trail No. 683**

Begin in meadows, climb a bit to the snowy and rocky crest of a ridge open to the sky, and wander for miles on the high line toward the lofty white mass of Mt. Baker. From a distance this trail appears to traverse a desolate pile of rocks, but when the snow is gone even the first rocky basin holds spectacular pockets of alpine flowers. Hidden from distant view are lush meadows, rock piles teeming with conies, and green slopes loud with whistling marmots. End the hike either at the informal area known as Camp Kiser or at an ice-bound unnamed lake. This hike has no single destination; a party may go a short way until stopped by snow or continue a long way to close-up views of the splendid Rainbow Glacier or accept the invitation of sidetrips. Everything is purely delightful.

But a note of warning: Ptarmigan Ridge is basically "climbers' country." Parts of this trail are snowbound until late August and some years the trail never melts out. *Do not attempt—do not even think about*—crossing a steep snowpatch. Turn back and try another year. In late summer of light-snowfall years, in good weather, hikers can venture into the wild and lonesome highland, but even then they must be

Cony drying winter food

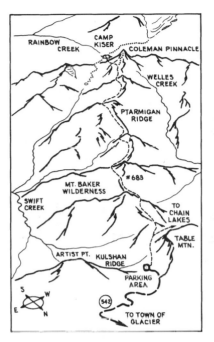

Mount Baker from Camp Kiser

well equipped and experienced. In fog, even skilled alpine navigators get confused; spur ridges may be mistaken for the main ridge and lead a party far astray.

Drive to the large Artist Point parking area, elevation 5100 feet, and hike the Chain Lakes trail 1 fairly level mile (Hike 17) to the Ptarmigan Ridge trail No. 683 junction, elevation 5200 feet.

At the junction go straight ahead on the Ptarmigan Ridge trail, dropping 200 feet into a basin that appears to be a moonscape of rock and snow. However, in mid-August there are bright patches of yellow and pink mimulus (monkeyflower) and bright green mosses. In the middle of the basin the trail splits. Go either way. Climb in volcanic rubble to the ridge line, the beginning of Ptarmigan Ridge. The trail improves, ascending into greenery. Traverse the south side of a very steep hillside; the trail has a neat fence of vegetation that gives a false sense of security, but a misstep could be extremely serious.

The farther one goes the greater the views as the trail traverses flower-covered hillsides and rockslides. At 3½ miles is a 5900-foot vista of the Rainbow Glacier, flowing from the top of Mt. Baker. A great place to break out the root beer and crackers, contemplate life, and swat flies.

From here the choice is between climbing another 300 feet in ½ mile to Camp Kiser or descending 300 feet in ½ mile to the gray-greenish, cold-looking "14-Goat Lake," only recently emerged from the Ice Age. The name (unofficial) was given by hikers who watched a band of mountain goats (fourteen of them) feeding there.

Elbow Lake

ELBOW LAKE

Round trip from road No. 38
    7½ miles
Hiking time 4 hours
High point 3600 feet
Elevation gain 1500 feet
Hikable mid-July through October

One day or backpack
Map: Green Trails No. 45 Hamilton
Current information: Ask at Mount
    Baker Ranger Station about
    trail No. 697

Three (well, really two-and-a-half) forest-ringed lakes in a narrow cleft of Sister Divide. Come alone and you'll find peace and quiet. There are two approaches: a 10-mile (round-trip) trail from the south and a 7½-mile (also round-trip) trail from the north. Both are interesting and worthwhile.

For the northern approach, drive Highway 542 and just short of milepost 17, at the hamlet of Welcome, turn right 5 miles on Mosquito Lake road. At Porter Creek, go left on road No. 38 for another 11.4 miles to trail No. 697, elevation 2100 feet.

Begin by descending to the river. Cross on a horse bridge, skirt a swampy area, and start a steady ascent along Green Creek. At 2 miles, in a grove of Alaska cedar, a view briefly opens up the valley to the reddish rock of Twin Sisters and Skookum Peak. Back in deep woods, the way parallels Hildebrand Creek, which goes dry in late summer.

At 3 miles, 3350 feet, cross Hildebrand Pass and small, marshy Lake (half a lake) Hildebrand. Continue ½ mile to much larger Elbow Lake, 3400 feet, with several small but comfortable campsites. From the far shore climb a small rise to Lake Doreen, boxed in by steep hillsides that make camping torturous.

For the southern approach, drive Highway 20 16.5 miles from Sedro Woolley and go left 12 miles to the national forest boundary. From there drive another 0.2 mile and go left on road No. 12, signed for Nooksack River and Mt. Baker National Recreation Area. In 14 miles go left 0.2 mile to Pioneer Camp and the Elbow Lake trailhead, elevation 2200 feet.

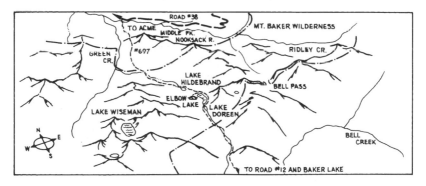

CATHEDRAL PASS

Round trip 19½ miles
Hiking time 8 hours
High point 4962 feet
Elevation gain 2900 feet in,
** 400 feet out**
One day or backpack
Loop trip 25 miles
Allow 2–3 days
High point 4962 feet
Elevation gain 5400 feet

Hikable mid-July through October
Map: Green Trails No. 45 Hamilton
Current information: Ask at Mount
** Baker Ranger Station about**
** trail Nos. 603, 690, and 697**

A little-used trail skims ridges and roams meadows to touch the very edge of the mighty glaciers on the south side of Mt. Baker. Why so little use? Because there's a much shorter approach via Schreibers Meadow (Hike 21, Park Butte—Railroad Grade). But why be in such a rush all the time? Half the fun of a hike is the getting there. The longer the trail, the more the fun. However, don't do this one until July 1; before that the entire upper valley of the South Fork Nooksack River is restricted, and the road gated, to let cow elks drop their calves undisturbed.

Drive the Baker Lake–Grandy Lake road and turn left on the Loomis-Nooksack road No. 12 (Hike 21). In 3.5 miles pass the Schreibers Meadow road but stay on road No. 12. At 14 miles go left 0.2 mile to the trailhead at Pioneer Camp, elevation 2200 feet (14.2 miles from the Baker Lake road).

Switchbacks ascend 3¾ miles to the beginning of the Bell Pass trail No. 603. Go right, leveling somewhat. At 6 miles cross the Sister Divide from the south to the north side at Bell Pass, 3964 feet, and enter Mount Baker Wilderness. Views extend west to the Twin Sisters Range, north over the chainsaw massacre of the Middle Fork Nooksack River, and east to the gigantic dazzlement of Mt. Baker.

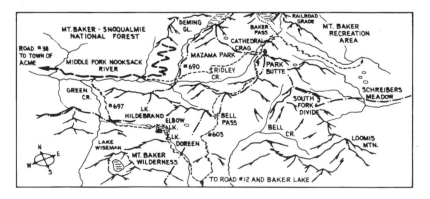

Mount Baker from Cathedral Pass trail

At 7 miles overlook Ridley Creek, then drop 400 feet to traverse beneath massive cliffs on the north side of Park Butte Lookout and into the beautiful meadows of Mazama Park. Here is the officially designated camping area for the Park Butte vicinity. At about 9 miles is the junction with Ridley Creek trail No. 690, 4400 feet.

The trail climbs steeply a final ¾ mile, rounding rocky Cathedral Crag and switchbacking to the narrow slot of Cathedral Pass, 4964 feet. A few feet farther the trail joins Railroad Grade (Hike 21), as the lateral moraine of Easton Glacier is called, for climax views of a volcano, a crater (perhaps steaming), and a world solely of snow and ice.

Loopers in the mood for a 25-mile day or backpack can descend Ridley Creek trail No. 690 to a crossing of the Middle Fork Nooksack River (perhaps on a skinny log) another ¼ mile to road No. 38, which in 1.7 miles reaches Elbow Lake trail No. 697 (Hike 19). Follow it over the Sister Divide past Elbow Lake and return to road No. 12 at Pioneer Camp.

21

PARK BUTTE— RAILROAD GRADE

Round trip to Park Butte 7 miles
Hiking time 6–8 hours
High point 5450 feet
Elevation gain 2250 feet
Hikable mid-July through October

One day or backpack; *no fires*
Map: Green Trails No. 45 Hamilton
Current information: Ask at Mount
Baker Ranger Station about
trail No. 603

Recommending any one hike in the parklands of Mt. Baker's southwest flank is like praising a single painting in a museum of masterpieces. There are days of wandering here, exploring meadows and moraines, waterfalls and lakes, listening to marmots and watching for mountain goats. The trail to Morovitz Meadow gives a good sampling of the country, with impressive near views of the glaciers of Baker, the towering Black Buttes (core of an ancient volcano), the Twin Sisters, and far horizons. This is the most popular hike on Baker's southern flanks. On weekends expect to meet hundreds of mountain climbers, hikers in

Mount Baker lost in clouds from Park Butte trail

street shoes and white shirts, little children, and—strangely enough—horses, encouraged by the Forest Service on the crowded trail.

Drive Highway 20 east from Sedro Woolley 14.5 miles and turn left on the Baker Lake–Grandy Lake road. In 12.5 miles, just past Rocky Creek bridge, turn left on Loomis-Nooksack road No. 12, at 3 miles go right on Sulphur Creek road No. 13, and follow it 6 miles to the end in a logging patch. Find the trail west of the road, near Sulphur Creek, elevation 3364 feet.

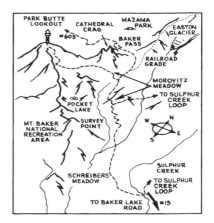

The trail immediately crosses Sulphur Creek into the heather and blueberries (in season) of Schreibers Meadow, passes frog ponds, and enters forest. In 1 mile is an interesting area where meltwater from the Easton Glacier has torn wide avenues through the trees. The drainage pattern changes from time to time; the creek is crossed on a bouncing cable bridge.

Beyond the boulder-and-gravel area the trail enters cool forest and switchbacks steeply a long mile to Lower Morovitz Meadow (*look out for horses*). At the last switchback the Scott Paul Trail (Hike 22) goes straight ahead. The grade gentles in heather fields leading to Upper Morovitz Meadow, 4500 feet.

At the trail junction in the upper meadow, go left to Park Butte, climbing to a ridge and in 1 mile reaching the 5450-foot summit. Views of Mt. Baker glaciers (and much more) are magnificent. Parties with spare time and energy may well be tempted to descend to the delightful basin of Pocket Lake or roam the ridge to 6100-foot Survey Point.

There is another direction to go from Upper Morovitz Meadow. Leave the trail near the junction and ramble upward on "the stairway to Heaven" to the intriguing crest of Railroad Grade, a moraine built by the Easton Glacier in more ambitious days. Look down the unstable wall of gravel and boulders to the naked wasteland below the ice. Walk the narrow crest higher and yet higher, closer and closer to the gleaming volcano. In late summer hikers can scramble moraine rubble and polished slabs to about 7000 feet before being forced to halt at the edge of the glacier.

From either Railroad Grade or Baker Pass, inventive walkers can pick private ways through waterfall-and-flower country to the edge of a startling chasm. Look down to the chaotic front of the Deming Glacier, across to stark walls of the Black Buttes. All through the wide sprawl of Mazama Park are secluded campsites, beauty spots to explore. Don't forget Little Mazama Lake or nearby Meadow Point.

Designated campsites, some among alpine trees, some in open gardens beside snowmelt streams, all are scenic.

69

SCOTT PAUL TRAIL

Round trip to Squak Glacier 7 miles
Hiking time 5 hours
High point 5800 feet
Elevation gain 2400 feet
Loop trip 8 miles
Hiking time 4 hours
High point 5200 feet
Elevation gain 2300 feet

Hikable mid-July through October
One day; *no fires*
Map: Green Trails No. 45 Hamilton
Current information: Ask at Mount Baker Ranger Station about trail No. 603.1

A looping route gives different perspectives on Mt. Baker, vistas of the North Cascades, looks down to the snouts of the Easton and Squak Glaciers, and a wide world of meadows to roam. A one-way trip to the Squak overlook gives a good share of the riches.

At press time this trail was not officially named, but tentatively it is referred to as the "Scott Paul Trail." It was named after the young ranger who nursed the trail through from conception to completion. Scott Paul died in 1993 in a forest-related accident.

Drive to the Schreibers Meadow parking area (Hike 21, Park Butte—Railroad Grade), elevation 3364 feet.

For the one-way trip to the Squak Glacier, follow the Park Butte

Clark's nutcracker

trail about 100 feet and turn right on the quite new Scott Paul Trail, which climbs steadily through forest, gaining 1200 feet in a scant 2½ miles to a 4600-foot saddle and the first views. To the right ¼ mile is a great campsite in view of Baker, Blum, and Shuksan, but no water after the snow is gone. A well-used way trail from the saddle steeply climbs meadows in ever-enlarging views of Mt. Shuksan, the Pickets, and south along the Cascade Range to Mt. Rainier. Directly above is the sharp point of Sherman Peak on the crater rim. The way trail runs out at about 5800 feet and a summit-climbers' route goes onto the Squak Glacier; this is the end of the line for hikers. Sit! Look! It is enough.

The loop is best done clockwise, starting on the Park Butte—Railroad Grade trail.

Mount Shuksan and North Cascades from Scott Paul trail

A short climb past the campsite turnoff, the Scott Paul Trail contours west through meadows, crosses streams to Metcalf Moraine, drops below the snout of the Easton Glacier, crosses Rocky Creek on a suspension bridge, and joins the Park Butte—Railroad Grade trail at the last switchback, closing the loop.

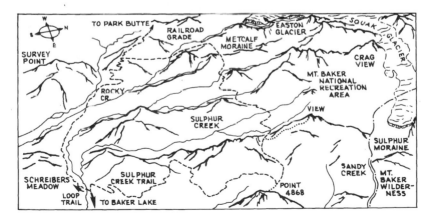

Mount Baker and Boulder Glacier from Boulder Ridge

23 BOULDER RIDGE

Round trip 8 miles
Hiking time 7 hours
High point 4500 feet
Elevation gain 1800 feet
Hikable July through October
One day or backpack

Map: Green Trails No. 46 Lake
 Shannon
Current information: Ask at Mount
 Baker Ranger Station about
 trail No. 605

A rough hike to one of the many alpine ridges radiating octopus-like from the white heap of Mt. Baker. The crest provides a magnificent overlook of the Boulder Glacier. Reconstruction in the next few years will be from the same trailhead, but the trail route will change. The old one is described here.

Drive Highway 20 east from Sedro Woolley 16.5 miles. Turn left on the Baker Lake–Grandy Lake road. At 12 miles enter the national forest and continue another 5.8 miles; 0.2 mile after crossing the Boulder Creek bridge, turn left on Marten Lake road No. 1130. In 2 miles go left on road No. 1131 for 3.5 miles to the road-end and trailhead, elevation 2700 feet.

Trail No. 605 has ups and downs, bogs, and waist-high huckleberry bushes, gaining only 300 feet in 2 miles. Then, ¼ mile after crossing a little stream, the tread vanishes in a small, marshy meadow; no formal trail ever existed beyond here. At the far right-hand end of the meadow is an obscure blaze and the start of a climbers' path angling to the left toward the ridge crest. The track is steep, sometimes among evergreen trees and occasionally through slide alder. Some 500 feet above the meadow the way bursts from timber onto a moraine grown up in knee-high firs and hemlocks.

There is now a choice: an easy ¾-mile hike, the route obvious, to the top of the moraine and a close view of Boulder Glacier, or an ascent of 500 feet in 1 mile to Boulder Ridge.

Weather-exposed but scenic camps are possible on the ridge; plan to cook on a stove; for water look for snowfield dribbles.

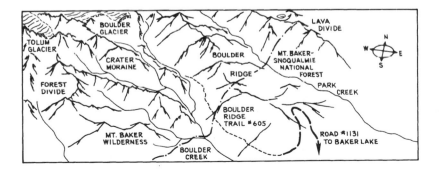

RAINBOW RIDGE

Round trip 4½ miles
Hiking time 3 hours
High point 4800 feet
Elevation gain 1200 feet plus ups and downs
Hikable August through mid-September

One day
Map: Green Trails No. 14 Mt. Shuksan (trail not shown)
Current information: Trail not listed; ask at Mount Baker Ranger Station about road No. 1130

The meadows are simply grand, the looks down to Avalanche Gorge are awesome, and the views of the spectacular south face of Mt. Shuksan across the valley and the crevasses of the Park Glacier close at hand can be a mystical experience. Moreover, the path was built solely by boots, is not maintained, is not shown on maps, and is barely visible on the ground, so the chances of solitude are much better than on the average Mt. Baker trail.

From Highway 20 drive the Baker Lake–Grandy Lake road to 0.2 mile beyond the Boulder Creek bridge. Turn left (Hike 23, Boulder Ridge) on Marten Lake road No. 1130 for 9.4 miles, to the end in a clearcut, elevation 3600 feet. The last 4 miles of this road get limited maintenance. Some years it is passable to the end; other times part must be walked—all the better for soaking in the splendid views.

The boot-built path, easy to lose, weaves around trees and over logs, across a massive blowdown, through huckleberry thickets. If you lose it, don't play guessing games—stop and backtrack to the last spot the trail was definite and try again. The way gains 800 feet in the first mile, to a small meadow with a tantalizing glimpse of Mt. Baker. In the next ¼ mile it gains 250 feet to meadows on the crest of Rainbow Ridge, 4400 feet, and views across the gulf of Swift Creek to the ramparts of Mt. Shuksan.

In fields of heather and alpine blueberries, alternating between views of Mt. Shuksan and Mt. Baker, the trail rides the ups and downs of the ridge crest to a 4800-foot high point. This is a great place to call it quits, to get out the watermelon and the freeze-dried pizza, to gaze a vertical 2000 feet down into Avalanche Gorge, to admire the snout of the Rainbow

Mount Shuksan from Rainbow Ridge

Snout of Rainbow Glacier from Rainbow Ridge

Glacier. The trail fades on the way to the next high point, then vanishes; one suspects the construction hereabouts was less by boots than goat feet.

Camps atop the ridge are sensational, watching the rosy sunset on Shuksan's cliffs and the pink sunrise on Baker's glaciers. However, the only water is from snowbanks, if any. So carry *two* watermelons. Either that or have supper at the car, hike to the ridge in twilight, and return to the car for breakfast. Camp near the trail so that if a low cloud slips in by night you can find the way down. The vicinity of a 2000-foot cliff is no place to be searching for goat tracks in the fog.

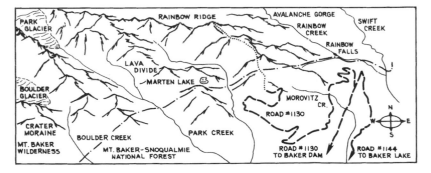

25   SWIFT CREEK

Round trip 4 miles
Hiking time 3 hours
High point 1600 feet
Elevation gain 400 feet in,
   200 feet out
Hikable May through October

One day or backpack
Map: Green Trails No. 14 Mt.
   Shuksan
Current information: Ask at Mount
   Baker Ranger Station about
   trail No. 607

Once upon a time, in days not so olden but that some folks still on the trails don't remember them fondly, the 10-mile trail from Baker Lake to Austin Pass was a major thoroughfare heavily trampled by the Old Rangers, the dirty miners in search of shining gold, and assorted bushwhackers. Nowadays, of course, the parking lot at Austin Pass is generally considered such small satisfaction for walking 10 uphill miles that the route is traveled the whole way mainly by fanatics who take joy in the fact the trail has been, in effect, abandoned by the Forest Service and let go back to nature.

However, the lower stretch of the trail offers so delightful a walk through magnificently virgin forest as to be extremely popular. It would be more so were the Forest Service to courageously confront Rainbow Creek, a raging glacial torrent that changes course every year or two, and do such engineering as would permit the route to dependably cross and proceed into the Mount Baker Wilderness.

From Highway 20 drive Baker Lake–Grandy Lake road 20 miles, to just opposite the entrance to Baker Lake Resort. Turn left on road No. 1144 for 3 miles to Swift Creek trail No. 607, elevation 1400 feet.

The trail drops some 200 feet in ½ mile through marvelous old forest to Rainbow Creek. If a logjam exists, proceed. If not, take a very slow pace back the ½ mile, the more fully to absorb the good juices from the primeval scene; the torrent is much too swift to wade, as is necessary to get to Swift Creek.

On the far side the trail follows within sound of Rainbow Creek, whose mists nourish the moss carpet of the forest floor, and enters Mount Baker Wilderness. After ¼ mile of minor ups and downs, it switchbacks up 300 feet in ½ mile, then levels off and plunges into

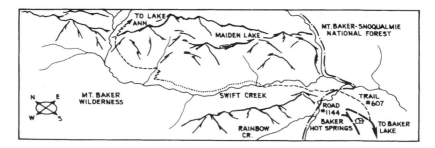

Crossing Rainbow Creek on a logjam

brush as high as a tall hiker's eye. The tread is as easy to find at night as in day; feet have to do it. At 2 miles, 1600 feet, the way touches the bank of Swift Creek. In early summer when the mountain's snow is being flushed back to the oceans to recharge them for the next winter's storms, the "creek" is a raging river. By midsummer, though, it has quieted to a delicious stream of clear, cool water and gravel bars that cry out to be camped on.

Mount Baker from Shannon Ridge

BAKER RIVER
Unprotected area

SHANNON RIDGE

Round trip 6 miles
Hiking time 5 hours
High point 4800 feet
Elevation gain 2300 feet
Hikable July through September
One day

Map: Green Trails No. 14 Mt.
Shuksan (trail not shown)
Current information: Ask at Mount
Baker Ranger Station about
trail No. 742

Heather-covered Shannon Ridge gives the really big picture of Mt. Baker, lofting high above the canyon depths of Swift and Shuksan Creeks, and the champion views across Baker Lake (Reservoir, that is) to glaciers on Hagan Mountain and Mt. Blum. Getting there demands much blood in fly time, a lot of sweat on hot days, and occasionally a fair number of tears.

Drive from Highway 20 on the Baker Lake–Grandy Lake road 23 miles (10.2 miles beyond the national forest boundary) to just opposite Shannon Creek Campground. Turn left on road No. 1152 for 4.5 miles. Go right on road No. (1152)014 another 1.4 miles, to where it becomes impassable, elevation 2500 feet.

Begin on an abandoned logging road overgrown with willows. At about 1 mile this road-trail enters a steep basin (see the meadows high above, keep the faith) and switchbacks twice. At 1½ miles the road ends and trail No. 742 (unsigned) begins, elevation 3200

Heather field near end of trail

feet. The trail climbs a steep, brush-covered clearcut made some 15 years ago and still not reforested, a heritage of the period when the College of Forestry taught that trees could be farmed to timberline.

Then, virgin forest (ain't Nature wonderful?). Alternating between steep and very steep, at about 2½ miles the trail gains the ridge top and with a little down and a lot of ups leaves forest for heather meadows. The recommended turnaround is some 3 miles from the car, at the boundary of the North Cascades National Park, 4700 feet. The views climax here and camping is possible on both sides of the boundary; sites on the inside have the best water and sleeping-bag spreads, but those on the outside don't require any paperwork.

A rude climbers' path leads to a 5400-foot pass directly above. The views there are nothing special and when snow-covered the route is slippery.

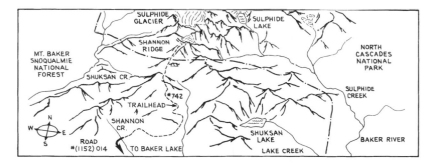

27 LITTLE SHUKSAN LAKE

Round trip 3 miles
Hiking time 5 hours
High point 4500 feet
Elevation gain 1800 feet in,
300 feet out
Hikable mid-July through
September

One day
Map: Green Trails No. 14 Mt.
Shuksan
Current information: Ask at Mount
Baker Ranger Station about
trail No. 608

Be warned, this hike is strictly for agile, experienced hikers. Don't be fooled by the mere 3 miles of the round trip. The boot-beaten path is as steep as a trail can get and not require climbing ropes and pitons. In spots it is nothing but a straight-up scramble route, badly eroded and on the descent wickedly treacherous. The hike to this beauty spot is short; the same can be said for climbing to the top of Seattle's Smith Tower—twice.

Drive from Highway 20 on the Baker Lake–Grandy Lake road 23.2 miles (10.4 miles beyond the national forest boundary). Turn left on road No. 1160, sign-described as "limited maintenance," so you won't be too surprised if there's a rockslide at about 2 miles that a passenger car may refuse to cross—or if you find other slides or slumpouts elsewhere. At a bit more than 4 switchbacking miles, the road makes a final zig to climb around a cliff on a narrow roadbed blasted from solid rock; the view of Mt. Baker above is spectacular and so is that of Baker Lake, a swandive below. At 4.7 miles the road abruptly ends in a space just big enough for a couple of cars to park and latecomers to turn around or go someplace else. Please don't block that turnaround; backing down this cliffhanger would be no picnic. The road-end is the trailhead, elevation 2900 feet.

Trail No. 608 is unmarked but obvious, starting in a huckleberry-covered clearcut. Sawn logs show that fishermen's boots have occasional help in maintenance. The path quickly enters virgin forest and

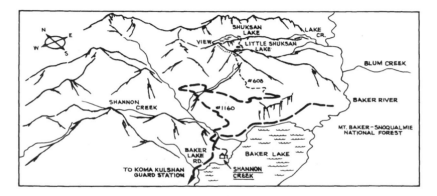

Little Shuksan Lake and Mount Blum

climbs steeply, and more steeply, gaining 1800 feet in a scant mile up a
very steep, very narrow ridge that gives a few views down to Baker
River, 3000 feet below.

At 4500 feet the way tops the ridge and Mt. Shuksan is framed by
foreground trees. The Sulphide Glacier is on the left of the summit
pyramid, Crystal Glacier and Ragged Ridge on the right. For views of
Mt. Baker follow the ridge ¼ mile farther to its highest point, a
heather meadow.

The trail drops 300 feet to Little Shuksan Lake, 4200 feet. The
fishermen's trail continues down to 3800-foot Shuksan Lake, with fish
(it darn well better have *something*) but few views.

The "Little" is ringed by clumps of trees, fields of heather, and acres
of blueberries. Though shallow, the lake has interesting bays and a
picturesque island. Campsites are numerous. By midsummer the outlet dries up and the water warms up (enough for swimming).

28 BAKER RIVER

Round trip to Sulphide Creek
  6 miles
Hiking time 3–4 hours
High point 900 feet
Elevation gain 200 feet
Hikable March through November
One day or backpack

Map: Green Trails No. 14 Mt.
  Shuksan
Current information: Ask at Mount
  Baker Ranger Station about
  trail No. 606
Park Service backcountry use
  permit required for camping

Luxurious rain forest, a lovely milky-green river, and tantalizing glimpses of glacier-covered peaks. Because of the very low elevation (and such low-altitude virgin valleys are now rare indeed in the Cascades), the trail is open except in midwinter and offers a delightful wildland walk when higher elevations are buried in snow. Even bad weather is no barrier to enjoyment, not with all the big trees, understory plants, and streams. For true lonesomeness, try the trip on a rainy day in early spring. It's also a good place to escape guns during hunting season, since the no-shooting North Cascades National Park is entered partway along.

Drive from Highway 20 on the Baker Lake–Grandy Lake road to the national forest boundary and 18 miles more to the road end; go left on road No. 1168 another 0.5 mile, to the start of Upper Baker trail No. 606, elevation 760 feet.

The first ¼ mile lies on and near old logging roads, then civilization is left behind. In ½ mile is the first view—up and up the far side of the river to glaciers of 7660-foot Mt. Blum. At 1 mile the trail climbs a few feet above the river, a beautiful sight, and drops again to go by large beaver ponds. In 2 miles, about where the national park is entered, see Easy Ridge at the valley head, and a little farther on, the sharp outline of 7574-foot Whatcom Peak, northern outpost of the

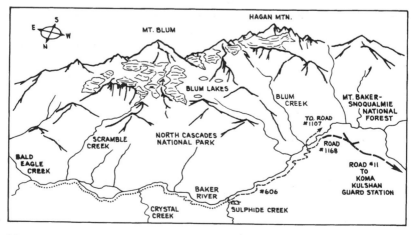

Pickets. In a scant 3 miles the way reaches raging Sulphide Creek, dominated by Jagged Ridge and its small glaciers. Partly hidden by trees is the huge expanse of the Sulphide Glacier on the south side of Mt. Shuksan.

If Sulphide Creek is high and a bridge is lacking, this is far enough for most hikers. The camp has four sites, elevation 900 feet.

The trail continues, sort of, 2 miles to Crystal Creek and once went 3 more miles to Bald Eagle Creek, 1100 feet. The upper section is now lost in brush and the best route beyond Crystal Creek is on gravel bars of the river.

Baker River

COW HEAVEN

Round trip 11 miles
Hiking time 8 hours
High point 4400 feet
Elevation gain 4000 feet
Hikable July through October
One day

Map: Green Trails No. 47
   Marblemount
Current information: Ask at Mount
   Baker Ranger Station about
   trail No. 763

Years ago, Skagit ranchers chased cows way up here to chew the alpine salads. Now only the occasional horse gobbles the flowers, so it's a heaven for hikers, with views from the Skagit Valley to the Pickets, Eldorado, Whitehorse, and countless peaks between. But the route to heaven lies through purgatory—gaining 4000 feet in 5½ miles. Moreover, from August onward a water shortage just about forces the trip to be done in a single grueling day, though in early summer snowmelt permits camping.

Drive Highway 20 to Marblemount. At the town edge turn north 0.7 mile to the North Cascades National Park ranger station. Inquire at the wilderness information center regarding where to park. The park personnel have easy access to the trail, but the public must walk the road by a barn and small house, ignoring sideroads and "No Trespassing" signs; these refer to cars—there is a legal easement to walk the road. The road climbs a bit, passes a large house with vicious-sounding but seemingly friendly dogs, a small creek, another building, and continues on the now-abandoned road. At ⅓ mile near Olson Creek spot the well-signed trailhead, elevation a meager, low-down 400 feet.

Queen's cup

The route is signed "Helen Buttes Trail 763, 4 miles." Don't believe it—the best views are at least 5½ miles. Eager to get the job done, the path wastes no time flirting but starts steep and stays steep. The initial 2 miles are in fine shape, the tread wide and edged by soft moss, cooled by deep shadows of virgin forest. A creek is crossed at 1 mile and recrossed at 1½ miles, the last for-sure water. At about 2½ miles the tread dips into a shallow ravine and for the next ½ mile often is gullied to naught. Just beyond 3 miles the way passes above an all-summer (usually) stream. Tall trees yield to short ones and at 4 miles to a dense tangle of mountain ash, white rhododendron, and huckleberry. At

Skagit Valley from Cow Heaven; Whitehorse Mountain in distance

4¼ miles, about 3600 feet, a brief flat with bits of heather invites camping but provides no lake, pond, river, creek, dribble, or spring for water purposes, only a snowfield that may last into July.

Maintained trail ends here, but a sketchy path, beaten out mainly by hunters, heads over the knoll on the skyline, climbing to the 4400-foot viewpoint. If aggrieved leg muscles and swollen tongue permit, continue up the alpine ridge to steadily broader views.

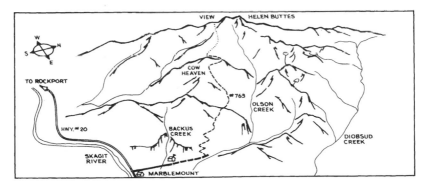

30 LOOKOUT MOUNTAIN— MONOGRAM LAKE

Round trip to Lookout Mountain
8½ miles
Hiking time 9 hours
High point 5699 feet
Elevation gain 4500 feet

Round trip to Monogram Lake
7½ miles
Hiking time 9 hours
High point 5400 feet
Elevation gain 4200 feet in,
550 feet out

Hikable mid-July through October
One day or backpack
Map: Green Trails No. 47
Marblemount
Current information: Ask at
Marblemount Ranger Station
Park Service backcountry use
permit required for camping
in park

Take your pick: a fire lookout with a commanding view of North Cascades peaks and valleys, or a cirque lake, a fine basecamp for roaming, nestled in the side of a heather-covered ridge.

Drive Highway 20 to Marblemount and continue east 7.3 miles on the Cascade River road to the trailhead between Lookout and Monogram Creeks, elevation 1257 feet.

The trail climbs steeply in a series of short switchbacks along the spine of the forested ridge between the two creeks, gaining 2400 feet in the 2½ miles to a campsite at the first dependable water, a branch of Lookout Creek at 3600 feet. At 2¾ miles is a junction, elevation 4100 feet.

Lookout Mountain. Go left from the junction, shortly emerging into meadow and switchbacking relentlessly upward. The tread here may be hard to find and difficult to walk. In 1½ miles from the junction, gaining 1500 feet, the 5699-foot summit is attained.

Flowers all around—and views. Look north and west to the Skagit River valley, southeast and below to the Cascade River. Mountains everywhere, dominated by giant Eldorado Peak. About ¼ mile below the summit, in a small flat, is a spring that runs most of the summer. Magnificent camps here for enjoyment of the scenery in sunset and dawn—but disaster camps in a storm.

Monogram Lake. Traverse right from the junction on a steep, lightly timbered hillside. The trail leaves trees for meadow and in a mile crosses a creek, climbs to a 5400-foot crest with broad views, and descends to 4873-foot Monogram Lake, usually snowbound through July. Designated no-fire campsites around the meadow shores.

The lake is a superb base for wanderings. For one, climb open slopes to the southeast and then follow the ridge northerly to a 5685-foot knoll looking down into Marble Creek and across to the splendor of 8868-foot Eldorado—a closer and even better view of the peak than that from Lookout Mountain. Continue on the ridge for more flowers, then drop through gardens to the lake. For a more ambitious tour, as-

Lookout Mountain and Eldorado Peak

cend meadows on the southern extension of Teebone Ridge and ramble
to the 6844-foot south summit of Little Devil Peak, with looks down to
small glaciers. Climbers can continue on and on along the rocky-and-
snowy ridge, but hikers must stop when the terrain gets too rough for
party experience.

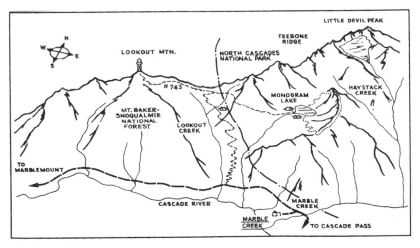

31 HIDDEN LAKE PEAKS

**Round trip to Sibley Creek Pass
6 miles
Hiking time 5 hours
High point 6100 feet
Elevation gain 2700 feet
Hikable mid-July through October**

**Round trip to Hidden Lake
Lookout 8 miles
Hiking time 8 hours
High point 6890 feet
Elevation gain 3500 feet
Hikable August through October**

**One day or backpack
Maps: Green Trails No. 48 Diablo
Dam, No. 80 Cascade Pass
Current information: Ask at Mount
Baker Ranger Station about
trail No. 745
Park Service backcountry use
permit required for camping
at Hidden Lake**

Flower fields, heather meadows, ice-carved rocks, and snow-fed waterfalls on an alpine ridge jutting into an angle of the Cascade River valley, an easy-to-reach viewpoint of North Cascades wilderness from Eldorado through the Ptarmigan Traverse to Dome Peak.

Drive Highway 20 to Marblemount and continue east on the Cascade River road 10 miles (2 miles past the Marble Creek bridge) to Sibley Creek road No. 1540. Turn left 4.7 miles to road-end (the way rough but passable to suitably small and spry cars) in a clearcut, elevation 3600 feet.

Trail No. 745 begins in the brush that 30 years after the logging still doesn't look much like a "renewable resource," entering virgin forest in ¼ mile and switchbacking upward 1 mile. The way then emerges from trees into lush brush and crosses Sibley Creek. (Some years avalanche snow may linger in the creek bottom all summer, in which case look for obvious trail cut through very steep sidehill greenery.) The trail switchbacks up alder clumps and deep grass and flowers to a recrossing of Sibley Creek at 2½ miles, 5200 feet. Note, here, the abrupt transition from metamorphic to granitic rocks, the first supporting richly green herbaceous flora, the other dominated by heather. Just past the crossing is a minimal campsite.

From the second crossing the trail traverses wide-open heather-and-waterfall slopes (several nice good-weather camps), then rounds a corner and climbs. One snow-

Hidden Lake Lookout

Boston Peak and Sahale Peak, center, *and Hidden Lake*

filled gully may be too treacherous for hikers lacking ice axes. If so, don't attempt to cross, but instead go straight uphill to find a safe detour, or turn back and visit Sibley Creek Pass. The trail may be snow-covered at other points but by proceeding straight ahead the tread can be picked up. At 3½ miles is a tiny basin, a lovely non-storm campsite. The abandoned lookout cabin can now be seen atop cliffs. Continue a short way, usually on a gentle snowfield, to the 6600-foot saddle and look down to Hidden Lake and out to a world of wild peaks.

Though it's only ½ mile and 300 feet from the saddle to the broader views of the 6890-foot lookout (maintained by volunteers), parts of the trail may be lost in extremely dangerous snow, suited only for trained climbers. Even without snow the final section of trail is airy.

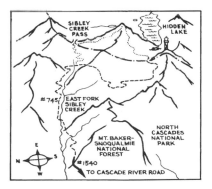

From the saddle an easy walk over loose boulders leads to the 7088-foot highest summit of Hidden Lake Peak. Or descend rough talus to the 5733-foot lake, ordinarily snowbound through most of the summer. Designated no-fire campsites above the lake.

BOSTON BASIN

**Round trip to first high moraine
  7 miles
Hiking time 8 hours
High point 6200 feet
Elevation gain 3000 feet
Hikable July through October
One day or backpack; *no fires***

**Map: Green Trails No. 80 Cascade
  Pass (trail not shown)
Current information: Ask at
  Marblemount Ranger Station
Park Service backcountry use
  permit required for camping**

When Forbidden Peak was included in a book as one of the "50 classic climbs in North America," the meadowlands of Boston Basin were infested by climbers from all over North America lusting for the 50 Peak Pin. Since a normal hiker, finding him-/herself amid a throng of sixty or seventy peakbaggers clicking carabiners, is liable to start screaming, and since the trail is unmaintained and poor, and since the camping is lousy, why go? Well, on a Tuesday or Thursday in late October, when the classicists are back in school, a person might just sneak up to the basin for a day and find the solitude proper for savoring the contrast of yellowing meadows and gray moraines and white glaciers.

Drive Highway 20 to Marblemount. Go straight through town, cross the Skagit River, and follow the Cascade River road 23 miles to the junction with the former (bought by the Park Service) Value Mines sideroad. Parking for six to eight cars, elevation 3200 feet.

Walk 1 steep mile on the abandoned mining road. Just past the fourth switchback the views open up and the old road levels off. Watch carefully now: A few feet farther, near some boulders, is a switchback; for a short bit the way is true trail, then road again. At the end of the road the trail turns steeply up and deteriorates into a very difficult climbers' scramble-path (no wonder it is not on a map) that intersects

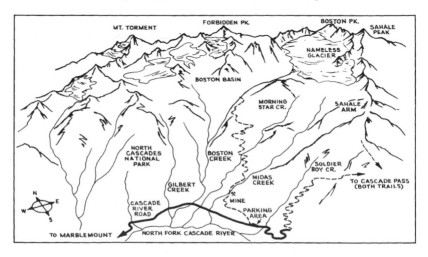

Mount Johannesburg from Boston Basin

an ancient miners' trail. Miners of old did neater work than modern climbers, so things improve. Vintage tread leads through a short bit of woods and then across a ½-mile-wide swath of avalanche greenery, down which tumble Midas Creek and Morning Star Creek. Next come switchbacks in deep forest to a broken-down mine cabin.

About ¼ mile from the cabin ruins the trail emerges from timber and swings around the foot of an open moraine to a raging torrent; boulder-hop across (the best crossing is upstream from where the trail meets the creek) and climb to a viewpoint atop the moraine. Look up to the fearsome cliffs and spires of Forbidden Peak and Mt. Torment, and to the glacier falling from Boston and Sahale Peaks, and across the valley to the mile-high wall of Johannesburg and its fingerlike hanging glaciers.

For one exploration of Boston Basin, traverse and climb westward over moraines and creeks to rich-green, marmot-whistling flower fields and beyond the waterfalls pouring down ice-polished buttresses under Mt. Torment. For another exploration, look for intermittent tread of an old miners' trail that ascends a moraine crest to tunnels and artifacts close under Sharkfin Tower, right next to the glacier falling from Boston Peak.

To conclude, there's a world of wandering in Boston Basin, if you can get there when the place isn't up to the scuppers in ropes and hard hats. However, absolutely no camping is allowed in the meadows. You must stay at the 5800-foot "climbers' camp," three sites, bouldery and wretched, just above timberline between the forks of Boston Creek, or up high on the snow or rock; if in doubt, go with the latter.

33 CASCADE PASS—SAHALE ARM

Round trip to Cascade Pass
  7 miles
Hiking time 5 hours
High point 5400 feet
Elevation gain 1800 feet
One day

Round trip to Sahale Arm 11 miles
Hiking time 10 hours
High point 6600 feet
Elevation gain 3000 feet
One day or backpack

Hikable mid-July through October
Map: Green Trails No. 80 Cascade
  Pass
Current information: Ask at
  Marblemount Ranger Station
Park Service backcountry use
  permit required for camping

A historic pass, crossed by Native Americans from time immemorial, by explorers and prospectors since early in the nineteenth century, and recently become famous as one of the most rewarding easy hikes in the North Cascades. But the beauty of the pass is only the beginning. An idyllic ridge climbs toward the sky amid flowers and creeklets of sparkling water and views that expand with every step.

Drive Highway 20 to Marblemount and continue east 23.5 miles on the Cascade River road to the road-end parking lot and trailhead, elevation 3600 feet.

In some thirty-three switchbacks, the 10 percent–grade "highway" climbs forest for about 2 miles, then makes a long, gently ascending traverse through parkland and meadows to Cascade Pass, 3½ miles, 5400 feet. Spectacular as the scenery is from road-end, the hiker runs out of superlatives before reaching the pass. The 8200-foot mass of Johannesburg dominates: hardly an hour goes by that a large or small avalanche doesn't break loose from its hanging glacier; several times a summer a huge section of ice roars all the way to the valley floor.

Cascade Pass retains its famous vistas, but during years of overuse

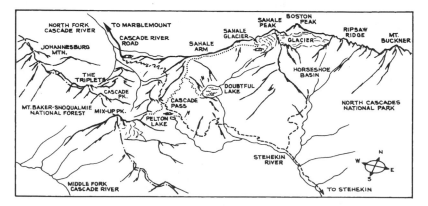

Eldorado Peak, and trail approaching Cascade Pass

the meadows were loved nearly to death. Camping and fires are now forbidden at the pass, and the Park Service has succeeded in rehabilitating the flower gardens. A few campsites are available below the pass to the east, in Pelton Basin, enabling a longer stay for extended sidetrips. (There also are several cozy pack-in sites close by the road-end—as scenic camps as one could want.)

One short ¼-mile sidetrip from the pass, easy and quick, is the wandering way south up the meadow crest of Mix-up Arm to a tiny tarn.

To explore the sky, climb north on a steep and narrow trail through meadows; find the start a few feet over the east side of the pass below a rock outcrop. In 1 mile and 800 feet the trail reaches the ridge crest and a junction. The right fork descends heather 800 feet in 1 mile to 5385-foot Doubtful Lake, a great hike in its own right, the shore cliffs riddled with old mines.

However, Sahale Arm calls. Walk the old prospectors' trail up and along the gentle ridge of flowers, and up some more. Look down to the waterfall-loud cirque of Doubtful Lake and east into the Stehekin River valley. Look west to Forbidden Peak and the huge Inspiration Glacier on Eldorado. Look south to nine small glaciers on the first line of peaks beyond Cascade Pass. Walking higher, see range upon range of ice and spires, finally including the volcano of Glacier Peak. To see it all in sunset and starlight and dawn, continue on and camp in the rocks at the toe of the Sahale Glacier. This is permitted.

34 THORNTON LAKES— TRAPPERS PEAK

Round trip to Lower Thornton
  Lake 9½ miles
Hiking time 6–8 hours
High point 5100 feet
Elevation gain 2600 feet in,
  400 feet out
Hikable mid-July through October

One day or backpack
Map: Green Trails No. 47
  Marblemount
Current information: Ask at
  Marblemount Ranger Station
Park Service backcountry use
  permit required for camping

Three deep lakes in rock basins gouged by a long-gone glacier. Close by are living glaciers, still gouging. All around are icy peaks on the west edge of the North Cascades National Park. From a summit above the lakes, a splendid view of Triumph and Despair and the Picket Range. Not realizing they are in a national park, many hikers come here with dogs and guns and without a permit, and sometimes go away with tickets. The camping is unpleasant to miserable and not recommended unless you're there for the fishing (which also is poor). Make it a day hike.

Drive Highway 20 to Marblemount and 11 miles beyond to Thornton Creek road; spot it between mileposts 117 and 118. Turn left 5 steep miles to a parking area, elevation 2500 feet.

The first 2 miles are on an abandoned logging road. Then begins the trail, which was never really "built" but just grew; it's very steep in places and mucky in others. Except for where the abandoned road crosses clearcuts, most of the way lies in forest. At a bit more than 1 mile from the abandoned road is an opening and a small creek to jump. The trail then switchbacks up a forested slope to the ridge crest.

Recuperate atop the 5000-foot ridge crest. Look down to the lake basin and out to Mt. Triumph. A miserable trail drops 500 miserable feet to the lowest and largest Thornton Lake. Across the outlet stream are poor campsites designated by posts; no fires allowed.

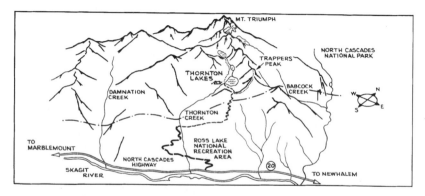

To reach the middle and upper lakes, traverse slopes west of the lower lake. The middle lake usually has some ice until the end of July; the upper lake, at 5000 feet in a steep-walled cirque, ordinarily is frozen until mid-August.

If views are the goal, don't drop to the lakes. Leave the trail at the 5000-foot crest and follow a faint climbers' track up the ridge to the 5966-foot summit of Trappers Peak. See the fantastic Pickets. And see, too, the little village of Newhalem far below in the Skagit Valley. The route is steep in places and requires use of the hands but is not really tough. Early in the season there may be dangerous snowpatches; go above or below them. Turn around content when the way gets too scary for plain-and-simple hikers.

Lower Thornton Lake and Mount Triumph

35 SOURDOUGH MOUNTAIN

Round trip to satellite dish 7 miles
Hiking time 7 hours
High point 4800 feet
Elevation gain 3900 feet
Hikable May through October
One day or backpack

Round trip to summit 11 miles
Hiking time 12 hours
High point 5985 feet
Elevation gain 5100 feet
Hikable July through October
One day or backpack

Loop trip 14 miles
Allow 2 days
High point 5985 feet
Elevation gain 4500 feet
Hikable July through October

Maps: Green Trails No. 48 Diablo
Dam, No. 16 Ross Dam
Current information: Ask at
Marblemount Ranger Station
Park Service backcountry use
permit required for camping

No other hike from the Skagit River can match these views of the North Cascades National Park. Look down to Diablo Lake and Ross Lake and out to forests of Thunder Creek. Look south to the ice of Colonial and Snowfield and southeast to Buckner and the sprawling Boston Glacier. Look east to the king of the Skagit, Jack Mountain, and north to Canada, and northwest and west to the Pickets.

There are two routes to Sourdough Mountain. One is an extremely steep trail—a strenuous day trip and not an easy weekend. The other is a loop, which can be done in an arduous 2 days.

Drive Highway 20 to the Seattle City Light town of Diablo. Go past the houses to the trailhead located beside the covered swimming pool. For a day hike park here, otherwise continue 0.3 mile and park in the main lot at the base of the dam, elevation 900 feet.

Summit–Satellite Dish Trail. The trail starts steep and stays steep; countless short switchbacks gain 3000 feet in the first 2½ miles before the way "levels off" to an ascent of 2000 feet in the final 4 miles to the summit.

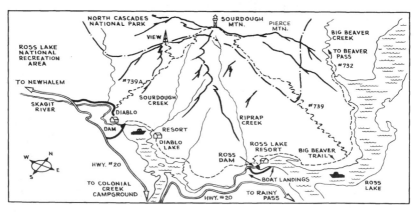

Diablo Lake from Sourdough Mountain

After 1½ miles of zigzags from the road up a forested hillside, an opening gives a sample of panoramas to come. At 3 miles is a junction. The left fork (good trail but easy to miss) climbs a steep ½ mile to a satellite dish serving Diablo. For most day-hikers this 4800-foot viewpoint is far enough, adding northern vistas to the southern. The way to this turnaround point often is free of snow in May, offering a spectacular springtime hike.

The main trail climbs from the junction, on a gentler grade than before, reaching a designated campsite at Sourdough Creek, 4 miles, elevation 5000 feet. (Water can be found at several places before this point, but it's thirsty travel at best.) In another 1½ miles the summit and fire-lookout cabin are attained, with all the previous views plus additional ones north up Ross Lake and west to the Pickets. Cross-country, no-fire camping is permitted on Sourdough Ridge.

Loop Trail. The loop is recommended counterclockwise due to routefinding problems. From the parking lot, hike the unmarked ½-mile trail to the top of Diablo Dam and take the Diablo Lake passenger boat to the base of Ross Dam. Climb the road 400 feet in 1 mile to the top of Ross Dam, cross the dam, and find the Big Beaver trail. In 3 miles is a junction. Turn left on Pierce Mountain Trail and climb 3000 feet in 4 miles to a designated campsite in Pierce Mountain saddle, then 1000 feet more in 1 mile to the 5985-foot lookout. Tread is indistinct or absent (the reason for counterclockwise direction) in the final rocky mile to the summit; watch for cairns. Descend to the parking lot via the "direct trail."

If two cars or a helper are available, a party can shortcut the loop by driving Highway 20 eastward from Colonial Creek Campground 3.8 miles to the parking lot of the Ross Lake trailhead, elevation 1800 feet, hiking the 1 mile down to Ross Dam, and exiting to a pickup at Diablo.

97

Pyramid Lake and Pyramid Mountain

36 PYRAMID LAKE

Round trip 4½ miles
Hiking time 3 hours
High point 2630 feet
Elevation gain 1550 feet
Hikable May through October

One day
Map: Green Trails No. 48 Diablo
   Dam
Current information: Ask at
   Marblemount Ranger Station

A popular trail, mostly in spindly forest, to a non-descript lakelet beneath the tower of 7182-foot Pyramid (actually, more cone-shaped) Peak. Climbers pass by this tiny lake on their way to and from ascents of Pyramid, Colonial, Paul Bunyan's Stump, and Snowfield; usually they do so before dawn and after dark, in a hurry. Fishermen don't come at all—no fish. No camping, either. So why the popularity? Because it is the first signed trail on the North Cascades Highway after leaving Newhalem.

Drive Highway 20 east from Newhalem to the Diablo (town) junction. Keep right on the highway, crossing Gorge Lake, and 0.8 mile from the junction spot the Pyramid Lake trailhead, elevation 1100 feet. Park on the opposite side of the highway.

The trail climbs a short cliff and then settles into a steady ascent of very young forest (from a not-long-ago fire) with a dense understory of salal. At about ¾ mile the vegetation becomes more exciting as the way enters a narrow valley of ancient giants, crosses a delightful creek, and continues uphill in a mixture of the young and the old, of the fir and the hemlock. At 2 miles note a monster of a Douglas fir leaning at such an impossible angle it surely can't last another day—as has obviously been true for a century or two.

At 2¼ miles is Pyramid Lake, 2450 feet. On two sides cliffs plunge to the water and keep right on going down; look deep into the blue-green water and see— not the bottom—but pale faces with dull, staring eyes.

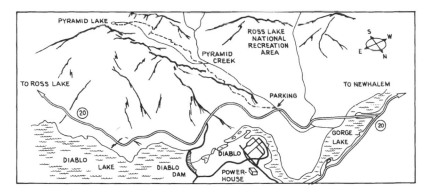

37 THUNDER CREEK

Round trip to McAllister Creek
  12 miles
Hiking time 5–7 hours
High point 1800 feet
Elevation gain 600 feet
Hikable April through November
One day or backpack

Maps: Green Trails No. 48 Diablo
  Dam, No. 49 Mt. Logan, No. 81
  McGregor Mtn.
Current information: Ask at
  Marblemount Ranger Station
Park Service backcountry use
  permit required for camping

Round trip to Park Creek Pass
  36 miles
Allow 3–5 days
High point 6040 feet
Elevation gain 5600 feet
Hikable late July through October

One of the master streams of the North Cascades, draining meltwater from an empire of glaciers. The first portion of the trail, easy walking, is nearly flat for miles, passing through groves of big firs, cedars, and hemlocks, in views of giant peaks. The route continues to a high pass amid these peaks; for experienced wilderness travelers, the trip from Thunder Creek over Park Creek Pass to the Stehekin River is a classic crossing of the range. Designated camps are scattered along the way, permitting travel by easy stages.

Drive Highway 20 to Diablo Dam and 4 miles beyond to Colonial Creek Campground, where the trail begins, elevation 1200 feet.

The trail follows Thunder Arm of Diablo Lake about 1 mile, crosses Thunder Creek on a bridge, and in another 1 mile comes to a junction with a trail climbing to Fourth of July Pass and Panther Creek (Hike 39). The Thunder Creek trail continues straight ahead on the sidehill, going up and down a little, mainly in big trees except at 4¼ miles, in a

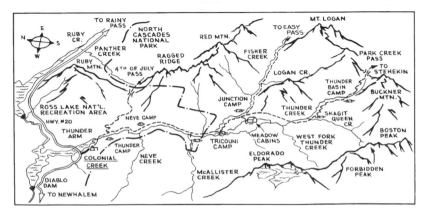

Thunder Creek trail

burn meadow from a lightning fire in 1971, and at 5 miles, in another from a 1970 fire; the openings give neck-stretching looks to the summits of Snowfield and Colonial. At about 2 and 2½ miles, respectively, are Thunder and Neve Camps.

At 5½ miles is the site of long-gone Middle Cabin, and ½ mile farther is the bridge to McAllister Creek Camp, a good turnaround for a day or weekend trip. The trail to here offers one of the best forest hikes in the North Cascades and is open to travel early in the season and late.

At 6 miles the way goes from national recreation area to national park; dogs must stop. At 7½ miles the trail crosses Fisher Creek to

Tricouni Camp and in ½ mile more begins a 1000-foot climb above the valley floor, which upstream from here becomes a vastness of swamp and marsh forbidden (by Nature) to human entry. Following Fisher Creek all the way, at 9 miles the trail levels out at Junction Camp, 3000 feet, and a junction with Fisher Creek trail (Hike 45). Off the trail a bit are grand views down to the valley and across to glaciers of Tricouni and Primus Peaks. Beyond the junction ¼ mile an obscure spur trail descends 1000 feet in 1 mile to the two Meadow Cabins, at the edge of the "Great Dismal Swamp," largest in the North Cascades and as wild as any scene this side of Mars. The main trail passes stunning viewpoints of the enormous Boston Glacier, Buckner and Boston and Forbidden thrusting above, drops steeply to the valley bottom at 2200 feet, and climbs to Skagit Queen Camp, 13 miles, 3000 feet, near where Skagit Queen Creek joins Thunder Creek. The way climbs steeply, gentles out somewhat in a hanging valley; at 15½ miles, 4300 feet, is the last designated campsite, Thunder Basin Camp. No fires. From here the trail ascends steadily up and around the meadow flanks of Mt. Logan to 6040-foot Park Creek Pass, 18 miles, a narrow rock cleft usually full of snow. To continue down to the Stehekin River, see Hike 49, Park Creek Pass.

Canadian dogwood, or bunchberry

38 BEAVER LOOP

Loop trip 26½ miles
Allow 3–5 days
High point 3620 feet
Elevation gain about 3500 feet

Round trip to Beaver Pass
27 miles
Allow 2–3 days
High point 3620 feet
Elevation gain 2000 feet

Hikable June through October
Maps: Green Trails No. 15 Mt.
Challenger, No. 16 Ross Lake
Current information: Ask at
Marblemount Ranger Station
Park Service backcountry use
permit required for camping

This loop hike from Ross Reservoir to close views of the Picket Range and back to Ross Reservoir offers perhaps the supreme dayslong forest experience in the North Cascades. The 27-mile trip up the Little Beaver Valley and down the Big Beaver Valley passes through groves of enormous cedars, old and huge Douglas firs and hemlocks, glimmery-ghostly silver fir, lush alder, young fir recently established after a fire (in 1926 enormous acreages of the Skagit country burned), and many more species and ages of trees as well. And there are brawling rivers, marshes teeming with wildlife, and awesome looks at Picket glaciers and walls. While the hike is recommended as a loop, the Big Beaver trail to Beaver Pass makes a great round trip (and does not en-

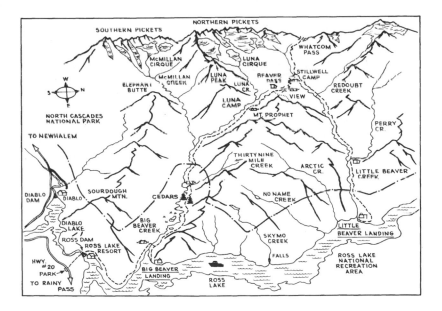

Big Beaver Valley

tail fords). The Park Service has a severely limited budget and some years is unable to brush out the trail.

Drive Highway 20 east to Colonial Creek Campground. Go another 3.8 miles and park at the Ross Lake trailhead. Walk the trail to Ross Lake Resort (Hike 42, Desolution Peak) and arrange for taxi service up the lake and a pickup at trip's end. The loop (or day or weekend hikes) can begin at either end; the Little Beaver start is described here.

After a scenic ride up Ross Reservoir, debark at Little Beaver Landing; a campground here, elevation 1600 feet. The trail starts by switch-backing 300 feet to get above a canyon, then loses most of the hard-won elevation. At 4½ miles is Perry Creek Camp, an easy ford-or-footlog crossing of several branches of the creek, and a passage along the edge of a lovely marsh. At 9 miles is Redoubt Creek; scout around for a footlog. At 11½ miles, 2450 feet, is a junction.

The Little Beaver trail goes upstream 6 miles and 2800 feet to What-com Pass (Hike 15). Take the Big Beaver trail, and *ford* Little Beaver Creek (beware—the creek isn't so little in early summer), pass a sidetrail to Stillwell Camp, and climb a steep mile to Beaver Pass, 3620 feet. The trail goes nearly on the level a mile to designated camp-sites at Beaver Pass Shelter (emergency use only), the midpoint of the loop, 13½ miles from Little Beaver Landing and 13 miles from Big Beaver Landing.

An hour or three should be allowed here for an easy off-trail sidetrip. Pick a way easterly and upward from the shelter, gaining 500–1000 feet through forest and brush to any of several open slopes that give a staggering look into rough-and-icy Luna Cirque; the higher the climb the better the view.

Passing Luna Camp on the way, descend steeply from Beaver Pass into the head of Big Beaver Creek; two spots on the trail offer impressive glimpses of Luna Cirque. At 6 miles from Beaver Pass Shelter (7 miles from Big Beaver Landing on Ross Lake), the Big Beaver tumbles down a 200-foot-deep gorge; a good view here of Elephant Butte and up McMillan Creek toward McMillan Cirque. The moderately up-and-down trail crosses recent avalanches that have torn avenues through forest, passes enormous boulders fallen from cliffs above, and goes by a marsh.

At 8 miles from Beaver Pass (5½ from Ross Lake), cross Thirtynine Mile Creek; campsite. The way now enters the glorious lower reaches of Big Beaver Creek, a broad valley of marshes and ancient trees, in-cluding the largest stand of western red cedar (some an estimated 1000 years old) remaining in the United States. Seattle City Light planned to flood the lower 6 miles of the valley by raising Ross Dam, but after an epic 15-year battle, in 1983 the plans were permanently dropped.

Passing one superb marsh after another, one grove of giant cedars after another, at 3 miles from Ross Lake the trail for the first time touches the banks of Big Beaver Creek, milky-green water running over golden pebbles. Finally the trail reaches Big Beaver Landing, from which a ¼-mile trail leads left to Big Beaver Camp. (This is a boaters' camp. Hikers should use Pumpkin Mountain Camp, 100 yards south of the bridge over Big Beaver Creek on the Ross Lake trail.)

There are two ways to return to Ross Dam. One is by hiking the 6-mile Ross Lake trail, which branches right from the Big Beaver trail at a junction ¼ mile before the landing. The second is to arrange in ad-vance with Ross Lake Resort to be picked up at Big Beaver Landing.

39 PANTHER CREEK— FOURTH OF JULY PASS

Round trip to Fourth of July Pass
11½ miles
Hiking time 6 hours
High point 3500 feet
Elevation gain 2000 feet
Hikable July through mid-October
One day or backpack

Maps: Green Trails No. 48 Diablo
Dam, No. 49 Mt. Logan
Current information: Ask at
Marblemount Ranger Station
Park Service backcountry use
permit required for camping

Rolling, bubbling, cascading, whirling, jumping, foaming, roaring, gurgling, singing—a whole thesaurus couldn't adequately summarize the lifestyle of this wondrous creek, deep in a verdant canyon between the glacial barrens of Ruby Mountain and Beebe Mountain. Follow the course for a single day of exploration or backpack to scenic camps just beyond Fourth of July Pass. If transportation can be arranged, plan a one-way trip ending at Colonial Creek Campground.

Drive Highway 20 east 8 miles from Colonial Creek Campground to the Panther Creek bridge and park at the East Bank trailhead, elevation 1850 feet.

Cross the bridge and walk the highway ⅓ mile to the Panther Creek trail and set out upward, switchbacking through open forest of lodgepole pine. In ¾ mile, at around 2200 feet, the trail levels off and then, to duck under a cliff, goes stark staring insane—turning back downvalley, losing several hundred feet of the hard-won elevation. The trail comes to the creek and turns back upvalley. The ferns are lush, the red cedars ancient. Pause often to watch the creek thrashing and splashing along its narrow course. At 3 miles the way crosses the creek on a sturdy bridge to a designated campsite, a good turnaround for day-hikers.

Proceeding onward, the trail soon crosses the first of several avalanche slopes and several small streams, passing from Ross Lake National Recreation Area into North Cascades National Park (Lassie, go home!). At 4¾ miles, 2700 feet, the route abruptly leaves the creek and in a forest mile climbs to Fourth of July Pass, 5¾ miles, 3500 feet.

The pass is fairly flat and wide for ⅓ mile, reflecting its past history as a glacier's trough. The forest is broken by small swamps. At the far end of the pass flat is an overlook of the inviting Panther Potholes. The trail then descends northward ¼ mile to Fourth of July Camp, which has a front-row seat for the big show of Colonial Peak, Neve Glacier, and Snowfield Peak.

One-way hikers are now not far from their pickup, via a quick 2½-mile drop to Thunder Creek trail and an easy 1½ miles to Colonial Creek Campground, 1240 feet, 10¼ miles from the Panther Creek trailhead.

Panther Creek

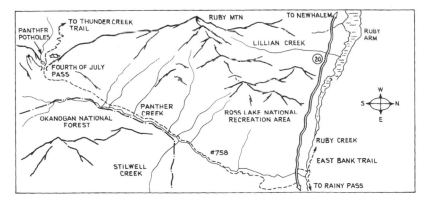

40 EAST BANK TRAIL

One-way trip from Panther Creek to Hozomeen 31 miles
Allow 3–5 days
High point 2853 feet
Elevation gain about 5000 feet
Hikable mid-June through October
Maps: Green Trails No. 48 Diablo Dam, No. 16 Ross Lake, No. 17 Jack Mtn.

Current information: Ask at Marblemount Ranger Station

Round trip from Panther Creek to Rainbow Camp 15 miles
Allow 2–3 days
High point 2600 feet
Elevation gain 900 feet in, 1250 feet out
Hikable May through October
Maps: Green Trails No. 16 Ross Lake, No. 17 Jack Mtn., No. 48 Diablo Lake

Park Service backcountry use permit required for camping in park

When full, the reservoir known as Ross "Lake" simulates nature and is, indeed, a veritable inland fjord. Unfortunately, draw-downs of water for power production expose dreary wastelands of mud and stumps. Because of the low elevation, the hike along the lake is especially attractive in spring, when most mountain trails are deep in snow; sorry

Lightning Creek bridge and Ross Lake

to say, that's when the "lake" is at its visual worst. Generally the reservoir is full from late June to October and at a lower level other months, the maximum draw-down of as much as 150 feet usually coming in March or April.

However, even when stumps are showing there still are grand views across the water to high peaks. To learn the valley in all its moods, to enjoy the panoramas from end to end, hike the East Bank Trail, mostly through forest, a little along the shore, and finally detouring inland to reach Hozomeen Campground. The complete trip can be done in several days or any portion selected for a shorter walk.

If only a portion of the trail is to be hiked, travel to Ross Dam and arrange with Ross Lake Resort for water-taxi service to the chosen beginning point and a pickup at trip's end (Hike 42, Desolation Peak).

To do the entire route drive Highway 20 the 8 miles from Colonial Creek Campground to the Panther Creek bridge and find the trailhead in the large parking area, elevation 1850 feet.

The trail drops 200 feet to the crossing of Ruby Creek and a junction beyond. Go left to Ruby Creek Barn, a scant 3 miles from the highway. The way leaves the water's edge to climb 900 feet over Hidden Hand Pass, returning to the lake near Roland Point Camp, 7½ miles.

The next 7½ miles to Lightning Creek are always near and in sight of the lake. Some stretches are blasted in cliffs; when the reservoir is full the tread is only a few feet above the waves, but when the level is down the walking is very airy. There are frequent boat-oriented camps, including the one at Lightning Creek, 16 miles from the highway.

Here the trail forks. The left continues 2 more miles up the lake, ending at the Desolation Peak trailhead (Hike 42).

For Hozomeen, take the right fork, switchback up 1000 feet to a glorious view of the lake, then lose all that elevation descending to a camp at Deer Lick Cabin (locked), 4 miles from the lake. The trail bridges Lightning Creek to a junction with the Three Fools Trail (Hike 80). Go left 7 miles to the junction with the abandoned Freezeout trail; go left on a bridge over Lightning Creek to Nightmare Camp, in a spooky cedar grove. The way leaves Lightning Creek and climbs to Willow Lake Pass at 2853 feet, 10 miles. Another 2 miles of some ups but mostly downs lead past a sidetrail to Hozomeen Lake and at last to the road-end at Ross Lake, 31 miles from the trailhead at Panther Creek.

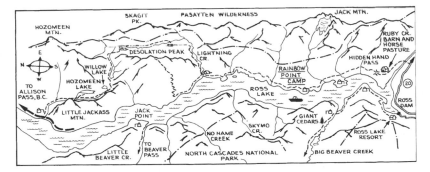

109

41 LITTLE JACK MOUNTAIN

Round trip to campsite 19 miles
Hiking time 9 hours
High point 6745 feet
Elevation gain 5097 feet
Hikable July through September
One day or backpack

Map: Green Trails No. 49 Mt. Logan
Current information: Ask at
Marblemount Ranger Station
Park Service backcountry use
permit required for camping

Few hiker-accessible vantages in the Ross Lake area offer gazing the likes of this: up and down the fjord-like sinuosity of Ross Reservoir; across to Elephant Butte and up the Big Beaver Valley to the heart of the Picket Range; west to Mt. Baker and Mt. Shuksan; and if that's not enough, south to such stars of the North Cascades show as Eldorado and Snowfield. So much for the good news. The trail is a bear—long, steep, and dry. Overnighters will find liquid in a small pond at Little Jack Camp but are advised not to drink it until they've used every water-purification procedure known to modern science—twice.

The trail begins at the Panther Creek bridge (Hike 39), elevation 1850 feet. Descend 200 feet to Ruby Creek and a junction. Go left 2½ nearly flat miles along Ruby Creek to a major junction, 1920 feet, where the trail branches into three. Take the far right, heading back upvalley and uphill in forest toward Little Jack.

The next 6 miles have more than sixty switchbacks, all up, though not steeply. At about 4 miles from the road views begin from the frequent openings. Progress can be measured by the dwindling size of cars streaming to and fro on Highway 20. At about 7½ miles from that thoroughfare, the path enters sweetly green meadows and turns east a final mile to Little Jack Camp, 6000 feet.

The camp is separated into hiker and horse areas on either side of a scummy little pond. Come early in the summer for the snowmelt.

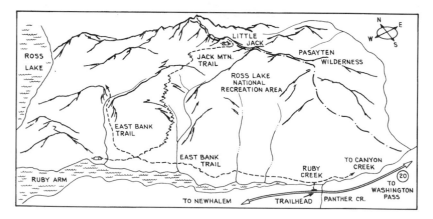

Just before the pond a vague sidetrail goes through a clump of trees and climbs to the ridge crest for a full panorama of Crater and Jack Mountains. This final mile of the main trail is strictly for diehards. The path disappears in heather and rich blueberry meadows. Take your choice of knoll summits. The views aren't any better here than before, they just feel better. Trail tread reappears, aiming toward Jack Mountain. Forget it. Once the route leaves the meadow it's for climbers only, and not many of those because the ascent is not so much interesting as nasty, and the "King of the Skagit" is mostly allowed to reign in lonesome splendor.

Crater Mountain from shoulder of Jack Mountain

DESOLATION PEAK

Round trip from Desolation Landing 9 miles
Hiking time 7 hours
High point 6085 feet
Elevation gain 4400 feet
Hikable mid-June through August

One day (from the lake) or backpack
Map: Green Trails No. 16 Ross Lake
Current information: Ask at Marblemount Ranger Station
Park Service backcountry use permit required for camping

A forest fire swept the slopes bare in 1926, giving the peak its name. In the late 1930s the lookout cabin on the summit was manned by the co-author's brother-in-law. But its fame in literary circles came after a summer's residence by the late Jack Kerouac, "beat generation" novelist and occasional Forest Service employee. Some of his best writing describes the day-and-night, sunshine-and-storm panorama from the Methow to Mt. Baker to Canada, and especially the dramatic close-up of Hozomeen Mountain, often seen from a distance but rarely from so near. Before and since Kerouac, the lookout frequently has been the summer home of poets. The steep trail is a scorcher in sunny weather; carry a lot of water.

The start of the Desolation Peak trail can be reached by walking 18 miles on the East Bank Trail (Hike 40) or by riding the water taxi. For the taxi, from home or while driving up the Skagit Valley, telephone Ross Lake Resort at (206) 386-4437 to learn the current price and make arrangements. For the latter, drive Highway 20 eastward from Colonial Creek Campground 3.8 miles to the parking lot of the Ross Lake trailhead, elevation 2200 feet. Then, from the trailhead, drop 450 feet to the dam and boat dock opposite the resort; here the resort boat will ferry you to your destination and return to pick you up at a prearranged time.

Jack Mountain (left) and Ross Lake from Desolation Peak

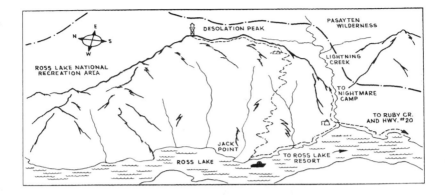

The trail starts steep and stays steep, climbing 1000 feet a mile. For such a desolate-appearing hillside there is a surprising amount of shade, the way often tunneling through dense thickets of young trees. This is fortunate because the sun can be unmerciful on the occasional barren bluffs.

Hozomeen Mountain from Desolation Peak

Views come with every rocky knoll. In ½ mile see a small grove of birch trees. In 2 miles there may be a spring. At 3 miles the trail enters steep, open meadows, and at 4 miles is the ridge crest. A high bump remains to be climbed over before the lookout is sighted. The flower fields include some species that properly "belong" on the east slopes of the Cascades.

The horizons are broad and rich. Only Mt. Baker stands out distinctly among the distant peaks, though those who know them can single out Shuksan, the Pickets, Colonial, Snowfield, Eldorado, and scores of other great mountains. Closer in, the spectacular glacier of 8928-foot Jack Mountain dominates the south. To the north rise the vertical walls of Hozomeen. West is the fjordlike Ross Reservoir, dotted by tiny boats of fishermen; beyond are the deep valleys of No Name Creek, Arctic Creek, and Little Beaver Creek. East are the high meadow ridges of the Cascade Crest and the Pasayten country.

A designated campsite (no fires) is in the trees just below the high meadows; water is from snowfields only and usually rare or nonexistent by late July. Because of the time spent getting to the trailhead, the best plan for a weekend trip is to travel the first day to Lightning Creek Camp, stay there overnight, and do the climb the second day.

43 CRATER–JACKITA RIDGE– DEVILS LOOP

**One-way trip to Devils Dome
  Landing 27 miles; complete
  loop 43 miles
Allow 5–9 days
High point 6982 feet
Elevation gain about 7300 feet
Hikable mid-July through
  October**

**Maps: Green Trails No. 16 Ross
  Lake, No. 17 Jack Mountain,
  No. 49 Mt. Logan
Current information: Ask at
  Methow Valley Ranger District
  about trail Nos. 738 and 752
Park Service backcountry use
  permit required for camping
  at Ross Reservoir**

Hoist packs and wander meadow ridges east of Ross Lake, encircling the far-below forests of Devils Creek and the cliffs and glaciers of 8928-foot Jack Mountain, "King of the Skagit," looking to peaks and valleys from Canada to Cascade Pass, the Pickets to the Pasayten. The trip is recommended as a loop, but for shorter hikes the climaxes can be reached from either end.

Drive Highway 20 eastward from Colonial Creek Campground 11 miles to Jackita Ridge (Canyon Creek) trailhead, elevation 1900 feet.

The way begins by crossing Granite Creek on a substantial bridge, going downstream a bit and crossing Canyon Creek on a commodious footlog.

Once across Canyon Creek the work begins—trail No. 736 gains 3400 feet in 4 miles. Fortunately, the labor is mostly shaded by big

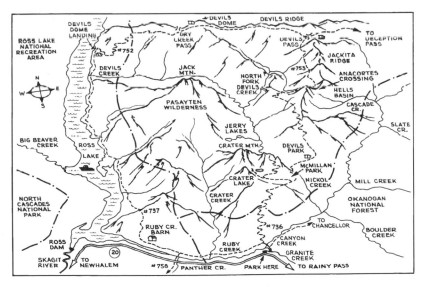

trees and there is water at several well-spaced points and ultimately glimpses of peaks. At 4 miles, 5280 feet, is a junction.

For a compulsory sidetrip, go left ¾ mile to the impressive cirque and shallow waters of 5800-foot Crater Lake. Just before the meadow-and-cliff-surrounded lake, a 2-mile trail climbs eastward to a lookout site on the broad, 7054-foot easternmost summit of Crater Mountain. From the lake a 2½-mile trail climbs westward to another lookout site on the 8128-foot main summit of Crater; the final ½ mile is for trained climbers only, but the panoramas are glorious long before difficulties begin. When this higher lookout was staffed, the final cliff was scaled with the help of wooden ladders and fixed ropes. Maintenance proved too difficult and summit clouds too persistent, causing installation of the lower lookout. Now both cabins are long gone.

From the 4-mile junction, go straight ahead on trail No. 738, descending the gently sloping table of McMillan Park to Nickol Creek, 4900 feet, then climb an old burn, loaded with blueberries in season, to Devils Park Shelter, 7 miles, 5800 feet. One can roam for hours in this plateau of meadows, clumps of alpine trees, and bleached snags.

The climb continues northward along Jackita Ridge into a larch-dotted basin at 8¾ miles, 6200 feet. Now commences a rollercoaster—up to a shoulder, down to a basin, up and down again, and again, at 13¼ miles coming to North Fork Devils Creek at 5500 feet.

The trail traverses sweeping gardens of Jackita Ridge, up some and down more, to Devils Pass, 15¼ miles, 5800 feet. The best camping is at Devils Pass Shelter, several hundred feet and ½ mile below the pass in a pretty meadow with a year-round spring, reached via the Deception Pass trail and then a sidetrail.

From Devils Pass head west on Devils Ridge trail No. 752, going through open woods near and on the ridge top, then climbing a lush basin to Skyline Camp, 18 miles, 6300 feet—a lovely spot for a star-bright sleep but waterless after the snows are gone. (In fact, there is no dependable water between North Fork Devils Creek and Dry Creek Pass.)

A flower-and-blueberry traverse and a short ridge-crest ascent lead, at 20 miles, to the 6982-foot site of the demolished Devils Dome Lookout, the trip's highest elevation. A descent into a basin of waterfalls and boulders and blossoms and a contour around the flowery slopes of Devils Dome leads at 21½ miles to a ¼-mile sidetrail to 6000-foot Bear Skull Shelter, the first possible camp if the loop is being done in the reverse direction and a long day—5½ miles and 4500 feet—above Ross Lake.

At last the highlands must be left. The trail goes down the crest a short bit to Dry Creek Pass, descends forests and burn meadows to the only dependable creek, at 23 miles, enters young trees of an old burn, crosses the East Bank Trail, and ¼ mile later, at 27 miles, ends at the lakeside camp of Devils Dome Landing.

To return to the start, either hike the East Bank Trail (Hike 40) or, by prearranged pickup, ride back in a boat of Ross Lake Resort (Hike 42, Desolation Peak).

Crater Mountain

CANYON CREEK—
CHANCELLOR TRAIL

**Round trip to Boulder Creek
7 miles
Hiking time 4 hours
High point 2400 feet
Elevation gain 500 feet**

**Round trip to Miners Creek
14 miles
Hiking time 8 hours
High point 2600 feet
Elevation gain 700 feet**

**Hikable June through October
One day or backpack
Map: Green Trails No. 49 Mt.
Logan
Current information: Ask at
Methow Valley Ranger District
about trail No. 754**

Walk a canyon-narrow valley through groves of giant trees, past waterfalls, and then on what obviously is the remnant of an ancient road, though one who didn't know there was such a thing as a specially made narrow-gauge truck would marvel what sort of vehicle ever traveled it. Once a main route from the Skagit Valley to goldfields of the Harts Pass area (the mother lode was—and still is—located in distant cities, worked by stock salesmen), lined by an almost continuous string of mining claims, many with cabins, the trail eventually reaches Chancellor, a thriving community in 1880, now a ghost town at the end of the road down from Harts Pass. If transportation can be arranged (and if the trail is known in advance to be passable the whole way), start at Chancellor and hike downstream. Otherwise, start at the lower end and hike upstream. The 3½ miles to Boulder Creek are a fine day hike. If backpacking, continue to Mill Creek, 7 miles, for campsites. But if the trail has slid out at the several spots where it is wont to do so, turn back.

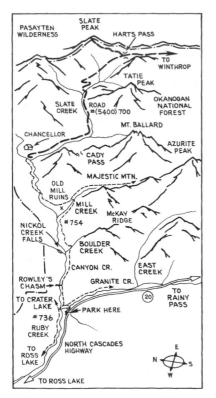

For the lower start, drive Highway 20 to Chancellor trail No. 754

(Hike 43, Crater–Jackita Ridge–Devils Loop). From the east side of the parking lot, follow Granite Creek upstream 100 feet to a bridge. Cross to a trail junction and take the right.

The big trees and the creek provide entertainment. So does keeping an eye out for collapsed cabins and rusty tools, though the generations of wet rot and green-jungling have left precious little evidence of the mining (prospecting, stock-selling) excitement. Conjure up a vision of Owen Wister and his bride riding down the trail on their honeymoon journey from the Methow Valley to Western Washington.

In a scant 2 miles take a 500-foot sidetrip to Rowley's Chasm, where the narrow walls almost touch; the chasm is spanned by a bridge scarcely 10 feet long, a giddy 100 feet and then some above nothing. Proceeding onward, look through trees to a good view of Crater Mountain and at 3 miles to the white splash of Nickol Creek Falls. At 3½ miles, 2400 feet, Boulder Creek may have to be forded, which at high water may be too neat a trick.

At 6 miles, 2600 feet, trail ends and narrow-gauge road begins at Mill Creek (the bridge may be missing). Campers will want to poke about such scant remains as may be found of the sawmill built to supply mine timbers.

At 9 miles from Highway 20, at 3000 feet, is Chancellor and the end of the road from Harts Pass (Hike 78, Grasshopper Pass).

A peek at Snowfield Peak from Canyon Creek trail

45 EASY PASS—FISHER CREEK

Round trip to Easy Pass 7 miles
Hiking time 7 hours
High point 6500 feet
Elevation gain 2800 feet
One day or backpack

One-way trip from Easy Pass to
Colonial Creek Campground
19 miles
Allow 3–4 days
High point 6500 feet
Elevation gain 5300 feet

Hikable mid-July through
September
Maps: Green Trails No. 48 Diablo
Dam, No. 49 Mt. Logan
Current information: Ask at
Methow Valley Ranger District
about trail No. 741
Park Service backcountry use
permit required for camping
in park

Dramatic the views are, but the trail definitely is not easy. Prospectors found this the easiest (maybe the only) pass across Ragged Ridge, and thus the name. However, the tread is rough, at times very steep, and in spots muddy. Finally, the pass area is very small and extremely fragile, and camping is not allowed.

Drive Highway 20 east 21.5 miles from Colonial Creek Campground or 6.2 miles west from Rainy Pass to a spur road and parking area, elevation 3700 feet.

In a scant ¼ mile the trail crosses Granite Creek on a footlog and then climbs 2 miles in woods to the edge of a huge avalanche fan, 5200 feet, under the rugged peaks of Ragged Ridge. The trail now may become elu-

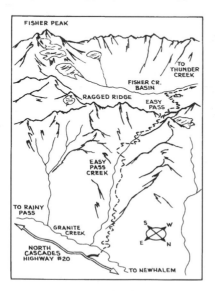

sive, buried in snow or greenery. (Make very sure not to lose the path; cross-country exploration here is agonizing.) The way goes over the avalanche fan and Easy Pass Creek and begins a long, steep ascent along the south side of the valley to the pass. Flower gardens. Small groves of trees. Watercourses. Boulder fields. Up, always up. The route crosses Easy Pass Creek twice more and at about 6100 feet comes within a few feet of a gushing spring, the source of the creek. Tread shoveled from a steep talus slope leads to the 6500-foot pass, a narrow, larch-covered saddle.

For the best views wander meadows up the ridge above the pass and look down 1300 feet into

Fisher Creek Basin and Fisher Peak

Fisher Creek Basin and out to glaciers and walls of 9080-foot Mt. Logan.

   To continue to Diablo Lake, descend 1½ miles to a designated no-fire camp in Fisher Basin, 5200 feet. At 5½ miles is Cosho Camp and, just beyond, a footlog crossing of Fisher Creek. At 10½ miles is Junction Camp, where is met the Thunder Creek trail (Hike 37), which leads to Colonial Creek Campground at 19 miles from the pass.

46 CHELAN LAKESHORE TRAIL

**One-way trip from Prince Creek
  17½ miles**
Allow 3–4 days
High point 1700 feet
Elevation gain perhaps 2000 feet

**One-way trip from Moore's Point
  6½ miles**
Allow 2 days
High point 1600 feet
Elevation gain about 900 feet

**Hikable late March through
  early June**
**Maps: Green Trails No. 82
  Stehekin, No. 114 Lucerne,
  No. 115 Prince Creek**
**Current information: Ask at Park
  Service–Forest Service
  Information Center about trail
  No. 1247**

The way to know Lake Chelan is to walk beside it, sometimes by waves slapping the shore, sometimes on high bluffs in sweeping views. There are green lawns atop rock buttresses, groves of old ponderosa pine and Douglas fir, glades of mystic aspen, slot gorges of frothing waterfalls. The views and trees and many of the creeks are grand in

Lake Chelan and McGregor Mountain from Hunts Bluff

any season but spring is the prime time, when the sun is dependable but not too weighty, cool breezes blow, and the flowers are in rich bloom. Early on, the trail is lined by trillium, chocolate lily, glacier lily, spring beauty, yellowbells, Johnny-jump-up, red currant, and more. Later on, the show features spring gold, prairie star, blue-eyed Mary, naked broomrape, primrose monkeyflower, death camas, balsamroot, miners lettuce, calypso, and more.

Note: By early summer the country gets so dry that wood fires within 1 mile of the shore are banned except where metal rings are provided—namely, at Prince Creek, Moore's Point, and Fish Creek Shelter. Carry a stove. You should've come earlier anyhow.

Drive to the town of Chelan or up the lake to Field Point and board the passenger boat *Lady of the Lake.* Contact the National Park Service–Forest Service Information Center in Seattle to learn the current schedule. The past pattern has been a single trip daily from mid-May to mid-September, uplake in early morning, downlake in early afternoon, and Sunday, Monday, Wednesday, and Friday trips the rest of the year (no Sunday boat in midwinter).

For a 2-day trip, hikers can start at Moore with day packs and have their overnight gear dumped on the dock at Stehekin to await them; this gives an afternoon on the trail and a morning poking around Stehekin.

To do the full 17½ miles from Prince Creek to Stehekin, the nice allowance is 4 days (including the going-home day) though 3 is tolerable. The map fails to say that though the trail never climbs higher than 1700 feet and generally is some several hundred feet above the shore (1098 feet above sea level), it irrationally manages to go uphill virtually the whole way.

At Prince Creek hikers have the choice of being put off downlake from the creek, perhaps to stay the first night at the campground there, or uplake (a campsite here, too) to save ½ mile of trail.

Since the debarkation at Prince Creek is about 11:00 A.M., most hikers camp the first night in the vicinity of Meadow Creek, 7 miles, after crossing Rattlesnake, Rex, Pioneer, and Cascade Creeks. The shelter cabin in the dark woods at Meadow Creek is unattractive except in a storm.

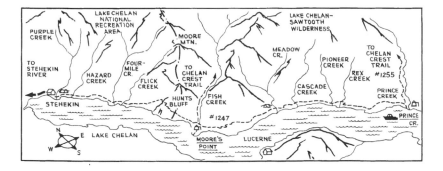

Lakeshore trail and Mount McGregor (Photo: John Spring)

By the nice plan, a relaxed second day attains the trail's high point at 1700 feet on a long, wide shelf, descends to Fish Creek, 10½ miles from Prince Creek, then takes the sidetrail ½ mile down the creek to Moore's Point, once a famous resort and now a spacious Forest Service campground. Spend the afternoon exploring the ancient orchard and the New England–like stone walls fencing a deer pasture.

The 6½ miles from Fish Creek to Stehekin are an easy morning for a 3-day trip. (Since the boat doesn't go downlake until afternoon, a party can finish the trip the morning of "boat day.") The way starts by climbing to 1600 feet on Hunts Bluff and its climactic views of lake and mountains. The trail then drops to the lake, crossing more creeks, and comes to Lakeshore (Flick Creek) Shelter, a choice camp on a jut of forest and rock out into the waves. It never again climbs high, wandering the base of cliffs and through woods to Flick Creek, Fourmile Creek, Hazard Creek, and finally Stehekin, 17½ miles. (To be technical, the sign here says "Fish Creek 6.6, Prince Creek 17.2.")

Overnight camping is permitted where the trail enters the Stehekin complex (this campground is designated "overflow") and ¼ mile up the road at Purple Point Campground.

47 RAINBOW LOOP

Loop trip 6 miles (with shuttlebus)
or 9 miles (without)
Hiking time 5 hours (or 7 hours)
High point 2600 feet
Elevation gain 1500 feet
Hikable March through November
One day or backpack

Map: Green Trails No. 82 Stehekin
Current information: Ask at
** Marblemount Ranger Station or**
** Park Service–Forest Service**
** Information Center**
Park Service backcountry use
** permit required for camping**

The high country of Stehekin is a long way up and for much of the year is up to a hiker's eyebrows in snow. The low country, on the other hand, offers relaxed walking almost year-round.

A favorite plan, especially among families with small children, is to take the boat to Stehekin (Hike 46, Chelan Lakeshore Trail), then the Park Service shuttlebus 5 miles up the Stehekin Road, and establish camp on the banks of the Stehekin River at Harlequin (formerly Company Creek) Campground, elevation 1195 feet. By walking the short bit out from the campground and across the Harlequin Bridge, a party can be whisked by shuttlebus up the Stehekin Road to any number of trailheads that provide nice day hikes: Agnes Gorge, Coon Lake, Flat Creek, Park Creek, and others. The party then can be whisked back to Harlequin for supper.

Lake Chelan from Rainbow Lake trail (Photo: Harvey Manning)

Stehekin River (Photo: Harvey Manning)

Contact the National Park Service Information Center in Seattle before the trip to learn the current bus schedule. The past pattern has been several round trips daily from spring to fall.

The bus isn't needed for the Stehekin River Trail, which takes off from the campground and in 4 flat and easy downstream miles of forest flowers and river vistas emerges at Weaver Point Camp, on the shore of Lake Chelan; the swimming is invigorating.

The bus also isn't needed, though it can be used, for the classic Rain-

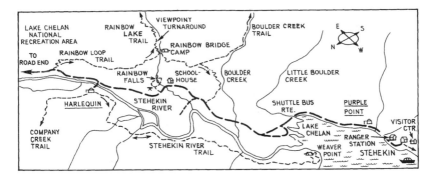

bow Loop. The upper and lower trailheads are a scant 3 miles apart on the Stehekin Road; the walk between them can be enlivened by a cooling sidetrip to Rainbow Falls and a tour of the historic Stehekin School.

Note: Rainbow has a reputation as the snakiest trail in the valley, but on none of his trips has the surveyor ever seen a rattler. However, standard precautions are in order while admiring the penstemon, cinquefoil, death camas, monkeyflower, naked broomrape, linear phacelia, salmon collomia, willow herb, broadleaf montia, balsamroot, lupine, stonecrop, lava alumroot, paintbrush, tiger lily, larkspur, suksdorfia, buckwheat, sandwort, luina, arnica, pinedrops, prairie star, snowbrush, and friends.

The recommended start is the upper trailhead, elevation 1240 feet, a long ½ mile up the valley road from Harlequin Bridge. Views through the forest grow steadily on the 2½-mile ascent to a junction, 2150 feet. The views here are very big, but don't be satisfied.

Sidetrip up the left fork, the Rainbow Lake trail, a long ⅓ mile to where it zigs right at 2600 feet. Zag left, out onto a bald slope of rock slabs and green grass. Find a piece of soft granite to sit on, break out the pickle sandwiches and the jug of orange juice, and gaze: across the valley to massive Si Si Ridge, crags of Devore Peak, the tower of Tupshin, but, especially, out to Lake Chelan, rippled by wind, sparkling in sun, and down the long fjord to Moore's Point, Domke Mountain, and the big peaks of Milham Pass.

Having returned from the sidetrip to the junction, descend 2½ miles to the lower trailhead, passing on the way: a few feet from the junction, Rainbow Creek, with a nice little woods camp; the Boulder Creek trail, branching left; a series of switchbacks on the naked valley wall, with more views of the lake and others straight down to the river, one meander picturesquely enwrapping Buckner's Orchard; Boulder Creek. The road is reached at 1160 feet, 2½ miles from Stehekin Landing.

If the trip schedule is meshed with the bus schedule, a party can ride back to Harlequin. However, it's only 2½ miles up the road. Halfway along are the Stehekin School and the short sideroad and path to Rainbow Falls, where sunburnt hikers have been known to sit in forest shadows and let the billows of spray wash over them until their pink skin turns a nice shade of blue.

48 NORTH FORK BRIDGE CREEK

Round trip to cirque 21 miles
Allow 2–3 days
High point 4200 feet
Elevation gain 2000 feet
Hikable early July through
  October
Map: Green Trails No. 81
  McGregor Mountain

Current information: Ask at
  Marblemount Ranger Station or
  Park Service–Forest Service
  Information Center
Park Service backcountry use
  permit required for camping

The North Cascades are distinguished by tall peaks—and also by deep holes. Among the most magnificent holes in the range is the huge cirque at the head of North Fork Bridge Creek, where breezes ripple meadow grasses beneath the ice-hung precipices of 9160-foot Goode Mountain, 8515-foot Storm King Peak, and 9087-foot Mt. Logan.

Travel by shuttlebus to Bridge Creek, 16 miles from Stehekin (Hikes 46, Chelan Lakeshore Trail, and 47, Rainbow Loop). Just before the creek is the trailhead, elevation 2200 feet.

The trail starts with a short, stiff climb of 400 feet, then goes up and down in woods, emerging to a view of Memaloose Ridge and reaching the bridge over Bridge Creek at 2½ miles, 2600 feet. Across the bridge and ¼ mile beyond is a junction; go left on the North Fork trail.

The way ascends steeply a bit and gentles out. From brushy openings in the forest are views of rugged cliffs, a promise of what is to come. To achieve fulfillment of the promise, it is necessary to camp somewhere in the North Fork. There are three choices: Walker Park Camp, 5½ miles, 3120 feet, a miserable, fly-ridden pit; Grizzly Creek Camp, about 6 miles, 3200 feet, in open woods near the stream; and Grizzly Creek Horse Camp, 6⅓ miles, 3180 feet.

The ford of Grizzly Creek is not life-threatening except in snowmelt season, yet neither are its wide, cold, rushing waters a novice's joy. Beyond the creek the way leaves woods and wanders along the valley bottom in cottonwood groves, avalanche brush, and patches of grass. Immense views continue, up and up the 6000-foot north wall of Goode to icefalls of the Goode Glacier and towers of the summit.

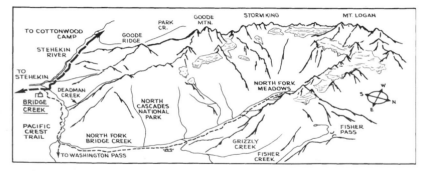

Mount Goode (Photo: Dick Brooks)

At 7¼ miles, about 1⅔ miles past Grizzly Creek, the maintained trail ends in North Fork Meadows. The old path continues, a bit less gentle. At about 9½ miles, 3800 feet, is the site of famous Many Water falls Camp, where camping is now banned. The scene is glorious with wide fields of hip-high grass, the roar of many waterfalls from hanging glaciers, and neck-stretching gazes to Goode and Storm King.

Paths here are confusing; climb the brushy knoll above to a resumption of tread amid small and sparse trees. In a stand of old alpine timber that has grown old by dodging avalanches is a heather-surrounded, rotted-out miner's cabin. The trail emerges into grass and flowers of the cirque, 10½ miles, 4200 feet, and fades away. The views of Goode are better than ever and Logan's walls are close above.

49 PARK CREEK PASS

Round trip to pass 16 miles
Allow 3–4 days
High point 6100 feet
Elevation gain 3900 feet
Hikable mid-July through
September
Map: Green Trails No. 81
McGregor Mountain

Current information: Ask at
Marblemount Ranger Station or
Park Service–Forest Service
Information Center
Park Service backcountry use
permit required for camping

A wild and alpine pass on the Cascade Crest between the 9000-foot summits of Mt. Buckner and Mt. Logan, dividing snow waters flowing east to the Stehekin River and Lake Chelan and snow waters flowing west to the Skagit River and the Whulge (the name by which the original residents knew "the saltwater"). The pass and its surroundings rank among the scenic climaxes of the North Cascades National Park. A base can be established at Buckner Camp for roaming, or a one-way trip made over the mountains from lowlands east to lowlands west. Keep in mind that there is no camping in the alpine areas around the pass. From the last permitted camp in Park Creek it is 5 miles, with a 2000-foot climb, over and down to Thunder Basin Camp.

Travel by shuttlebus (or walk) 18.5 miles from Stehekin (Hikes 46, Chelan Lakeshore Trail, and 47, Rainbow Loop) to Park Creek Campground and trailhead, elevation 2300 feet.

The trail switchbacks steeply from the Stehekin into the hanging valley of Park Creek, then goes along near the stream through forest and occasional open patches with views up to Goode Ridge. At 2 miles, 3200 feet, is a two-site designated camp and a footlog crossing of the creek. Beyond here the grade gentles, continuing mostly in trees but with openings that give looks to Park Creek Ridge. At 3 miles is an obscure junction with a rough-and-sketchy climbers' route to 7680-foot Goode Ridge and broad views; the scramble is for experienced hikers only, but well worth the effort.

Crossing numerous creeks in green avalanche tracks, views growing of high peaks, the trail ascends gradually to 4000 feet, 4½ miles. Now the way leaves the main valley of Park Creek, which falls from the glaciers of Mt. Buckner, and traverses and switchbacks steeply into a hanging side-valley, gradually emerging into parkland. At 7 miles, 5700 feet, the trail flattens out in a magnificent meadow laced by streams and dotted by clumps of alpine trees, the view dominated by the north wall of 8200-foot Booker Mountain.

A final wander in heather and blossoms leads to the rocky, snowy defile of 6100-foot Park Creek Pass, 8 miles from the Stehekin Road.

In order to preserve the fragile meadows, camping is not permitted in the area near the pass; however, fair basecamps for exploration are located in the forest at 5 miles (Buckner Camp) and 2 miles west of the pass in Thunder Basin.

Air view of Park Creek Pass: Mount Buckner (left) and Mount Logan (right)

For one wandering, with grand views of Buckner, Booker, Storm King, and Goode (tallest of all at 9160 feet, and third-highest nonvolcanic peak in the Cascades), find an easy, flowery route to the ridge southeast of the pass, overlooking the head of Park Creek. For another, descend west from the pass about ½ mile, leave the trail, and contour meadows and moraines to a jaw-dropping vista of the giant Boston Glacier and great peaks standing far above the valley of Thunder Creek.

If transportation can be arranged, a one-way trip can be made on down Thunder Creek to Diablo Lake (Hike 33, Cascade Pass and Sahale Arm).

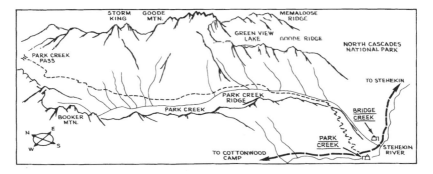

HORSESHOE BASIN (STEHEKIN)

Round trip from Cascade River road 18 miles
Allow 3–4 days
High point 4800 feet
Elevation gain 3000 feet in, 1800 feet out

Round trip from Cottonwood Camp 8 miles
Hiking time 5 hours
High point 4800 feet
Elevation gain 2000 feet
One day or backpack

Hikable July through October
Map: Green Trails No. 80 Cascade Pass
Current information: Ask at Marblemount Ranger Station or Park Service–Forest Service Information Center
Park Service backcountry use permit required for camping

Nine or more waterfalls tumble to the meadow floor of this cliff-ringed cirque. Above are glaciers on Sahale and Boston Peaks, both nearly 9000 feet, and the spires of Ripsaw Ridge. Wander the flowers and rocks and bubbling streams. The basin is well worth a visit in its own right and makes a splendid sidetrip on the cross-mountain journey described in Hike 51, Lake Chelan to Cascade River.

The Horseshoe Basin trail can be reached either from the west side of the Cascades or the east. For the west approach to the junction, as-

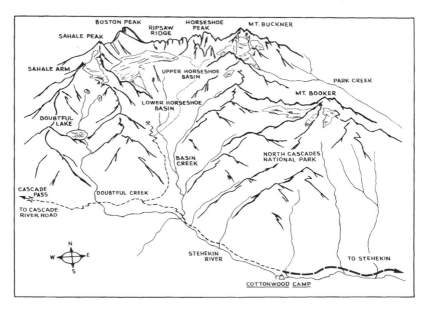

Glory Mountain (left) *and Trapper Mountain* (right) *from mine in Horseshoe Basin.*

cend to Cascade Pass (Hike 33) and descend 3 miles into the Stehekin valley. For the east approach to the junction, walk or ride the shuttle-bus to the end of the Stehekin River road at Cottonwood Camp, eleva-tion 2800 feet, and walk upvalley on the abandoned mining road 2 miles.

At an elevation of 3600 feet, the Cascade Pass trail goes left. The washed-out, bouldery, 1950s mining road switchbacks sharply in a rockslide, climbing around and up the mountainside to enter the hang-ing valley of Basin Creek. At 1½ miles the way emerges from brush and flattens out amid boulder-strewn meadows, 4200 feet. Impressive looks upward from flowery knolls to ice and crags, and a magical view and sound of white water on the glacier-excavated walls.

The road remnants continue ½ mile upward across the sloping floor of the basin to the Black Warrior mine tunnel at 4800 feet, close under the froth and splash of the falls. The Park Service has tidied up the mine to make explorations safe; bring a flashlight. Hours can be spent roaming the basin.

Experienced off-trail hikers can go higher. Cross the creek a short way below the mine and to the right of the vertical walls, scramble brushy slopes, amid small cliffs, to the upper cirque of Horseshoe Ba-sin. The ascent is not easy but doesn't require the ropes and other gear of mountain climbers; traces of an old miners' trail may be found, sim-plifying progress. Once on the high shelf under Mt. Buckner and Rip-saw Ridge, the way is open for extended explorations, always looking down waterfalls to the lower basin and out to peaks beyond the Stehekin.

51 LAKE CHELAN TO CASCADE RIVER

One-way trip from Cottonwood
  Camp to Cascade River road
  9 miles
Hiking time 6 hours
High point (Cascade Pass)
  5400 feet
Elevation gain 2600 feet
One day

One-way Boy Scout hike from
  Prince Creek to Cascade River
  50 miles
Allow at least 6 days
Elevation gain 5900 feet,
  loss 2600 feet

Hikable mid-July through
  mid-October
Maps: Green Trails No. 80 Cascade
  Pass, No. 81 McGregor Mtn.
Current information: Ask at
  Marblemount Ranger Station or
  Park Service–Forest Service
  Information Center
Park Service backcountry use
  permit required for camping

A classic and historic cross-Cascades route from the Columbia River to Puget Sound, the trip can begin from either side of the range, but for a well-ordered progression of soup, salad, main course, and finally dessert (rather than the reverse) the approach from the east is recommended. The journey can be a quick-and-easy 9 miles or, by starting at Prince Creek, a Boy Scout "50-mile hike."

Voyage Lake Chelan, elevation 1098 feet (Hike 46, Chelan Lakeshore Trail).

Begin the 50-mile hike at Prince Creek on the 17½-mile-long Chelan Lakeshore trail (Hike 46), then walk the quiet road from the Stehekin boat landing to Cottonwood Camp, 2800 feet, 23 miles from Stehekin

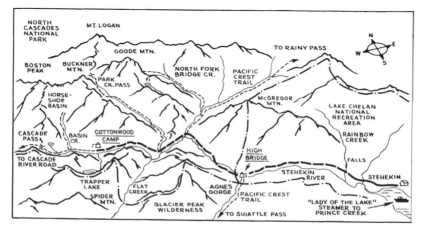

Stehekin Valley and McGregor Mountain from Cascade Pass trail

and the end of automobile traffic. Hikers who don't need a merit badge may ride the shuttlebus this far (Hike 47, Rainbow Loop).

At Cottonwood Camp the way emerges from woods into avalanche greenery and goes along the valley bottom, views of ridges above, to the grassy-and-bouldery avalanche fan at the crossing of Basin Creek, 3100 feet, 1½ miles from Cottonwood; campsite here. In another ¾ mile, at 3600 feet, is the junction with the route into Horseshoe Basin (Hike 50).

Excellent trail climbs an enormous talus to Doubtful Creek, 4100 feet, ¾ mile from the Horseshoe Basin junction. The ford can be difficult and extremely dangerous in high water, and falls above and below forbid any easy detour. Now the trail rises into a hot slope of slide alder, ascending in twelve gentle switchbacks to the crest of the wooded ridge above Pelton Basin and views. In the basin at 4820 feet, 5 miles, the Park Service has installed wooden tent platforms to allow camping in meadows without destroying them. This is a superb base for easy explorations.

A scant mile more leads to 5400-foot Cascade Pass and broader views. A supertrail descends 3¾ miles to the end of the Cascade River road, 3600 feet (Hike 33, Cascade Pass and Sahale Arm).

Forest, alpine meadows, and mountains along the Chelan Crest trail from side of South Navarre Peak

LAKE CHELAN—STEHEKIN RIVER
Partly in Lake Chelan–Sawtooth Wilderness

 CHELAN SUMMIT TRAIL

One-way trip 38 miles
Allow 5–9 days
High point 7400 feet
Elevation gain about 8500 feet
Hikable early July through
  September

Maps: Green Trails No. 115 Prince
  Creek, No. 83 Buttermilk Butte,
  No. 82 Stehekin
Current information: Ask at Park
  Service–Forest Service Information
  Center about trail No. 1261

A miles-and-miles and days-and-days paradise of easy-roaming ridges and flower gardens and spectacular views westward across the deep trench of Lake Chelan to the main range of the Cascades. Snow-free hiking starts earlier and the weather is better than in the main range, which traps many winter snows and summer drizzles. Only twice before the final plunge does the trail dip as low as 5500 feet, in forest; eight times it climbs over passes or shoulders, the highest 7400 feet; mainly it goes up and down (a lot) through meadows and parkland on the slopes of peaks that run as high as 8795-foot Oval Peak, in the Sawtooth Group. Good-to-magnificent camps are spaced at intervals of 2–3 miles or less. Sidetrips (on and off trails) to lakes, passes, and peaks are so many that one is constantly tempted; for that reason a party should allow extra days for wandering.

The trail can be sampled by short trips from either end or via feeder trails from Lake Chelan on one side or the Methow and Twisp Rivers on the other. (For examples of the latter, see Hikes 54, Foggy Dew Creek, and 56, Eagle Lakes—Boiling Lake.) The perfect dream trip is hiking the whole length to Stehekin, but this requires either a two-car switcharound or a very helpful friend to do drop-off and pickup duty. Further, the road routes range from rude to disgusting. Some years cars simply can't get there. Most parties thus settle for a nearly perfect dream trip that starts on a feeder trail from the lake and uses the *Lady of the Lake* (Hike 46, Chelan Lakeshore Trail) to handle the drop-off and pickup.

Thanks (no thanks) to the maddening motorcycles still permitted on the south end of the Summit Trail, experienced hikers will opt to by-pass part of it on the rough and steep Summer Blossom Trail (Hike 53). Beginners, however, had best take ear plugs and dust masks and sedatives and set out where the wheels do—notebook in hand to compose the letter of complaint that will be sent to a congressperson after the trip, with a copy to the Forest Service.

The Summit Trail has two trailheads other than the Summer Blossom alternate—from South Navarre Campground and Safety Harbor Creek. Because some years the final 2 miles of road to the former generally are too rough for a family car, the Safety Harbor Creek trail is described here. (Check at the Park Service–Forest Service Information Center.)

Drive the North Shore Road from Chelan past Manson and turn right on Grade Creek road, signed "Antilon Lake," at this point becoming road No. 8200. At 36 miles from Chelan go left on road No. (8200)150, signed "Safety Harbor Trailhead," and continue 2 miles to the end and trailhead, elevation 4400 feet.

Safety Harbor trail No. 1261 follows an abandoned pipeline a scant 2 miles and then turns uphill. At 4 miles, 5700 feet, it intersects Chelan Summit Trail No. 1259, which has just descended 600 feet in 3 miles from the South Navarre Campground. The Summit Trail now climbs to meadows of Miners Basin (5 miles) and a ridge crest. A traverse above headwater meanders of Safety Harbor Creek in Horsethief Basin leads to a 7400-foot pass (6½ miles) to East Fork Prince Creek. At the pass is a junction with the Summer Blossom Trail, which has come here in 6 miles from the road.

The way drops 700 feet to the broad meadow basin of the East Fork and makes a big swing around it, under the foot of 8321-foot Switchback Peak to a 7120-foot pass (8 miles) to Middle Fork Prince Creek. Down and around another wide parkland at 10 miles are the junction with the Middle Fork Prince Creek trail and a basecamp for sidetrips to Boiling Lake and Hoodoo Pass and all.

Note: The Middle Fork Prince Creek trail is the best feeder for a tidy

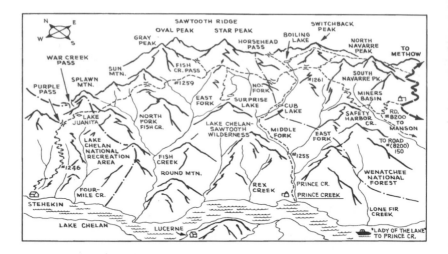

loop. Have the *Lady* drop you at Prince Creek, on the uplake side (Hike 46, Chelan Lakeshore Trail), and gain 5500 feet in 12 miles. Camps at 4, 6, and 8 miles from the lake.

The trail climbs to Chipmunk Pass, the 7050-foot saddle (11½ miles) to North Fork Prince Creek, and here enters the Lake Chelan–Sawtooth Wilderness, the end of motorcycles. It descends to a 5560-foot low point in forest (14 miles) and climbs to flowers again and the 7400-foot pass (18½ miles) to East Fork Fish Creek. In odd-numbered years, sheep that have been driven up Buttermilk Creek here graze northward, devouring the flowers and fouling the water. (That's *another* letter for you to write your congressperson, with another copy to the Forest Service.)

A short, steep drop leads to a 6800-foot junction with the trail to Fish Creek Pass (the sheep route). From a camp here, sidetrips include a stroll to larch-ringed Star Lake beneath the great wall of Star Peak and scrambles to the summits of 8690-foot Star Peak and 8392-foot Courtney Peak. On the other hand, if camp is made after a meadow traverse to Twin Springs Camp in Horseshoe Basin, there are sidetrips to Tuckaway Lake, Gray Peak, and Oval Lakes.

The way ascends to the 7400-foot pass (22 miles) to North Fork Fish Creek, descends to 5520-foot woods (24½ miles), and climbs through gardens (camps off the trail, near Deephole Spring) to a 7250-foot pass (27½ miles) to Fourmile Creek. A descent and an upsy-downsy traverse lead to Lake Juanita, 6665 feet, 30 miles. The quick and terrific sidetrip here is to Boulder Butte, 7350 feet, one-time lookout site.

At 30½ miles is 6880-foot Purple Pass, famous for the gasps drawn by the sudden sight—5800 feet below—of wind-rippled, sun-sparkled waters of Lake Chelan, seeming close enough for a swandive, and except for one brief glimpse earlier, the first view. Hundreds of switchbacks take your poor old knees down Hazard and Purple Creeks to Stehekin, 38 miles, and the ice cream.

138

53 SUMMER BLOSSOM TRAIL

One-way trip to Chelan Summit
   Trail 6 miles
Hiking time 4 hours
High point 7850 feet
Elevation gain 1800 feet in,
   600 feet out

Round trip to North Navarre
   viewpoint 5 miles
Hiking time 4 hours
High point 7850 feet
Elevation gain 1400 feet

Hikable mid-July through
   September
One day or backpack
Map: Green Trails No. 115 Prince
   Creek
Current information: Ask at Park
   Service–Forest Service
   Information Center about trail
   No. 1258

You say horse manure ruins your lunch? Motorcycles convince you
there's a bright side to nuclear extinction? The south end of the Chelan
Summit Trail weakens your belief in a Benign Creation? Is that what's
bothering you, Bunky? Be of good cheer! Take the Summer Blossom
Trail! Sniff the blossoms in peace on a "hikers-only" trail! Enjoy the
horizons unobstructed by the blue haze of exploding hydrocarbons! But
note that this Utopia is for experienced backpackers, not beginners.

The ancient sheepherders' driveway, recently resurrected and lov-
ingly renamed, parallels the Sum-
mit Trail for 6 miles, traversing
gardens in sky-high views. There
are two problems. The first is
driving to the trailhead. The second is that the path is steep, in
part rough, and in part hardly
there at all. However, if the
trailhead can be reached, the
route provides a magnificent day
hike to the top of North Navarre
Peak, or a gorgeous 2- or 3-day
round trip, or the start of a week-
long journey along the Sawtooth
Ridge and on down to Stehekin.

The road (if such a cliffhanger
deserves the name) often is impassable to ordinary passenger
cars; before setting out, check at
the Park Service–Forest Service
Information Center. One approach
is via Grade Creek road (Hike 52,
Chelan Summit Trail); however,
the 2 miles beyond Safety Harbor
trailhead to South Navarre Camp-

Daisies

Summer Blossom trail on side of North Navarre Peak

ground are some years sporty for jeeps but a misery for the Family Circus Wagon, though the 2 final miles from the campground to the Summer Blossom trailhead are quite decent. The least bad approach is from the Methow Valley. From Pateros on the Columbia River drive the Methow Valley Highway 17 miles toward Twisp. Just before crossing the Methow River the seventh time turn left on Gold Creek Road. In 1 mile turn left on road No. 4340, and in 1 mile more left again on road No. 4330. At about 5.5 miles from this junction is another; go right, following the sign "Cooper Mountain Road 7." These 7 miles grow steeper. The junction with Cooper Mountain Road is in a scenic parkland saddle on the divide between the Methow River and Lake Chelan. Turn right 9 miles on road No. 82, sliced just far enough into the flowery sidehill for two hikers to walk side by side comfortably. At 23.5 miles from the Methow Valley Highway is Summer Blossom trailhead, elevation 6440 feet.

The wheel-free, horse-free, narrow, sometimes meager trail ascends "Narvie Basin," as old-timers pronounce "Navarre," then the ridge of North Navarre Peak. At about 1½ miles it rounds a knob, crosses fields of boulders and blossoms of arid-land flowers, and at about 2½ miles tops out on a 7850-foot shoulder that is a quick stroll away from the summit of North Navarre, 7963 feet; on shoulder as on summit, the views are from snow giants of the Cascade Crest to open steppe of the Columbia Plateau. For a day hike, this is a most spectacular turnaround.

The trail continues to be steadily and wildly scenic as it loses about 450 feet in tight switchbacks and a scary use-your-hands balcony traverse under a cliff, then roams open meadows on the very crest of Sawtooth Ridge and swings around the slopes of a 7751-foot peaklet. At 4½ miles it drops to a tiny basin with water and luscious camps in early summer, then ascends a bit and contours to a junction with the Summit Trail at the 7400-foot pass between Horsethief Basin and East Fork Prince Creek headwaters, attained at 6 miles from the Summer Blossom trailhead.

For the first campsite with guaranteed water (providing the sheep haven't been there first) go another ½ mile down into the lush basin at the headwaters of the East Fork.

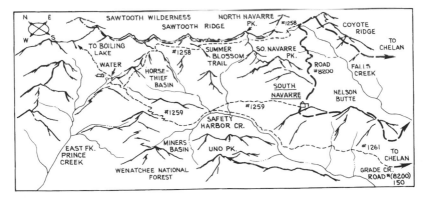

54 FOGGY DEW CREEK

Round trip to Sunrise Lake
   13 miles
Allow 2 days
High point 7228 feet
Elevation gain 3700 feet
Hikable July through early October

Map: Green Trails No. 115 Prince
   Creek
Current information: Ask at
   Methow Valley Ranger District
   about trail No. 417

The name has magic for those who love the folk song, and the scene
has more. Maybe the stiff climb of 3700 feet doesn't usually stir the
poetry in a hiker's soul, but the loud waters of Foggy Dew Creek do,
and the lake in a horseshoe cirque amid meadows, cliffs, and parklike
larch and alpine firs. Try it in late September when the larch has
turned to gold. However, since hunters are here then, maybe you'd prefer the midsummer solitude, caused in no small measure by the fish-
less condition of the shallow lake. A party could spend many days
happily here, exploring the sidetrails on both sides of the divide and,
as well, the Chelan Summit Trail (Hike 52), to which this trail leads.

From Pateros on the Columbia River, drive the Methow Valley High-
way 17 miles toward Twisp. Just before crossing the Methow River for
the seventh time, turn left on a narrow country road signed "Gold
Creek Loop." At 1 mile turn left on road No. 4340 signed "Foggy Dew."
If coming from Twisp drive 15 miles toward Pateros. Just before crossing the Methow River for the third time, turn right on narrow Gold
Creek Loop road. In 1.5 miles turn right on the above-mentioned road
No. 4340. Whichever way you reach it, from this point drive North
Fork Gold Creek road No. 4340 for 5 miles and turn left on road No.
(4340)200 for another 3.7 miles. At 9.1 miles are the road-end and
trailhead, elevation 3490 feet, 8.8 miles from the county road.

Foggy Dew trail No. 417 starts in selectively logged (all the big pines
selected) forest, climbs steadily, and at 2½ miles passes Foggy Dew

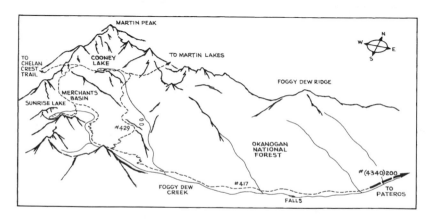

Foggy Dew Falls

Falls, something to sing about. At 3½ miles the valley and trail turn sharply right. At 4 miles cross a small tributary and at 5 miles come to a junction with Martin Peak trail No. 429 and the end of the motorcyclists.

At 5½ miles, 6400 feet, steepness lessens and the path ascends moderately in ever-expanding meadows. At 6 miles reach Merchants Basin and a junction with a way trail to Sunrise Lake. From here the Foggy Dew trail to the Chelan Summit is little traveled.

The Sunrise Lake trail climbs ½ mile to the shores at 7228 feet, 6½ miles from the road. Explorations abound but campsites are limited; Merchants Basin is a nice base.

For a different way back, adding to the round trip an extra 2 miles, 1200 feet, more meadows, and another lake, at the trail junction in Merchants Basin take the path climbing toward an unnamed 8000-foot pass to the north. From the path the trail switchbacks above a rockslide 1½ miles to Cooney Lake; return to Foggy Dew trail by trail No. 429.

55 COONEY LAKE

Round trip 16 miles
Hiking time 10 hours
High point 7241 feet
Elevation gain 3750 feet
Hikable mid-July through
September

One day or backpack
Map: Green Trails No. 115 Prince
Creek
Current information: Ask at
Methow Valley Ranger District
about trail Nos. 417 and 429

The jewel of the Sawtooths, that's what many hikers call Cooney Lake, located just at timberline, the shores sprinkled with lovely larches, the waters mirroring cliffs of the cirque.

You might very well call it a crime that the Forest Service has let a hundred-odd ORV drivers drive away thousands of hikers from the

Cooling off in Cooney Lake after a strenuous backpack

Cooney vicinity while nearby Oval Lakes (Hike 61) are in wilderness and thus are being trampled by those hundreds and hundreds of feet. Beauty is in the eye of the beholder, but Cooney Lake, Sunrise Lake, Martin Lakes, Boiling Lake, Eagle Lakes, both Crater Lakes, and their surrounding meadows are—in the eye of these here surveyors—more beautiful than the three Oval Lakes. But because of the possible encounters with motorcycles, most hikers shun these beauties like the plague.

Now, contrarily, you may call this a blessing, and indeed it is when there are no motorcycles around to harass hikers. In fact, few motorcyclists actually use the Gold Creek trails, which add up to only a 2-hour ride, not worth unloading their machines. Even fewer bother to get off their machines to walk the short distance to the lakeshores. Hikers who brave the trails may find a whole lake to themselves.

Drive to Foggy Dew trail No. 417 (Hike 54), elevation 3490 feet. Ascend the Foggy Dew trail 5 miles to a junction, 6000 feet, and go right on Martin Creek trail No. 429. The way switchbacks upward 3 miles, gaining 1200 more feet, crossing two forks of Foggy Dew Creek. At 8 miles from the road the Martin Creek Motorcycle Expressway on which you have been jaywalking goes right and a hiker/horse path crosses the creek, enters a meadow, and reaches the shore of Cooney Lake, 7241 feet.

To help the Forest Service revegetate the shore, don't camp here, but continue on the trail above the left side of the lake to areas less brutalized.

For extra stimulation, add a loop trip to the basic trip, and a sidetrip from the loop to Sunrise Lake (Hike 54, Foggy Dew Creek). Stay on the trail from Cooney Lake as it climbs over a low cliff on the south side, past a shallow (maybe dry) pond, and steeply switchbacks to an 8000-foot pass. Descend to Merchants Basin and proceed down the Foggy Dew trail, past the sidetrail to Sunrise Lake, to the starting point. The loop adds 2 miles and 1000 feet of elevation gain, plus the numbers for the sidetrip.

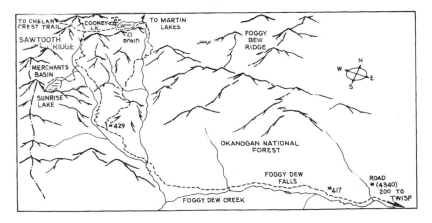

Boiling Lake

LOWER METHOW RIVER
Unprotected area

EAGLE LAKES— BOILING LAKE

Round trip 17 miles
Allow 2 days
High point 7600 feet
Elevation gain 2900 in,
600 feet out
Hikable July through September

Map: Green Trails No. 115 Prince
Creek
Current information: Ask at
Methow Valley Ranger District
about trail No. 431

Pretty Eagle Lakes under beetling crags. A 7590-foot pass across the Chelan Summit to Boiling Lake. A bushel of byways to meadow nooks. Easy-roaming routes to peaks with views over forests and sagebrush to ranches in the Methow Valley, over the Lake Chelan trench to ice giants of the North Cascades.

The "National Recreation Trail" (whatever that is) has been rebuilt smooth and wide, with banked corners. For the benefit of racing hikers? Galloping horses? Not at all. For the motorcyclists who burrowed into the state gas-tax money and—making sure to keep the plot from hikers—turned the former foot trail into a machine speedway. To avoid dust and danger and aggravation, it is recommended you do this trip in late June or early July when snowpatches still stop wheels but not feet. Take note of the mint of money the Forest Service spent to "improve" the trail for motorcycles and the obviously costly maintenance. Note, too, that for the benefit of horse-riders, who in the beginning were the earliest to do battle against the invasion by wheels, the Forest Service has installed at the trailhead a water system for horses, several corrals, and picnic tables. This is called "multiple use," or "something for everybody." For hikers it means dodging hot wheels and finding a safe place to pass horses. (Have *you* written *your* letter to your congressperson, with a copy to the Forest Service?)

Drive North Fork Gold Creek road No. 4340 (Hike 54, Foggy Dew Creek). At 5 miles pass the Foggy Dew road. At 6.7 miles is a junction. Turn left on road No. (4340)300, signed "Crater Creek," another 4.6 miles (at 3.7 miles keep left on a switchback where a spur road takes off) to Eagle Lake trail No. 431, elevation 4700 feet, 11.3 miles from the county road.

The first mile is fairly level, then a steady ascent begins. Pass the Crater Lake trail (Hike 57) and the Martin Creek trail (Hike 58). At 4½ miles, 6600 feet, a hiker-only sidetrail goes off left, dropping 120 feet in ½ mile to lower Eagle Lake, elevation 6490 feet; good camping. The main trail proceeds to campsites near a small tarn and then, at 7000 feet, a short sidetrail to Upper Eagle Lake, 7 miles, 7110 feet.

At 7½ miles the main motorcycle raceway slices through the Sawtooth Ridge at Horsehead Pass, 7590 feet, between two 8000-foot peaks of the crest. The wheel-easy switchbacks descend 1 mile to 6950-foot Boiling Lake, not (as the name implies) a hot puddle in a sunbaked desert, but a cool pool in green meadows, ringed by widely scattered and pleasant campsites. (The "boiling" is bubbles of air rising from bottom mud.) The trail continues down a bit more to join the Chelan Summit Trail (Hike 52). Via that thoroughfare and its offshoots, or the old sheep trails from the lake, restless souls may wander to any number of flower gardens (early July is most colorful) and summit views.

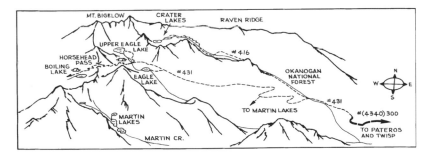

57 CRATER LAKES

Round trip 8 miles
Hiking time 5 hours
High point 6841 feet
Elevation gain 2100 feet
Hikable mid-June through
September

One day or backpack
Map: Green Trails No. 115 Prince
Creek
Current information: Ask at
Methow Valley Ranger District
about trail Nos. 416 and 431

Oh yes, the Gold Creek scenery is terrific and the greenery is luscious, but the wheels wheels wheels razzing this way and that! The cavalry regiments beating the trails to dust! Who can handle it? Cheer up, hiker, because in the middle of the uproar lies an oasis of clean peace, a trail to two alpine lakes ringed by rugged peaks, surrounded by groves of neat trees and patches of pretty meadow. Motorcycles are prohibited—the trail is too steep for them. Horses are not—but the trail is too short and mean to please the heavy cavalry. So don't complain about the steepness. If the trail were improved it would become just another half-hour sidetrip for the wheel-spinners.

Drive to Eagle Lake trail No. 431 (Hike 56), elevation 4700 feet.

Hike the dusty Eagle Lakes razzerway No. 431 a long ½ mile to a junction at about 4900 feet, just past Crater Creek. Go right on Crater Lakes trail No. 416, signed "No Motorcycles." The hiker is immediately struck by the fact the tread is covered not by inches of dust, as on ORV trails (roads), but needles. Ah, wilderness! In a long ½ mile (1 mile from the road), the path bridges Crater Creek. Several very steep stretches have been badly chewed up by the few horses that venture here. Otherwise the tread is in fair shape considering the gain of 2000 feet in 3 miles. The hiker will want to take the excuse of two viewpoints to pause, inhale deeply, and gaze across rolling hills to Methow ranches.

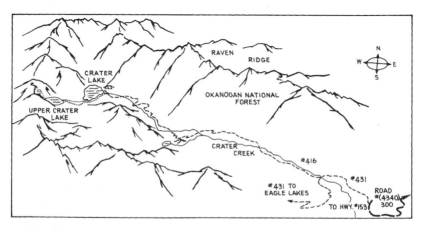

At 3¼ miles from the Eagle Lakes trail (4 miles from the road), 6814 feet, is the first of the two Crater Lakes. The horse camp is ¼ mile below the lake, but horse manure and hoof pits in campsites at the little meadow at the lakehead show that horses don't care.

The upper Crater Lake has no formal trail. At the lower lake go right, around the shore, cross an inlet stream in the lakehead meadow, and continue to the second stream rushing down the mountainside. Cross it and follow the course up. A person who stays close to the tumbling water can't get lost but will have numerous windfalls to dodge. In ½ mile, at 6969 feet, is the shallow upper lake. The ragged ridge to the south is a nameless spur of Mt. Bigelow. To the north is an extension of Raven Ridge. The surveyor found no horse souvenirs in the camps.

Upper Crater Lake

Lower Martin Lake

LOWER METHOW VALLEY
Unprotected area

 MARTIN LAKES

Round trip 14 miles
Hiking time 8 hours
High point 6800 feet
Elevation gain 2400 feet in,
400 feet out
Hikable July through September

One day or backpack
Map: Green Trails No. 115 Prince
Creek
Current information: Ask at
Methow Valley Ranger District
about trail Nos. 429 and 431

Beneath the cliffs of 8375-foot Martin Peak nestle two small lakes, the shores lined with larch trees; late September, when the needles turn golden before falling, is an especially fine time for a visit. But

150

the flowers of early July are nothing to sneeze at either, unless you're allergic.

Drive to Eagle Lake trail No. 431 (Hike 56), elevation 4700 feet.

Hike the Eagle Lakes Obstacle Course (you being one of the obstacles), pass the Crater Lakes trail at ½ mile, and continue to another junction at 2 miles, 5700 feet. Turn left onto Martin Creek Expressway No. 429, dropping 400 feet in a bit less than 1 mile to a crossing of Eagle Creek. Watch out for runaway motorcycles doing 20 miles per hour.

In long switchbacks suitably banked for speeding, ascend Martin Creek valley, never near the creek, thanks to a wonderful old-growth forest, views are few to the outside world. At about 6½ miles from the road is a junction, 6400 feet. Go right on Martin Lake trail No. 429A. See the sign "No Motorcycles," and make a happy face. Then make a different face on stretches of steep tread

Grouse

torn up by motorcycles (don't blame the machines—they can't read). At 7 miles, 6729 feet, is the first Martin Lake. Settle in to enjoy the peace under the larches. However, before your trip check with the State Wildlife Department on the bag limit for illegal motorcycles.

A way trail along the shore leads in a scant ¼ mile to the second lake.

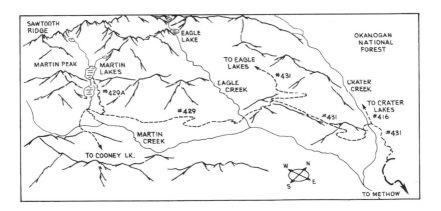

59 GOLDEN LAKES LOOP

Loop trip 23 miles
Allow 3 days
High point 8000 feet
Elevation gain 4200 feet
Hikable mid-July through
September

Map: Green Trails No. 115 Prince
Creek
Current information: Ask at
Methow Valley Ranger District
about trail Nos. 431, 434, and
429

The Enchantment Lakes have gained wide and well-deserved fame, so much that the Forest Service has put forth a long list of restrictions to preserve the quality of the land and the recreational experience. Trembling on the brink of comparable fame is the Golden Lakes Loop, a route that goes through miles of meadows, passes five lakes and looks down to three others, and tops ridges with views from the Columbia Plateau to the Cascade Crest. The trip is a glory in summer, the grass lushly green and the flowers many-colored. In fall it's absolutely mystical, the larch trees turned to gold, giving the name by which this tour will become famous.

The hiker who takes the 3-day introduction will want to return for a week—for many weeks over many years. The first trip also will stimulate strong letters to congresspersons (as well as copies to the Forest Service), asking how come the Enchantments are treated so tenderly as to exclude dogs and limit the number of hikers, yet in this companion piece of wonderland the motorcycles are permitted—more accurately say, officially encouraged.

Drive to Eagle Lake trail No. 431 (Hike 56), elevation 4700 feet.

The description here is counterclockwise; clockwise is just as good. Either way start on the Eagle Lake trail, at 2 miles passing Martin

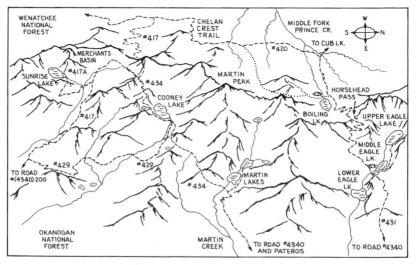

Headwater basin of East Fork Prince Creek

Creek trail (Hike 58), the final leg of the loop return. At 7 miles, 7110 feet, on a short spur from the main trail, is Upper Eagle Lake, with camps for the first night.

The second day's 6 miles, mostly above timberline, could keep a party of explorers happy for a week. Cross 7590-foot Horsehead Pass to Boiling Lake (Hike 56). (The Forest Service plans to reopen, for hikers only, an old sheep drive from Boiling Lake south over a 7500-foot pass to join the Chelan Summit Trail, avoiding several miles of ORVs.) If not so signed, continue from Boiling Lake a mile down into open forest. At 9½ miles from the road is a junction with the Chelan Summit Trail (Hike 52), 6600 feet. Turn left on it, climbing back to meadows, passing nice campsites, to a 7100-foot saddle.

Contour from the saddle about ½ mile into the broad headwaters basin of East Fork Prince Creek and an unmarked junction of the Switchback Peak trail. The one and only real difficulty is finding the exact spot where the way goes from lush sidehill onto a vast boulder field on the slopes of "Switchback Peak" (called this locally for generations). Look for tread, cairns, and/or horse manure heading off to the left and slanting up the meadows. Maintenance has been next to nothing in the near-century since sheepherders completed the engineering feat; some rocks have fallen onto the tread.

The switchbacks lead to a 8000-foot high point on the shoulder of the 8321-foot peak, tremendously scenic. The way sidehills above Merchants Basin to the ridge above Cooney Lake. Switchbacks drop (steep snow here may force the unequipped to turn around or die) to a campsite bench near the upper end of Cooney Lake (Hike 55), at 7241 feet.

The third day is mostly downhill. From Cooney Lake follow the outlet stream a few hundred feet to a junction with the Martin Creek trail. The right fork descends to the Foggy Dew trail; take the left, switchbacking down into forest and a junction with the sidetrail to Martin Lakes (Hike 58). Stay with the Martin Creek trail down to the crossing of Eagle Creek and up the 500 feet to the Eagle Lake trail, reached at a point just 2 miles from the trailhead.

60   LIBBY LAKE

Round trip 11 miles
Hiking time 6 hours
High point 7618 feet
Elevation gain 3200 feet
Hikable July through September
One day or backpack

Maps: Green Trails No. 83
   Buttermilk Butte, No. 115
   Prince Creek
Current information: Ask at
   Methow Valley Ranger District
   about trail No. 415

Massive rockslides dramatically ring the lake on three sides. On the fourth are giant larch trees that turn golden in fall. A connoisseur might judge the scene not quite as beautiful as the nearby Oval Lakes—unless he brought his nose into the evaluation, since the Ovals typically entertain up to half a hundred horses a weekend, while Libby rarely sees a horse wading out from the shore and letting a souvenir drop. The reason is that the trail is so steep in places as to be a notorious horse-killer. However, lest hikers rejoice to excess, the Forest Service plans to rebuild the trail to horse standards when funds can be found.

Drive Highway 153 from the Columbia River toward Twisp. Just 1.2 miles east of Carlton turn south (left) on the county road signed "Black Pine Lake." At 2.5 miles go left on road No. 43, again signed "Black Pine Lake." At 7.7 miles from the highway road go left on road No. 4340, signed "North Fork Gold Creek." In another 1.2 miles go right on road No. (4340)700, signed "Libby Lake," then left on (4340)750, signed "Libby Creek," to the road-end and trailhead, about 12.4 miles from the highway, elevation 4400 feet.

Evening grosbeak in an abandoned campfire site

Logging has messed up the start of Libby Lake trail No. 415. The route goes very steeply up a cat track to the old tread, which contours the ridge slopes and then, with some ups and downs (more ups than downs), levels off and enters the Lake Chelan–Sawtooth Wilderness. In about 2½ miles the trail crosses North Fork Libby Creek to a pleasant camp. It climbs into a forest of pine and larch and glacier-polished slabs, at 5 miles passing remnants of a falling-down cabin. Several rocky stretches (undoubtedly why there are no horses to speak of) lie along the way to the shores of the lake, 7618 feet, 5½ miles from the road.

Libby Lake

The shore has very little flat ground. At the outlet is a rock-filled dam, evidently built by farmers long ago and also forgotten long ago. (Golly knows what they had in mind. Irrigation?) A few hundred feet below the lake are some decent campsites.

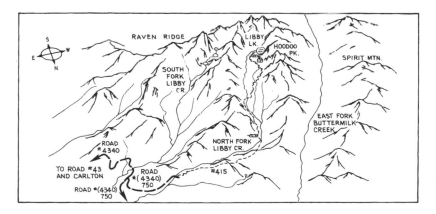

61   OVAL LAKES

**Round trip to West Oval Lake
16 miles**
Allow 3–5 days
High point 7000 feet
Elevation gain 4000 feet

**Round trip to Middle Oval Lake
21 miles**
Allow 3–5 days
High point 7700 feet
**Elevation gain 4700 feet in,
1000 feet out**

Hikable mid-July through October
Backpack
**Map: Green Trails No. 83
Buttermilk Butte**
**Current information: Ask at
Methow Valley Ranger District
about trail Nos. 410 and 410A**

Three mountain lakes, each in its own pocket scooped in the side of
Sawtooth Ridge. The lakes are not quite as pretty as the ones in the
Gold Creek area, which are little visited, but not having motorcycles,
Oval Lakes are the most popular destination in the Twisp Ranger District. The use is equally divided between hikers and horse-riders. During
a dry summer the horses pound the trail to inches-deep powder; better
go early while the ground is still damp. However, don't go too early because during snowmelt season the crossing of Eagle Creek is extremely
difficult. If the parking lot is jammed up by a dozen or two dozen horse-
trailers, each built for eight or more beasts, you would be well advised
to go elsewhere.

From the center of Twisp, drive Twisp River road 14.5 miles, go left
on War Creek road No. 4430, and in another 0.3 mile go left on road
No. 4420, signed "Eagle Creek Trail," for 0.8 mile, then sharply right
1.5 miles on road No. (4420)080 to the road-end and trail No. 410, elevation 3000 feet.

The first 1½ miles gain 1800 feet to a junction and the wilderness
boundary. The right-hand trail follows Eagle Creek to the crest of the

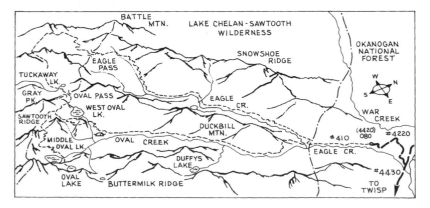

Sawtooth Range, the recommended route for a loop. For a round trip to Oval Lakes, take the trail straight ahead. In ¼ mile cross Eagle Creek, which early in the season is formidable for hikers. Scout upstream and down a hundred or two feet for a safe crossing.

From Eagle Creek the trail gains another 800 feet in a long ¾ mile and moderates, gaining 1200 feet in the next 3½ miles to a nice streamside campsite in a large meadow, 5800 feet. The next 1½ miles climb 1100 feet to a junction. Go right ¼ mile to West Oval Lake, 6860 feet.

For Middle Oval Lake go left, steeply at times, first in forest, then meadowland, and finally up barren slopes to a 7700-foot shoulder of Gray Peak. Drop 1000 feet to Middle Oval, 6695 feet. A way trail leads to East Oval Lake.

A loop is possible but not recommended for novices. The trail is not dangerous but often invisible. In fact, experienced highland roamers, aided by maps, are surprised to find traces of tread. To do it, follow Eagle Creek 6 miles from the Oval Lake junction to 7300-foot Eagle Pass and drop 800 feet to Summit Trail No. 1259. Climb back to 7000 feet and at a four-way junction go left on a sketchy trail to Tuckaway Lake, over 7000-foot Oval Pass to join the Middle Oval Lake trail. The loop totals 21 miles, elevation gain of 5500 feet.

The few nice campsites at West Oval Lake are so fragile that the Forest Service asks people to camp at Middle Oval Lake, too far for a day hike. If Middle Oval is the destination, plan to hike 5¾ miles to a first-night camp at the 5800-foot meadow.

Oval Peak from between West and Middle Oval Lakes

Larch trees and Scatter Lake

SCATTER LAKE

Round trip 9 miles
Hiking time 7½ hours
High point 7047 feet
Elevation gain 3900 feet
Hikable mid-July through October

Backpack
Map: Green Trails No. 82 Stehekin
Current information: Ask at
   Methow Valley Ranger District
   about trail No. 427

If you want a definition for "grueling," try this, and don't be fooled by the mere 4½ miles of hiking because they gain 3900 feet, unmercifully hot in the midday summer sun. Why do it, then? You'll know when you get there. From the cirque walls in the side of 8321-foot Abernathy Peak the sterile brown talus, streaked with mineralized yellow and red, slopes to the shore of a stunning blue gem ringed by larches, their delicate green a striking contrast to vivid colors of the rock.

Drive the Methow Valley Highway to Twisp and turn west on the Twisp River road, signed "Twisp River Rec. Area," 22 miles (pavement ends at 14 miles). After crossing Scatter Creek go off right on a side-road 500 feet, passing a corral, to the start of Scatter Creek trail No. 427, elevation 3147 feet.

The route begins on a cat track dating from selective logging (all the big pines were selected). In ¼ mile the way becomes a regular footpath and briefly joins the Twisp River trail. The first mile makes long, gentle switchbacks above the Twisp valley. The second mile traverses and switchbacks high above Scatter Creek. At 2½ miles the creek is close.

At this point whoever built the trail apparently got tired of switchbacks; from now on when the hill is steep so is the path. At 3½ miles cross the Scatter Lake fork of Scatter Creek and follow the right side of the stream. At 4 miles is a delightful camp in sound of a waterfall. The trail climbs above the falls, levels out, passes a tiny tarn, and reaches the shore of Scatter Lake, 7047 feet. It was worth it. Numerous pleasant camps but not much wood.

The highest point of the cirque wall is Abernathy. The summit is to the left of the point with a red cap.

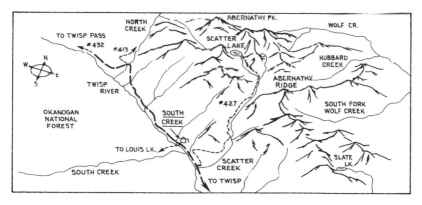

63   LOUIS LAKE

Round trip 10½ miles	**One day or backpack**
Hiking time 5½ hours	**Map: Green Trails No. 82 Stehekin**
High point 5351 feet	**Current information: Ask at**
Elevation gain 2600 feet	**Methow Valley Ranger District**
Hikable mid-July through October	**about trail Nos. 401 and 428**

Beneath one of the most serrate stretches of Sawtooth Ridge is Louis Lake, large for this part of the Cascades, lying under terrific cliffs of 7742-foot Rennie Peak on the left and a nameless 8142-foot peak on the right. So narrow is the gash of a valley that even in midsummer the sun touches the floor only a few hours a day.

Drive the Methow Valley Highway to Twisp, turn west on the Twisp River road 22.5 miles, and just beyond South Creek Campground find the start of South Creek trail No. 401, elevation 3200 feet.

Cross the Twisp River on a bridge, pass the Twisp River trail, and ascend in sound of South Creek cascading down a slot canyon. At 2 miles, 3800 feet, is a junction. The main trail continues up South Creek another 5½ miles to the national park and a junction with Rainbow Creek trail. Go left on Louis Lake trail No. 428, dropping a bit to camps and a bridge over South Creek. South Creek Butte can be recognized by its red crest.

At about 3½ miles the path enters Louis Creek valley; a hiker has the dark suspicion she's entering a trap, a cul-de-sac with no escape through precipices. The trail contours high above Louis Creek with many ups and a few downs. At 4 miles, where the way parallels the stream, an opening appears in the otherwise unbroken expanse of high walls and the route proceeds through it to the lake, 5351 feet.

The setting is spectacular. On the far shore is a small, tree-covered island. The lake surface is largely choked with enormous masses of driftwood from gigantic winter avalanches. Camping at the lake is very

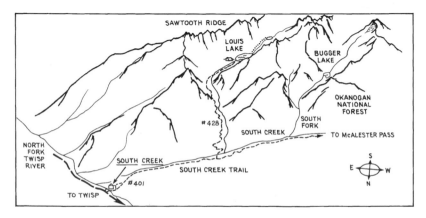

Louis Lake

limited and best not done at all; instead, use the sites several hundred
feet before reaching the shore.

A second lake, tiny, is 1 mile away and 500 feet higher, which
sounds like an easy amble, but it ain't, the access mostly over broad
bad fields of big boulders. If determined to get there anyhow, find a
trail of sorts that goes around a thicket of slide alder, then parallels
the shore.

64 TWISP PASS— STILETTO VISTA

Round trip to Twisp Pass 9 miles
Hiking time 6–8 hours
High point 6064 feet
Elevation gain 2400 feet
Hikable late June through October
One day or backpack
Map: Green Trails No. 82 Stehekin

Current information: Ask at
Methow Valley Ranger District
about trail No. 432
Park Service backcountry use
permit required for camping
at Dagger Lake

Climb from Eastern Washington forest to Cascade Crest gardens, glacier-smoothed boulders, dramatic rock peaks, and views down to Bridge Creek and across to Goode and Logan. Then wander onward amid a glory of larch-dotted grass and flowers to an old lookout site with horizons so rich one wonders how the fire-spotter could ever have noticed smoke. For a special treat do the walk in autumn when the air is cool and the alpine country is blazing with color.

Drive the Methow Valley Highway to Twisp and turn west on the Twisp River road, signed "Twisp River Rec. Area," 25 miles to the end. A short bit before the road-end is a large trailhead parking area, elevation 3650 feet.

The trail begins by ascending moderately through woods, with occasional upvalley glimpses of pyramid-shaped Lincoln Butte. At 2 miles are a junction with Copper Pass trail No. 426 and the last well-watered campsite for a long, hot way. Cross the North Fork Twisp River on a footlog and continue fairly steeply on soft-cushioned tread to 3 miles; stop for a rest on ice-polished buttresses, the views down to valley-bottom forest and up to the ragged ridge of Hock Mountain, above the glaciated basin of the South Fork headwaters. The trail emerges from trees to traverse a rocky sidehill, the rough tread sometimes blasted from cliffs. At about 4 miles the route enters heather and flowers. A final ¼ mile climbs to Twisp Pass, 6064 feet, 4½ miles, on the boundary of the North Cascades National Park. The pass is so fragile the Park Service prohibits camping on its side and the Forest Service wishes you wouldn't.

The trail drops 450 steep feet in 1 mile to Dagger Lake camps at 5508 feet and 4 more miles to Bridge Creek and a junction with the Pacific Crest Trail.

For wider views ascend meadows north from the pass and look down to Dagger Lake and Bridge Creek and across to Logan, Goode, Black, Frisco, and much more.

Don't go away without rambling the crest south from the pass about ¼ mile to the foot of Twisp Mountain and a magical surprise—a hidden little lake surrounded by grass and blossoms and alpine forest, a mountain sanctuary.

The open slopes north of the pass demand extended exploration. And here is another surprise. Hikers heading in the logical direction toward

Dagger Lake from Twisp Pass

Stiletto Peak will stumble onto sketchy tread of an ancient trail, fairly obvious the first mile, then less so. Follow the route up and down highlands, by sparkling creeks, to a green shelf under cliffs of 7660-foot Stiletto Peak, a fairy place of meandering streams and groves of wispy larch. Then comes a field of photogenic boulders, a rocky ridge, and the 7223-foot site of the old fire-lookout cabin. Look north over Copper Creek to Liberty Bell and Early Winter Spires, northwest to Tower, Cutthroat, Whistler, Arriva, and Black, southwest to McGregor, Glacier, and Bonanza, and south to Hock and Twisp—and these are merely a few of the peaks seen, not to mention the splendid valley. This vista is only 2 miles from Twisp Pass, an easy afternoon's round trip.

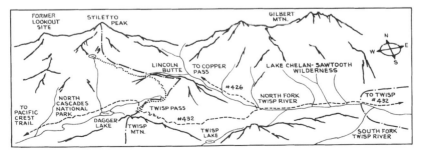

Copper Pass

65 COPPER PASS

Round trip to pass 10 miles
Hiking time 6 hours
High point 6760 feet
Elevation gain 3100 feet
One day
Loop trip 21 miles
Allow 2 days
High point 6760 feet
Elevation gain 5500 feet
Hikable July through mid-October
Map: Green Trails No. 82 Stehekin
Current information: Ask at
Methow Valley Ranger District
about trail Nos. 432 and 426

The climb to the heathery pass is steep, but the color is worth it. Try the trip in July when glacier lilies and yellowbells are blooming, or in August for asters and cow parsnip and paintbrush and a few tucked-away gentians, or in late September when larch trees turn to gold.

The prospectors' trail of olden days connected the Twisp River to the Stehekin via Bridge Creek. Unused for decades, in 1981 and 1982 it was reopened to the pass by volunteers from the Sierra Club and Outward Bound. The trail down to Bridge Creek has not been brushed but can be found and used for a 3-day loop trip, returning via Twisp Pass (Hike 64). This alternative requires a backcountry permit for the North Cascades National Park, obtainable at the Twisp Ranger Station.

Drive the Twisp River road to the end, elevation 3700 feet (Hike 64).

Hike Twisp River trail No. 432 for 2 miles to a junction just before crossing North Fork Twisp River (dwindled to a creek); go straight on

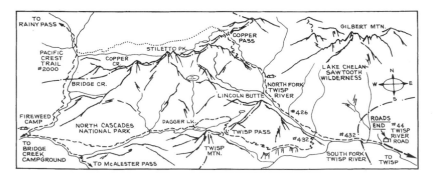

North Fork Twisp River near old prospector's cabin

trail No. 426, signed "Copper Pass." With more ups than downs the way follows the North Fork, mostly in woods. At 3½ miles cross the stream to a nice campsite, 5200 feet.

There's nothing now but up. In ¼ mile is a view of a double waterfall, and a bit farther, ruins of an old cabin. Scarcely deigning to switchback, the trail aims at the sky, partly in trees and partly in meadows.

At 6700 feet, 5 miles, is the sky—which is to say, Copper Pass, where herbaceous meadows yield to heather meadows. Day-hikers may gaze down Copper Creek, across to the rocky ridge of Early Winters Spire, out to faraway, ice-clad Goode Mountain, eat lunch, and go home satisfied.

Loopers can readily see the trail dropping steeply to green meadows at the head of Copper Creek. A bit of searching at the far edge of the boggy meadow may be needed to find the resumption of tread in forest. In about 4 miles from the pass the path intersects the Pacific Crest Trail. Follow it down Bridge Creek 1 mile to enter North Cascades National Park, then 1 more mile to Fireweed Camp, 3600 feet. From Fireweed, 4 long, steep miles climb to Twisp Pass, 6064 feet, and 4 shorter miles drop to the trailhead, completing a loop of 21 miles with an elevation gain and loss of 5500 feet.

66 WOLF CREEK

Round trip to end of trail 23 miles
Allow 2–3 days
High point 5700 feet
Elevation gain 3400 feet
Hikable mid-June through
October

Maps: Green Trails No. 51 Mazama,
No. 83 Buttermilk Butte
Current information: Ask at
Methow Valley Ranger District
about trail No. 527; if exploring,
also ask about trail No. 527A

For the hiker who wants to be alone, really alone, try Wolf Creek (but not in hunting season). It's a long walk up a long valley to meadows, old mines, and abandoned sidetrails to golly knows where. Adventure! Get lost—or at least bemused.

From the center of Winthrop drive Highway 20 east across the Methow River bridge and go right, past the school, on a road signed "Sun Mountain Lodge." At 1.3 miles turn right on Wolf Creek road 4.3 miles, then left on a road signed "L. Fork Wolf Creek." At 4.7 miles from Winthrop turn right on a road signed "Wolf Creek Trail," and at 8.4 miles go straight ahead to the large, road-end parking area and trail No. 527, elevation 2400 feet, 9 miles from Winthrop.

In the first easy ½ mile the trail enters the Lake Chelan–Sawtooth Wilderness. At about 4¼ miles is the crossing of North Fork Wolf Creek. In another ¼ mile is the unsigned and abandoned North Fork trail No. 528 (if it can be found), which goes 5 miles to the 6000-foot divide between McKinney Mountain and Storey Peak. Somewhere on this trail is an old stock driveway going east past Milton Mountain to Gardner Meadows; Milton Mountain is a former lookout site, so it must have a trail.

On the main Wolf Creek trail at 5½ miles from the road-end, a short spur goes left to campsites near an old patrol cabin. The trail becomes more rugged with a few steep pitches. At 8½ miles is the abandoned South Fork Wolf Creek trail, dead-ending in 2 miles. At 9

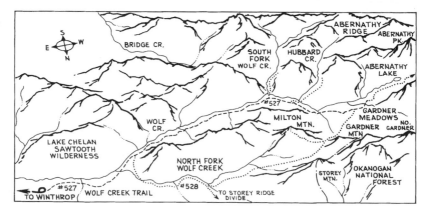

miles abandoned Hubbard Creek trail No. 527A climbs high to a cirque on Abernathy Ridge.

By 9 miles, 5700 feet, the Gardner Meadows have shaped up nicely, giving a good look at Abernathy Ridge. The maintained trail ends about 11 miles, 5800 feet. An abandoned trail, lost in vegetation, continues another 2 miles to a long-ago mining operation in 7400-foot meadows below the bare cliffs of Abernathy Ridge. A cross-country explorer could visit Abernathy Lake, 6357 feet.

Gardner Meadows and Abernathy Ridge

DRIVEWAY BUTTE

Round trip 8 miles
Hiking time 6 hours
High point 5982 feet
Elevation gain 3000 feet
Hikable late May through
September

One day
Map: Green Trails No. 50
    Washington Pass
Current information: Ask at
    Methow Valley Ranger District
    about trail No. 481

The former lookout site has views down the Methow Valley to ranches and towns and across to the Pasayten Wilderness, south to Gardner Mountain and the glaciers on Silver Star Mountain, and west to peaks of the Cascade Crest. There's a price to pay—sweat, much sweat. Be advised. Don't try the trip in the heat of day; the route has very little shade. Snow melts early on the south-facing slopes, making the hike possible in late May or early June when fields of sunflowers (balsamroot) are in full bloom. However, snow lingers in the high timber until middle or late June, halting a party not prepared to cope. Except during hunting season the trail is almost deserted.

Of the three routes to Driveway Butte, two haven't been maintained for 20 years: trail No. 450, from Early Winters Campground; and trail No. 481, from Rattlesnake Campground, beginning with a difficult ford of the Methow River. The way described here is by the latter trail but from its other terminus, at Klipchuck Campground.

Drive North Cascades Scenic Highway 20 east 12.6 miles from Washington Pass or 2.9 miles west from the Forest Service's Early Winters Information Center. Turn onto road No. (5310)300, signed "Klipchuck Campground," and drive 1 mile to the campground entrance; park here. A few feet back from the entrance find a gated forest road. Walk it about 500 feet to the start of Driveway Butte trail No. 481, elevation 3000 feet.

The trail sets out in a selective-logging area. (See the big stumps.) The grade is moderate at first but soon slants steeply up open fields of

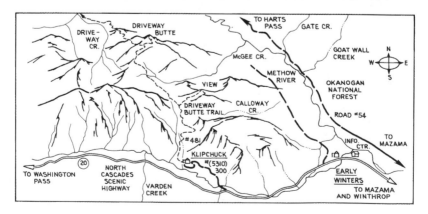

Silver Star Mountain from Driveway Butte trail

bright yellow balsamroot, with only occasional shade trees. After climbing 2100 feet in approximately 1¾ miles (that seem like 3), the path levels a bit, enters a dense forest, and comes to a junction. The campsites here have no water after the snow melts in middle or late June. If snow covers the main trail, which forks left, take the right fork steeply to the top of a 5545-foot nameless butte. A window in the trees gives a spectacular view of Silver Star Mountain.

From the junction the angle of the main trail moderates but the tread grows rougher, at times is obscured by brush, and at about 3½ miles disappears. A few rock cairns lead across open slopes of Driveway Butte. Take careful note of the point where the tread vanishes; you'll want to find this point on your way home. Should you lose the trail on the way up, simply zig and zag to the summit. Marvel how completely the old horse trail has vanished on the slopes, only to reappear 100 feet from the top.

The history of fire-watching from Driveway Butte began long, long ago with a platform in a tree. This was replaced in 1934 by a building on a 30-foot tower. In 1953 it was torn down and burned. Bits of glass and a scattering of rusty nails remain. So does the view.

68 ABERNATHY PASS

Round trip 18 miles
Allow 2 days
High point 6400 feet
Elevation gain 3400 feet
Hikable July through October

Maps: Green Trails No. 50
    Washington Pass, No. 51 Mazama
Current information: Ask at
    Methow Valley Ranger District
    about trail No. 476

Finding the trails too peopled for your solitudinous tastes? Try Cedar Creek. Climb splendid forests, first in a narrow V valley and then in a broad U trough between Silver Star and Gardner Mountains, which do not present themselves in sweeping panoramas but through many peeking-type windows. Proceed to Abernathy Pass for the big picture. Or strike off through the open woods and get really lonesome and very high on slopes of the Big Kangaroo.

Drive North Cascades Scenic Highway 20 west 3.5 miles from Early Winters Campground or east 13 miles from Washington Pass and turn

Cedar Creek Falls

onto road No. 200, signed "Cedar Creek Trail." At the road-end in 0.9 mile, turn right at the sign "Trailhead" into a large gravel pit. Cedar Creek trailhead No. 476 is atop the bank to the left, elevation 3000 feet.

Though the trail starts 400 vertical feet higher than the creek, to stay above the wild torrent it gains 500 feet in a short 2 miles to Cedar Falls, a spectacular twin waterfall, the destination of most hikers, many of whom stay at the camp here overnight despite the danger to their hearing.

The way continues to climb steeply to keep dry. At about 3 miles is a window view of the craggy summit of North Gardner Mountain. At 4 miles the post-glacial notch is left behind and the U-shaped glacial trough entered, with a consequent flattening of the grade. The path crosses occasional aspen-dotted meadows that give looks at the impressive shoulders of Silver Star right and Gardner left, and far up the valley to a wall of mountains, part of the Abernathy Peak massif.

The pleasant forest walk is enlivened by creeks that may or may not be log-bridged and in snowmelt time may or may not be easy to cross. Campsites are scattered along the way, including one at West Fork Cedar Creek and another, the best and the last, a scant mile farther at Middle Fork, 7 miles, 5000 feet. (The old mile markers predate the Sandy Butte road, so subtract a mile.)

The valley head appears to be a cul-de-sac, no possible route through the solid wall of granite peaks. The 2 miles and countless switchbacks that climb 1400 feet to Abernathy Pass, 6400 feet, therefore seem a magic trick. The summit of the pass is a narrow cleft and the trail immediately drops to North Creek and the Twisp River. For views, scramble the granite knobs west from the pass, on architecturally handsome ledges and slabs and buttresses, in picturesque pines and larches. The climax knob is ¾ mile, 7002 feet. Look north to Snagtooth Ridge and Silver Star Mountain and south across North Creek to Gilbert Mountain and pyramid-shaped Reynolds Peak, and back down the long valley whence you came.

The greatest hiking hereabouts is on paths beaten out by climbers. In open forests aromatic with Labrador tea and white rhododendron ("skunkbush"), and boggy glades dotted with insect-eating butterwort, then on steep heather meadows and rockslides, follow Middle Fork Cedar Creek to the south end of Kangaroo Ridge, or West Fork to the north end. Since this country has some of the most famous granite in the Cascades, watch out for Yellow Helmets chalking their fingers and snapping their carabiners.

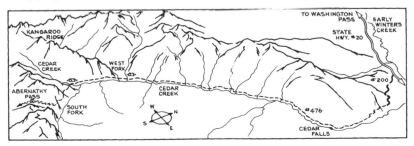

SILVER STAR

Round trip to Mudhole Lake
  9 miles
Hiking time 8 hours
High point 6600 feet
Elevation gain 3800 feet in,
  400 feet out
Round trip to viewpoint 10 miles
Hiking time 10 hours
High point 6919 feet
Elevation gain 4300 feet in,
  600 feet out

Hikable mid-June through
  September
One day or backpack
Maps: Green Trails No. 49
  Washington Pass, No. 50 Mazama
  (trail not shown)
Current information: Ask at
  Methow Valley Ranger District
  about trail No. 467A

A tiny lake, grand views, and a mountain lake nestled in a glacial cirque under the towering cliffs and glacier of Silver Star Mountain. Before putting on your hiking boots and grabbing your pack, be warned that this is not a hike for everyone. In fact, it is almost not a hike for anyone. The information block tells it all, a 4300-foot elevation gain to the best viewpoint. However, except for horse use during hunting season, the difficulties almost assure solitude. Fill a large canteen; there is no water on this trail.

Drive the North Cascades Highway to the Cedar Creek trailhead (Hike 68, Abernathy Pass), elevation 3000 feet.

Walk the Cedar Creek trail 200–300 feet and turn abruptly right on Varden Creek trail No. 467A. The way gains elevation rapidly, some 2500 feet in the first 2 miles to a shoulder of Silver Star, mostly steep and often rocky. Occasional glimpses down to Cedar Creek and out to the upper Methow Valley and across to Goat Peak grow to views up

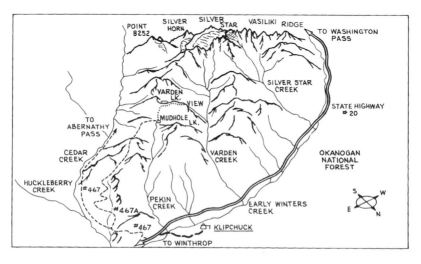

Cedar Creek valley from Varden Creek trail

Cedar Creek to Kangaroo Ridge and across the valley to North Gardner Mountain.

At approximately 3 miles the trail reaches a 6100-foot high point and then drops 120 feet, climbs 100 feet over the next high point, descends a bit, and climbs another 500 feet to 6600 feet, there leaving the ridge and dropping to tiny tree-ringed Mudhole Lake, 6400 feet, the official end of the trail, 4½ miles from the car.

A boot-beaten path leads to open meadows and a 6919-foot viewpoint under the towering cliffs of Silver Star. To the west are peaks in the Golden Horn Roadless Area, north are others in the Pasayten Wilderness, and 500 feet below is sparkling Varden Lake.

70 CUTTHROAT PASS

**Round trip from Cutthroat Creek
   road-end to Cutthroat Pass
   12 miles**
Hiking time 6–8 hours
High point 6800 feet
Elevation gain 2300 feet

**One-way trip from Rainy Pass to
   Cutthroat road-end 10½ miles**
Hiking time 6–7 hours
High point 6800 feet
Elevation gain 2000 feet

**Hikable July through
   mid-October**
One day or backpack
**Map: Green Trails No. 50
   Washington Pass**
**Current information: Ask at
   Methow Valley Ranger District
   about trail Nos. 483 and 2000**

A high ridge with impressive views, among the most scenic sections of the Pacific Crest Trail. If transportation can be arranged, a hike can start at Rainy Pass and end at Cutthroat Creek, saving 400 feet of elevation gain. However, because a short sidetrip to sparkling Cutthroat Lake makes a refreshing rest stop, the trail is described starting from Cutthroat Creek.

Drive North Cascades Scenic Highway 20 east from the Skagit Valley over Rainy and Washington Passes, or west from the Methow Valley 14 miles from Winthrop to Early Winters and 11 miles more to Cutthroat Creek. Beyond the bridge turn right on the Cutthroat Creek road 1

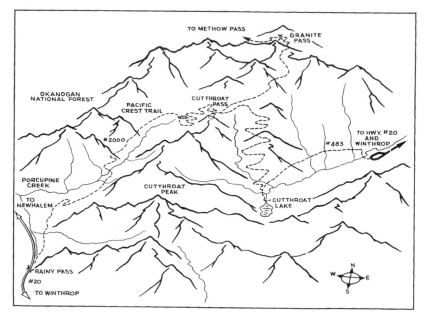

Mountain goats at Cutthroat Pass

mile to the road-end and trailhead, elevation 4500 feet. The upper regions are dry, so have a full canteen.

The trail quickly crosses Cutthroat Creek and begins a gentle 1¾-mile ascent amid sparse rainshadow forest to a junction with the Cutthroat Lake trail. The 4935-foot lake is ¼ mile away, well worth it, and the last practical campsites.

The next 2½ miles climb through big trees and little trees to meadows and a campsite (no water in late summer). A final scant 2 miles lead upward to 6800-foot Cutthroat Pass, about 6 miles from the road-end.

It is absolutely essential to stroll to the knoll south of the pass for a better look at the country. Cutthroat Peak, 7865 feet, stands high and close. Eastward are the barren west slopes of Silver Star. Mighty Liberty Bell sticks its head above a nearby ridge. Far southwest over Porcupine Creek is glacier-clad Dome Peak.

If time and energy permit, sidetrip 1 mile north on the Pacific Crest Trail to a knoll above Granite Pass and striking views down to Swamp Creek headwaters and across to 8444-foot Tower Mountain, 8366-foot Golden Horn, and Azurite, Black, and countless more peaks in the distance. This portion of the Crest Trail may be blocked by snow until mid-August.

From Cutthroat Pass the Crest Trail descends Porcupine Creek, past several campsites, a pleasant 5 miles to Rainy Pass, the first 2 miles in meadows and the rest of the way in cool forest by numerous creeks. The trail ends a few hundred feet west of the summit of 4840-foot Rainy Pass.

175

71 MAPLE PASS

Round trip to pass 6½ miles
Hiking time 4½ hours
High point 6600 feet
Elevation gain 1800 feet
Loop trip 7 miles
Hiking time 5 hours
High point 6850 feet
Elevation gain 1950 feet
Hikable mid-July through mid-October

One day
Maps: Green Trails No. 49 Mt. Logan, No. 50 Washington Pass, No. 81 McGregor Mtn., No. 82 Stehekin
Current information: Ask at Methow Valley Ranger District about trail No. 740

Lakes, little flower fields, small meadows, a loop, and big views sum up this delightful hike. The Forest Service built the trail to the pass (over the objection of the Park Service), intending it to be a segment of the Pacific Crest Trail, only to discover what had been obvious to the Park Service, that the impact on fragile meadows by hundreds of hikers—and especially by horses—led there by construction of the trail—would be disastrous.

Drive North Cascades Scenic Highway 20 east from the Skagit Valley or west from the Methow Valley to Rainy Pass and park at the south-side rest area. Find trail No. 740, signed "Lake Ann–Maple Pass." Elevation 4855 feet.

Elevation is gained at the obnoxiously easy grade typical of the freeway. At 1½ miles, 5400 feet, is a spur to the right to Lake Ann, destination of most hikers. The ½-mile path goes along the outlet valley, nearly level, by two shallow lakelets, around marshes, to the shore. Due to the dense population, camping is prohibited within ¼ mile of the lake.

The main trail ascends across a large rockslide well above Lake Ann. At 2¼ miles is 6200-foot Heather Pass; from a switchback, look west to Black Peak, Lewis Peak, and the cirque of Wing Lake, out of sight under the peak. A way trail traverses steep hillsides of heather, snow,

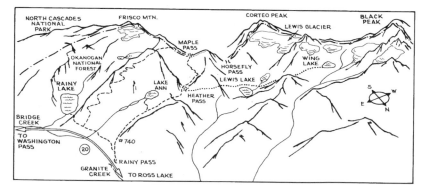

and boulders to Lewis Lake and Wing Lake; camping at the latter.

The main trail continues from Heather Pass, contouring over the top of cliffs 1000 feet above Lake Ann to Maple Pass at 3⅓ miles, 6600 feet.

For the loop and more views, a safe but primitive trail follows the ridge crest eastward to a 6850-foot shoulder of Frisco Mountain and then descends, steeply at times, the ridge between the spectacular cirques that surround both Lake Ann and Rainy Lake. The trail joins the Rainy Lake trail ½ mile from its starting point.

Corteo Peak from Maple Pass

72 GOLDEN HORN

Round trip 23 miles
Allow 2 days
High point 6900 feet
Elevation gain 2700 feet in,
600 feet out
Hikable August through September

Map: Green Trails No. 50
Washington Pass
Current information: Ask at
Methow Valley Ranger District
about trail No. 2000

Several explanations are in order. First, three drainages are traversed on this spectacular section of the Pacific Crest Trail; the designation of "Early Winters" is arbitrary. Second, the hike is not to the summit of Golden Horn (Mountain), but to the Snowy Lakes, filling cirques scooped in the side of Golden Horn. Third—and not for us to explain—is why it is not in a national park or wilderness. When the North Cascades National Park was being proposed, pompous state and federal officials deigned to do a flyover and—from 10,000 feet— declared the area to be "not of national park caliber." Walk the ground. Make up your own mind.

Now, why do we call the trip "Golden Horn"? Because aside from rugged peaks and green meadows and groves of larch that turn gold in fall, the most distinctive feature of the region is the rock, which due to the complex mineralogy has a lovely pinkish-goldish hue. Geologists have dubbed it the "Golden Horn Granodiorite," and we think the rock alone gives the vicinity national park caliber.

Drive North Cascades Scenic Highway 20 to Rainy Pass, and park in the north trailhead area, elevation 4800 feet.

At a grade that refuses to exceed a horsey 10 percent, the two-horses-wide Crest Trail ascends through forest to big and bigger meadows. At 4 miles pass a campsite; at 5½ miles reach Cutthroat Pass, 6800 feet (Hike 70). The way continues up meadows and rockslides to a 6900-foot high point with a view of needlelike Tower Mountain and the golden horn of Golden Horn, then drops 600 feet to Granite Pass; snow may linger on the tread until August in this vicinity, at a steepness that will force hikers lacking ice axes to turn around. From the pass the freeway-wide trail has been dynamited in cliffs and gouged out of steep unstable slopes for a long 2 miles across Swamp Creek headwaters. Due to slides this section is often impassable to horses and scared hikers. At about 2 miles from Cutthroat Pass, the trail reaches a small stream, 6300 feet, in a meadow flat not yet recovered from the devastating impact of the construction crew that camped here just a single summer in the 1960s. See if you can find their horseshoe pits. Nevertheless, this is the place to camp. If you reach a switchback you have gone too far.

An unmarked way trail climbs steeply ½ mile to Lower Snowy Lake, 6735 feet, and a bit more to Upper Snowy Lake, 6839 feet, miraculously located precisely in the summit of Snowy Lakes Pass. Thoughtless hikers and horse-riders have contributed their share of damage to

Upper Snowy Lake and Mount Hardy

the acres of fragile meadows. Cowboys and cowgirls, leave your horses near the Crest Trail and walk; don't take them to dig post holes in the soft turf. Pedestrians, spread your sleeping bags by the Crest Trail, not on the heather or fragile meadows near the lakes.

The view from Snowy Lakes Pass is straight up Golden Horn and Tower Mountain and out across Methow Pass to the spires of Mt. Hardy, above headwaters of the West Fork Methow River. The determined hiker can scramble onto slopes of Golden Horn Mountain, but the feldspar crystals are just as stunning throughout the batholith.

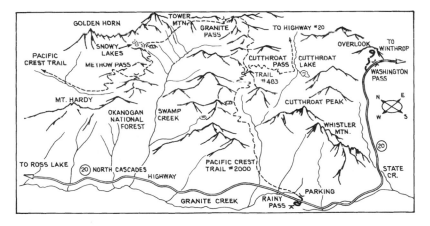

Silver Star Mountain from Goat Peak

73 GOAT PEAK

Round trip 5 miles
Hiking time 6 hours
High point 7001 feet
Elevation gain 1400 feet
Hikable June through October

One day
Map: Green Trails No. 51 Mazama
Current information: Ask at
  Methow Valley Ranger District
  about trail No. 457

A commanding view of the Methow Valley and the north face of Silver Star Mountain, the most spectacular peak in the area. Most of the way is on a south slope, and all the way is hot and bone-dry, so start early and carry buckets of water.

Drive North Cascades Scenic Highway 20 west 12 miles from Winthrop. Just before crossing the Methow River, go right on county road No. 1163 toward Mazama. At 6.2 miles turn right on road No. 52. From this intersection go another 3.7 miles and turn left on road No. 5225. At 8.3 miles from the Mazama road go right on road No. (5225)200, and at 11.2 miles reach a saddle and trailhead, elevation 5600 feet.

Goat Peak trail No. 457 takes off south, sometimes tree-shaded, sometimes in open, sparse meadows, sometimes on rocky ridges with great views. If often steep and rough, the tread is quite decently walkable as it switchbacks to the lookout building atop Goat Peak, 7001 feet.

Though 9 miles distant, 8901-foot Silver Star easily dominates the scene. North Gardner Mountain, 8956 feet, highest in the region, is a little to the south. Farther away is the precipice of Washington Pass peaks. Northward rise the rolling, high ridges of the Pasayten Wilderness; this view of their south slopes makes them seem barren and unimpressive, very unlike the reality encountered by hikers.

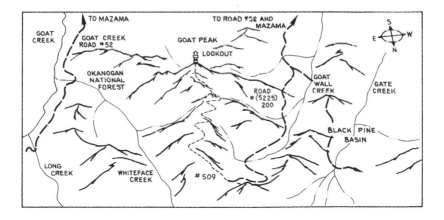

74 LOST RIVER

Round trip 8 miles
Hiking time 4 hours
High point 2700 feet
Elevation gain 600 feet in,
   300 feet out
Hikable mid-May through October

One day or backpack
Maps: Green Trails No. 50
   Washington Pass, No. 51 Mazama
Current information: Ask at
   Methow Valley Ranger District
   about trail No. 484

A river-loud trail ambles along through forest and across rockslides to pleasant camps at the mouth of the legendary Lost River Gorge, a part of the Pasayten Wilderness which is as wild as it was a century ago and likely to be so a century from now. Look all you want, and maybe even touch, if you dare.

Drive North Cascades Scenic Highway 20 east of Early Winters Campground 1.5 miles and turn left, cross the Methow River, and go 0.4 mile to the hamlet (post office, gas station, grocery) of Mazama and turn left again, upvalley, on the Harts Pass road. Cross the Lost River and at 7.2 miles from Mazama turn right 0.3 mile to a parking lot, signed "Monument Creek trail No. 484," elevation 2400 feet.

The wide and soft tread, next thing to flat, pokes along in forest 2 miles to the high point of 2700 feet. The next 2 miles are generally rough, in an alternation of trees and rocks. At about 3¼ miles (much too far up the valley, all of which belongs there) enter the Pasayten Wilderness. At 4 miles is the dramatic confluence of two gorges, Eureka Creek from the left, Lost River from the right. A sturdy bridge crosses Eureka Creek to choice campsites located a bit upstream beside the Lost River at 2650 feet.

The usual plan is to loiter here for lunch or overnight, then loiter on back to the car. The trail does something perfectly awful—climbs 4600 feet up the hogback between the two canyons to 7300-foot Pistol Pass, and nary a drop to drink, then drops 2800 feet into Monument Creek, a tributary of Lost River. In the latter's gorge the hand of trail-constructing humans never has set foot. Ascending the brutal path to hot-as-a-Pistol Pass is as recommendable as a Fourth of July picnic in Death

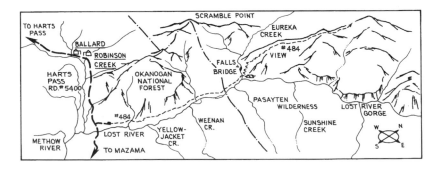

Lost River near Eureka Creek

Valley. However, it's worth huffing up ½ mile to a great view down-river toward Gardner Mountain.

At no point can a trail-walker see more than the awesome exit of the Lost River Gorge. The few doughty explorers who venture into its mysteries usually do so in late summer, when the river is low. They mostly wade, silently praying that no cloudbursts occur while they are in the chasm.

Slate Peak and Robinson Pass

UPPER METHOW RIVER
Pasayten Wilderness

75 ROBINSON PASS

Round trip 18 miles to pass
Allow 2 days
High point 6200 feet
Elevation gain 3600 feet
Hikable late May through October
Loop trip 43 miles
Allow 5–7 days
High point 7500 feet
Elevation gain 10,100 feet

Hikable mid-July to October
Maps: Green Trails No. 50
  Washington Pass; for loop add
  No. 18 Pasayten, No. 51 Mazama
  Peak, No. 19 Billy Goat
Current information: Ask at
  Methow Valley Ranger District
  about trail Nos. 478, 474,
  and 484

The geography here is not of the big glacier-monster crag sort characteristic of the North Cascades National Park, but spectacular it is—

high, massive, shaggy ridges, naked and cliffy, reminding of Montana, and enormous U-shaped glacial-trough valleys, and awesome swaths of climax avalanches sweeping down from crests thousands of feet to bottoms and hundreds of feet up the other sides. Also, lovely streams rush through parkland forests. And among the greatest appeals, trips in what the local folk call the "Wilderness Wilderness" are like taking a ride in a time machine back to the 1930s. Solitude! Though Robinson Creek is a main thoroughfare into the heart of the Pasayten Wilderness, and a favorite with horse people, most come in the fall hunting season. Summer is lonesome even on the main trail and on byways one can roam a hundred miles and maybe never see another soul.

Drive the Harts Pass road upvalley from Mazama (Hike 74, Lost River). At 7 miles pavement ends. At 9 miles cross Robinson Creek and turn right into a small campground, parking area, and trailhead, elevation 2600 feet.

The trail follows the creek ¼ mile, then switchbacks a couple hundred feet above the water. At 1½ miles enter the Pasayten Wilderness and shortly cross a bridge over Robinson Creek. Partly in rocky-brushy opens, partly in forest of big ponderosa pines, then smaller firs, the way climbs steadily, moderately, at just short of 3 miles crossing a steel bridge over Beauty Creek, which waterfalls down from

Bridge over Robinson Creek

Cow parsnip

Beauty Mountain, at 4 miles recrossing Robinson Creek on a bridge. The avalanche country has been entered, wide aisles cut in the forest, huge jackstraws piled up; from here on the way is a constant garden.

At 6 miles are a log crossing of Robinson Creek, now much smaller, and Porcupine Camp, in the woods and unappealing except in a storm. To here, avalanche meadows have broken the forest. From now on strips of forest break the ridge-to-creek meadows. A nice camp is located in the first broad meadow above Porcupine; an even better one in the second, at 6½ miles, 4900 feet, by the creek in a grove of large spruce trees; and a third just before Robinson Pass, in the trees 300 feet below the trail.

The trail sidehills through flower fields, rock gardens, and avalanche gardens, to Robinson Pass at 9 miles, 6200 feet, a great broad gap through which the continental glacier flowed. Long-ago forest fires cleared the big timber and now the wildflowers blaze.

The pass is a trip in itself, but also is the takeoff for longer journeys. To begin, the open slopes above the pass invite easy roaming—to the left, up to big views from Peak 6935 and onward to Slate Pass, just 2 miles from Robinson Pass, and another mile to Slate Peak, or the other way on the long, lonesome heights of Gold Ridge; to the right, up to Peak 7720, and maybe along the ridge a mile to Devils Peak, or (climbers only) 2 miles more to 8726-foot Robinson Mountain, the neighborhood giant.

If trail-walking is preferred, descend Middle Fork Pasayten River, through gaspers of avalanches from Gold Ridge, the most impressive series of swaths in the Cascades; 15 miles from the pass is Soda Creek, and in another 8 miles, Canada. The classic long loop of the region is as follows: down the Middle Fork 6 ½ miles; up by Freds Lake to a 7100-foot pass, down by Lake Doris and around the headwaters of Eureka Creek, under Osceola, Carru, and Lago, three peaks between 8585 and 8745 feet, and up to Shellrock Pass, 7500 feet, 8 miles from the Middle Fork trail; 8½ miles down forests of Monument Creek and up by Lake of the Woods to Pistol Pass, 7100 feet; and 10¾ infamous miles down, down, and down, hot and thirsty, to the Lost River and out to the Methow road, reached at a point 2 miles from Robinson Creek. Total loop, 43 miles, elevation gain about 10,000 feet. Allow a week.

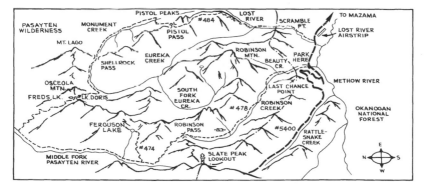

West Fork Methow River

UPPER METHOW RIVER
Unprotected area

76 WEST FORK METHOW RIVER

Round trip 12 miles
Hiking time 6 hours
High point 3600 feet
Elevation gain 900 feet plus ups
  and downs
Hikable late May through
  mid-October

One day or backpack
Map: Green Trails No. 50
  Washington Pass
Current information: Ask at
  Methow Valley Ranger District
  about trail No. 480

Early in the season, when the highlands are of no use to anyone but skiers, is the happy time to walk this trail, sometimes beside the West

Fork Methow River, always in sound of the roar, with look-ups through the trees to the country where the flowers will not appear for months. But they're already blossoming here.

Drive to Mazama (Hike 74, Lost River) and proceed upvalley on the Harts Pass road 8.8 miles to a junction. Keep left on road No. (5400)060, signed "Riverbend Campground," 0.8 mile to the road-end and trailhead, elevation 2700 feet.

The trail crosses Rattlesnake Creek (yes, keep an eye out) and ambles up and down in forest and around and across giant rockslides. At about 2 miles it crosses Trout Creek on a log bridge and passes a campsite. At about 3 miles a delightful camp is located beside the river. At 4 miles the way ascends above the water and doesn't come back down for a mile. At 6 miles, 3600 feet, it leaves the river for good; time to go home.

The West Fork trail goes on, of course. At 7 miles, 4100 feet, it intersects the Pacific Crest Trail. Turning right (north) isn't recommended; Grasshopper Pass is better reached from Harts Pass.

Elephanthead, a member of the figwort family

Turning left might be considered, because in that direction lie Methow Pass, Snowy Lakes Pass, and Golden Horn (Hike 72).

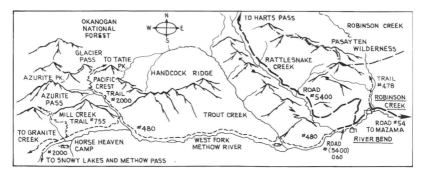

Flower fields in Trout Creek valley

UPPER METHOW RIVER
Unprotected area

TROUT CREEK

Round trip 6 miles
Hiking time 4 hours
High point 5425 feet
Elevation gain 100 feet in,
    800 feet out
Hikable July through September
One day or backpack

Map: Green Trails No. 50
    Washington Pass (trail not
    shown)
Current information: Ask at
    Methow Valley Ranger District
    about trail No. 479

When the meadows of the Harts Pass (very) highlands are engulfed in clouds, why fight the mists? Settle for a lower level, the (still quite) highlands, the vast meadows of South Fork Trout Creek. The trail

doesn't get much maintenance, so it's rough and brushy in spots. In the meadows where the grass and flowers grow to a hiker's hips it can scarcely be seen or even found by probing feet. On a wet day this is an ideal place to test the claims of the manufacturers of those expensive rain pants.

Drive to Mazama (Hike 74, Lost River) and proceed upvalley on the Harts Pass road. Abruptly ascend from the valley floor up the Big Hill, past Dead Horse Point. At about 18 miles from Mazama (just 2.3 miles short of Harts Pass) find Trout Creek trail No. 479, elevation 5425 feet.

The trail wanders up and down, seemingly without aim, the first ¼ mile. In the next ¼ mile it drops 250 feet from a rocky knoll. The next ¼ mile descends more moderately to a crossing of North Fork Trout Creek. The way continues down in woods, over several large boulder fields. At 2½ miles is the low point, 4600 feet, at the edge of meadowland.

The path now tilts slightly up, following the South Fork. In early July the tread might be findable another mile but by the end of the month, forget it. On the far side of the meadow are possible campsites.

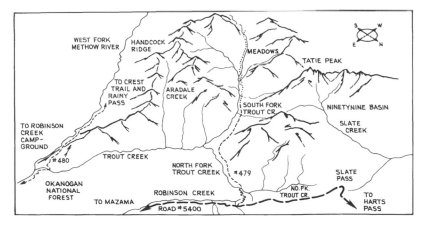

78 GRASSHOPPER PASS

Round trip 11 miles
Hiking time 6 hours
High point 7000 feet
Elevation gain 1000 feet in,
 1000 feet out
Hikable July through October

One day or backpack
Map: Green Trails No. 50
 Washington Pass
Current information: Ask at
 Methow Valley Ranger District
 about trail No. 2000

Wide-open, big-sky meadow ridges, grand views of giant peaks and forested valleys. The entire hike is above timberline, contouring hillsides, traversing gardens, and sometimes following the exact Cascade Crest.

Drive to Mazama (Hike 74, Lost River). Continue 20 miles upvalley to 6198-foot Harts Pass. From the pass turn left on the Meadow Campground road 2 miles, keeping right at a fork, to the road-end and trailhead, elevation 6400 feet.

The Pacific Crest Trail immediately leaves the trees, going along an open slope below diggings of the Brown Bear Mine and above a pretty meadow. The first mile is a gentle ascent to the 6600-foot east shoulder of a 7400-foot peak. The way swings around the south slopes of this peak to a saddle, 7000 feet, overlooking Ninety-nine Basin at the head of Slate Creek, then contours 7386-foot Tatie Peak to another saddle, 6900 feet, and a magnificent picture of Mt. Ballard.

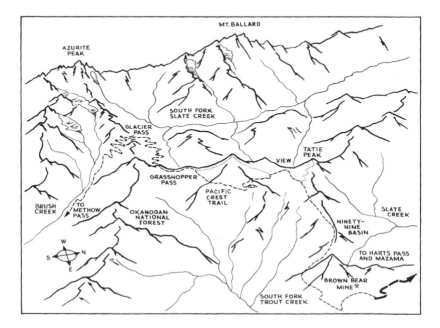

Azurite Peak and Grasshopper Pass

A moderate descent, with a stretch of switchbacks, leads around a 7500-foot peak. In a bouldery basin at 4 miles, 6600 feet, is the only dependable water on the trip, a cold little creek flowing from mossy rocks through a flower-and-heather meadow ringed by groves of larch. Splendid camps.

The trail climbs gradually a final mile to the broad swale of 6700-foot Grasshopper Pass. (Fine camps in early summer when snowmelt water is available.) But don't stop here—go ¼ mile more and a few feet higher on the ridge to a knob just before the trail starts down and down to Glacier Pass. The views are dramatic across Slate Creek forests to 8440-foot Azurite Peak and 8301-foot Mt. Ballard. Eastward are meadows and trees of Trout Creek, flowing to the Methow.

Each of the peaks contoured by the trail invites a sidetrip of easy but steep scrambling to the summit, and the wanderings are endless amid larches and pines and spruces, flowers blossoming from scree and buttress, and the rocks—colorful shales, slates, conglomerates, and sandstones, and an occasional igneous intrusion.

79   WINDY PASS

Round trip 7 miles
Hiking time 5 hours
High point 6900 feet
Elevation gain 500 feet in,
   1000 feet out
Hikable early July through October
One day or backpack

Maps: Green Trails No. 18
   Pasayten Peak, No. 50
   Washington Pass
Current information: Ask at
   Methow Valley Ranger District
   about trail No. 2000

In all the hundreds of miles of the Pacific Crest Trail in Washington, this ranks among the easiest and most scenic segments. The hike starts in meadows and stays high the entire way, contouring gardens thousands of feet above the trees of Slate Creek, magnificent views at every step.

Drive to Harts Pass (Hike 78, Grasshopper Pass) and turn right on the Slate Peak road about 1.5 miles to the first switchback and a small parking area at the trailhead, elevation 6800 feet.

If the trip is being done in early July, don't be discouraged if the road beyond Harts Pass is blocked by snow and the trail beginning is

Pacific Crest Trail in Benson Basin; Mount Ballard in distance

blinding-white; snow lingers here later than on any other portion of the hike, and mostly clear trail can be expected after a frosty start.

The Pacific Crest Trail gently climbs a meadow shelf the first ½ mile, contours steep slopes of Slate Peak, and drops into lovely little Benson Basin, a creek and nice camps a few hundred feet below the tread. The way swings up and out to a spur ridge, contours to Buffalo Pass and another spur, and then descends above the gorgeous greenery of Barron Basin to 6257-foot Windy Pass and delightful camps in flowers and larch trees.

Sad to say, the wreckers have been here. Barron Basin is one of the most magnificent easy-to-reach glorylands in the Cascades, but it is mainly "private property" and the "owners" have raised havoc, gouging delicate meadows with bulldozers, dumping garbage at will. This hike is bound to convert any casual walker into a fierce enemy of the ultrapermissive federal mining laws, which make it next to impossible for the Forest Service to protect the land. Some of the desecration is very new but much is nearly a century old—note how long Nature needs to restore ravaged meadows.

Sidetrips from the pass will make a person want the basin to be reclaimed for the public domain and placed within the Pasayten Wilderness, the boundary of which follows the divide, excluding the miner-mangled slopes to the west and the entire route thus far of the Pacific Crest Trail. Wander meadows north to the panoramas from 7290-foot Tamarack Peak, or walk the Crest Trail a short mile into Windy Basin, offering the best (and most heavily used) camps.

Views on the way? They start with Gardner Mountain, the Needles, Silver Star, Golden Horn, Tower Mountain, and especially the near bulks of Ballard and Azurite. Westerly, Jack and Crater dominate, but part of Baker can also be seen, and many more peaks. Easterly is the Pasayten country, high and remote.

Before or after the hike, take a sidetrip to the fire lookout on the 7440-foot summit of Slate Peak, formerly the highest point in Washington State accessible to automobiles; the road is now gated ¼ mile from the summit, and that's a help.

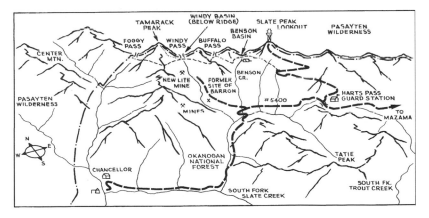

THREE FOOLS TRAIL

One-way trip from Castle Pass to Ross Reservoir 27 miles
Allow 3–5 days
High point 7000 feet
Elevation gain about 10,000 feet
Hikable mid-July through September

Maps: Green Trails No. 50 Washington Pass, No. 18 Pasayten Peak, No. 17 Jack Mtn., No. 16 Ross Lake
Current information: Ask at Methow Valley Ranger District about trail Nos. 2000 and 749

One-way trip from Harts Pass to Ross Reservoir 54 miles
Allow 7–9 days

One-way trip from near Allison Pass (Canada) to Ross Reservoir 38 miles
Allow 5–7 days

A classic highland wander from the Cascade Crest to Ross Reservoir, up and down a lonesome trail through some of the wildest valleys, ridges, and meadows in the range. A one-way trip is recommended, starting at Harts Pass (or near Manning Park headquarters in Canada) and ending at the reservoir. (See note on border crossings in Hike 100, Pacific Crest Trail.) Special transportation arrangements are required: a drop-off at Harts Pass (or near Manning Park headquarters—see Hike 82, Cascade Loop Trail and Monument 83); a pickup by boat from Ross Lake Resort (Hike 39, Panther Creek and Fourth of July Pass), though a party can, if desired, exit via the East Bank Trail.

Drive to Harts Pass (Hike 78, Grasshopper Pass) and go right on the Slate Peak road about 1½ miles to the first switchback and trailhead.

Hike the Pacific Crest Trail (Hike 100) 27 miles from Harts Pass (or 11 miles from near Manning Park headquarters) to Castle Pass, elevation 5451 feet. Turn west on the Three Fools Trail (officially, Castle Pass trail No. 749), climbing steeply in forest, then meadows. At 3 miles, 6000 feet, enter a little basin with a welcome creeklet, the first dependable water since before Castle Pass, and the last for several more miles. Tread ascends from the basin, swings around a spur, descends meadows to a saddle, and climbs the crest to a 6534-foot knob

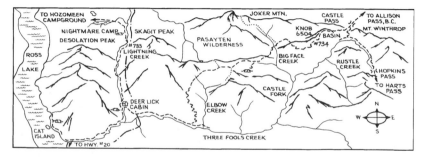

Three Fools Peak from Lakeview Ridge (Photo: Harvey Manning)

which ranks among the most magnificent viewpoints of the region. Look north across the headwaters of Castle Creek to Castle Peak, Frosty Mountain in Canada, and Mt. Winthrop; look south across forests of Three Fools Creek to peaks along and west of the Cascade Crest; look in every direction and look for hours and never see all there is to see. The way drops from the knob and climbs ridge-top heather and parklands to 6 miles, 6400 feet, and a grandly scenic camp—but the only water, if any, is from snowmelt.

The trail angles down across a broad, steep flower garden, then switchbacks through avalanche-wrecked forest to Big Face Creek, beneath the impressive wall of Joker Mountain. (At 6½ miles is a tumbling creek; below the trail here is a campsite on a tiny, wooded shelf.)

Woody Pass Peak from side of Three Fools Peak (Photo: Harvey Manning)

At 8 miles, 5200 feet, the path reaches the valley bottom. For a mandatory sidetrip, fight through a bit of brush and climb the open basin to a high saddle with views out to Hozomeen and the Chilliwacks and below to a snowy cirque lake draining to Freezeout Creek.

The trail goes gently downstream in trees to a crossing of Big Face Creek at 8¾ miles, 4840 feet, then turns right in a gravel wash to the ford. A possible camp here on gravel bars.

A long climb begins up forest to avalanche greenery; when tread vanishes in the grass go directly uphill, watching for sawn logs. The ascent continues in trees, opens to meadows, and at 11½ miles, 6350 feet, tops out in the wide green broad-view pass between Big Face and Elbow Creeks. A sidetrail drops ¼ mile to a campsite and meandering stream in the glorious park of Elbow Basin. The main trail—tread missing for long stretches—contours and climbs north around the basin to a grassy swale (and a scenic camp, if snowmelt is available) near the ridge crest at 13 miles. Be sure to walk to the 6687-foot plateau summit of the ridge and views: east to the Cascade Crest; south to Jack Mountain; west to the Pickets, Chilliwacks, Desolation, and especially the nearby towers of Hozomeen; north into Canada.

The trail descends near and along the crest, giving a look down to the tempting cirque of Freezeout Lake (accessible via a steep scramble), passing through a spectacular silver forest. A stern drop commences down and down hot and dry burn meadows and young trees. The mouth grows parched, the knees floppy. At 18 miles, 2350 feet, the trail at last touches Three Fools Creek and a possible camp; stop for an orgy of drinking and foot-soaking and an understanding of why this trip is not recommended to begin at Ross Reservoir.

Hopes of an easy downhill water-grade hike are quickly dashed by a 1000-foot climb. The trail then goes down, goes up, and down and up, and finally on a forest bench to Lightning Creek at 23 miles, 1920 feet. Just before the crossing is a junction with the trail north to Nightmare Camp and Hozomeen (Hike 40, East Bank Trail). Just beyond the ford is Deer Lick Cabin (locked) and a campsite.

Again the trail climbs 1000 feet and goes down and up, high on the side of the Lightning Creek gorge, coming at last to a superb overlook of Ross Reservoir a thousand feet below. The conclusion is a switchbacking descent to the shore and Lightning Creek Camp, 1600 feet, 27 miles from Castle Pass.

Grouse

Silver Lake trail high above Middle Fork Pasayten River valley

UPPER METHOW RIVER
Pasayten Wilderness

SILVER LAKE

Round trip 10 miles
Hiking time 7 hours
High point 7000 feet
Elevation gain 1200 feet in,
    2000 feet out
Hikable mid-July through
    September

One day or backpack
Maps: Green Trails No. 50
    Washington Pass, No. 18
    Pasayten Peak
Current information: Ask at
    Methow Valley Ranger District
    about trail No. 498

Miles of alpine meadows dotted with flowers and trees, like Christ-mas trees, leading to a shallow lake surrounded by mountains. Half of the way is a romp on a wide, smooth trail. The other half is a different

story. Some parts are rough and some are downright mean. Make the trip in late July when the meadows are green or in late September when the larch trees have turned golden.

From Mazama drive 20 miles to Harts Pass. Go right on Slate Peak road (5400)600. At the second switchback, 1.7 miles from Harts Pass, find Buckskin Ridge–Silver Lake trail No. 498, elevation 6900 feet.

A short but steep climb to a saddle is followed by a long switchback 400 feet down to meadowland high above the Middle Fork Pasayten River Valley, the beginning of miles of green parkland. These are not the massed flower fields of Mt. Rainier but pretty colors dot the meadows.

In a long half-mile is a junction. To the right the trail drops to the Middle Fork Pasayten Valley trail. Stay high on the Buckskin Ridge trail for 2 mostly parkland miles. With some ups and downs the trail regains its lost elevation and rounds a rib, only to drop 300 feet into another valley. Three times the trail climbs to 6800 feet, three times to lose 200–300 feet. At 4½ miles the trail steeply loses another 400 feet to an unmarked junction. Go left on an almost level ⅕ mile to Silver Lake, 6256 feet. Camping there and several places along the way.

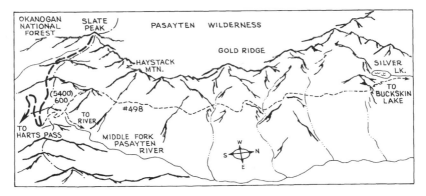

82 CASCADE LOOP TRAIL AND MONUMENT 83

Loop trip 34 miles
Allow 2–3 days
High point 6550 feet
Elevation gain 4900 feet
Round trip to lookout 20 miles
Hiking time 12 hours
High point 6500 feet
Elevation gain 2800 feet

Hikable late June through
   October
Map: Green Trails No. 18
   Pasayten Peak (US only)
Current information: Ask at
   Methow Valley Ranger District
   about trail Nos. 533 and 2000

When built in the 1920s the fire lookout at Monument 83 probably was the most remote in the Cascades. It still is if approached from the United States via Slate Peak, West Fork Pasayten River, the pass near Dead Lake, and the Boundary Trail—a wilderness walk of nearly 30 miles that is well worth the doing, especially if part of a loop that returns down the Pacific Crest Trail. However, since construction of Trans-Canada Highway 3 across Manning Provincial Park in Canada, Monument 83 is only 10 miles from a road and lies on the very popular Cascade Loop Trail, featuring miles of splendid forest, climaxes of al-

Old and new lookout buildings at Monument 83

202

pine meadows, and the thrill of (technically illegal) international travel.

Drive Highway 3 from Hope, British Columbia, across Allison Pass to Manning Provincial Park administration office, lodge, and visitors center (Nature House), where U.S. Forest Service wilderness permits (no longer needed) used to be available for camping in the Pasayten Wilderness. Park here, at the end of the loop hike, in order to have your car waiting, or drive 1.8 miles farther to the Monument 83 parking lot on the right side of the road, elevation 3700 feet.

The "trail" to Monument 83 is a rough, seldom-used service road, closed to public vehicles. In ¼ mile the way crosses the Similkameen River, then ascends gradually in forest along Chuwanten Creek and Monument Creek. At about 9 miles pass a sidetrail signed "Cathedral Lakes" and continue on the service road to the flowery little meadow of Monument 83, 10 miles, 6500 feet.

In the 1920s the U.S. Forest Service built the small log cabin on the highest point, which happens to lie in Canada. In 1953 the tower, tall enough to see over the foreign hill, was erected in the United States. The grave marker memorializes a pack mule that broke its leg and had to be shot.

From the lookout the now-true trail goes ¾ mile to join trail No. 533, which descends 4½ miles along Chuchuwanteen (the American spelling of "Chuwanten") Creek to a campsite at the Frosty Creek crossing and a junction with trail No. 453, 4500 feet, 15 miles from Highway 3. Go right, upstream on Frosty Creek, to a camp ¼ mile past tiny Frosty Lake at 5345 feet. The trail steepens and switchbacks to meadows of 6550-foot Frosty Pass, 21 miles, then drops 1½ miles to Castle Pass, 5451 feet, and a junction with the Pacific Crest Trail. Head north, passing water and a campsite in ½ mile. The Crest Trail descends gently above Route Creek, then Castle Creek, 3 miles to the border at Monument 78, then 7½ miles more along Castle Creek to Manning Park Headquarters.

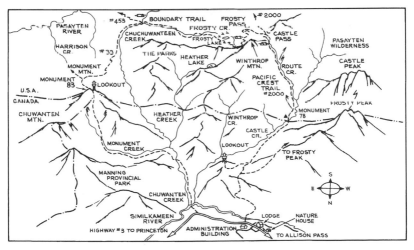

83 COPPER GLANCE LAKE

Round trip 6 miles
Hiking time 6 hours
High point 6400 feet
Elevation gain 2600 feet in,
   300 feet out
Hikable June through October

One day or backpack
Maps: Green Trails No. 19 Billy
   Goat Mtn., No. 51 Mazama
Current information: Ask at
   Methow Valley Ranger District
   about trail No. 519

Beneath the cliffs of Isabella Ridge and 8204-foot Sherman Peak, ringed by fields of boulders and clumps of larch trees, sits Copper Glance Lake, a drop of snowmelt that by itself might scarcely be considered worth the walk. But, the walk is short. This is not to say it's *quick*. The trail gains 2500 feet in 3 miles. Some stretches are quite flat. All the worse; as any student of mountain mathematics understands, when a route that climbs this high is not very steep, a bit farther on it's going to have to be extremely steep to make up the difference. The spectacular scenery is worth the sweat. So are the meadows.

Drive North Cascades Scenic Highway 20 to Winthrop. There are two ways to reach the trailheads radiating from the Chewuch River Valley. From the center of town the shortest way is to follow the East Chewuch River road signed "Pearrygin Lake." Pass the sideroad to Pearrygin Lake State Park, and in 6.5 miles cross the Chewuch River and reach a junction with the West Chewuch River road. If coming from the west or wishing to stop at the Winthrop Ranger Station for maps and information, the West Chewuch River road is best. The road starts at the west side of town opposite the city park and large parking area. Pass the sideroad to the ranger station and at 7 miles reach the aforementioned junction with the East Chewuch River road. In a short distance the road enters the national forest and becomes road No. 51. From the junction drive 2.5 miles and go left on Eightmile Road No. 5130 for 12.5 miles and find Copper Glance trail No. 519 at a gate on the lefthand side, elevation 3800 feet.

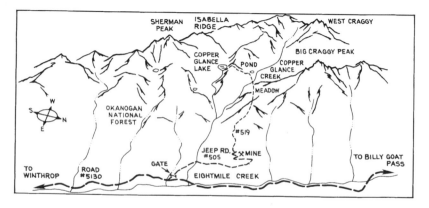

Copper Glance trail

The trail starts on a steep mining road (gated) suitable only for jeeps. At about 1 mile, just after the second switchback, note remains of a log cabin. At 1½ miles is a mine shaft, 5200 feet, and the end of the mining road. True trail climbs on, at about 2 miles entering large, lush meadows dotted in season with lupine, aster, paintbrush, columbine, and valerian. The way returns to the woods, at 2¾ miles passing a small pond. That flatness has to be made up, and it is, by a supersteep ascent of a rockslide, topping out at 6400 feet. To loosen up the knees, the way descends 300 feet to the shore of the lake, 6100 feet.

84 PARSON SMITH TREE— HIDDEN LAKES

Round trip to Big Hidden Lake
  35 miles
Allow 3 days
High point 5800 feet
Elevation gain 2200 feet in,
  2700 feet out

Hikable late June through September
Map: Green Trails No. 19 Billy Goat
  Mtn.
Current information: Ask at
  Methow Valley Ranger District
  about trail No. 477

> *I've roamed in many foreign parts my boys*
> *And many lands have seen.*
> *But Columbia is my idol yet*
> *Of all lands she is queen.*
>
> Parson Smith, June 8, 1886

From the middle of the nineteenth century, miners passed through the Pasayten on their way to Canadian goldfields. A few stopped to poke around. After all this time there is virtually no evidence of their

Gully used by early travelers over Eightmile Pass

passage except for Allen L. Smith, known as Parson Smith, prospector, sometime trapper, artist, and poet, who on a return trip from Canada camped for a few days on the Pasayten River. There, on a pine tree just 12 feet from the U.S.–Canadian border, he carved the preceding poem.

Parson Smith's poem was first seen in 1903 when men from the International Boundary survey crew cleared a 10-foot swath on each side of the boundary line. The men noted the work of art but soon forgot it. It was rediscovered in 1913 by Rangers Frank Burge and George Wright. The tree was next seen in 1926 by Ranger Bill Lester. In 1965 the tree was dead and a shelter was built over the stump. In 1971 the stump was placed on the National Register of Historic Places. However, the shelter wasn't saving the wood from rot and the last straw was when a bear chewed up the stump. In 1980 this stump was moved to Early Winters Visitor Center, where it is on display.

Today's hikers can see for themselves the pioneering route taken by Parson Smith. From Winthrop drive (Hike 83, Copper Glance Lake) to the union of the East and West Chewuch River roads (which becomes road No. 51). Drive another 3.5 miles and go left on Eightmile Creek road No. 5130 (Hike 83) 16.7 miles to the end at the hikers' parking area, elevation 4600 feet.

Parson Smith Tree in Early Winters Visitor Center

The trail follows a mine road about 100 feet; keep right. In ¼ mile, at Billy Goat Pass junction, keep left on Hidden Lakes trail No. 477. At 1¼ miles is a good view of Eightmile Pass and the steep gully Parson Smith may have descended. At 1½ miles cross the 5400-foot pass and drop to a campsite and bridge over Drake Creek, 4 miles from the road, 4600 feet. This is the last campsite with reliable water for the next 6 miles.

Passing Drake Creek trail, hikers have a choice of how to climb 1200

Lost River valley from Lucky Pass

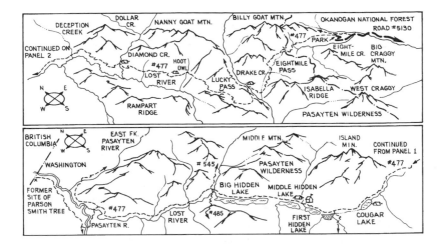

feet to Lucky Pass, 5800 feet. It can be in one long switchback on a 5 percent grade, or a quick but steep 15–20 percent trail. At 8 miles pass Hoot Owl Camp (doubtful water supply) and at 10 miles reach a campground at the crossing of Diamond Creek, 4300 feet, lowest point of the trip.

Beyond Diamond Creek the trail climbs 300 feet, with ups and downs to dodge cliffs. Pass Deception Creek (underground most of the summer). At about 13 miles the trail finally comes close to Lost River and enters a fine old-growth forest that was spared by the great fire of around 1920. At 14 miles, 4300 feet, is lovely Cougar Lake and camp-sites. At 15½ miles is usually dried-up Island Lake, and at 16 miles First Hidden Lake. Beyond are two Forest Service patrol cab-ins and separate campsites for horses and hikers. Next is Middle Hidden Lake, a slight rise, and the crossing-over to Pasayten drainage. The trail soon reaches 1½-mile-long Big Hidden Lake, 4300 feet, 17½ miles from the road.

Most hikers are content to turn around here, but in 1½ miles, at the far end of Big Hidden Lake, wonders are to be seen: a large shelter and a rusted grader. A fi-nal 7½ miles lead to the Canadian border, where Parson Smith carved his tree; however, don't look for it there; go instead to the Early Winters Visitor Center.

Middle Hidden Lake

85 BILLY GOAT PASS—BURCH MOUNTAIN

Round trip 10 miles
Hiking time 5 hours
High point 7782 feet
Elevation gain 3000 feet
Hikable late June through October
One day

Map: Green Trails No. 19 Billy
Goat Mtn.
Current information: Ask at
Methow Valley Ranger District
about trail Nos. 502A and 538

Hike to the edge of the Pasayten Wilderness, climb toward an old lookout site, and see miles and miles of broad valleys and open ridges. Carry plenty of water and start early before the sun gets hot. This is big-scale country, often with long stretches between points of scenic interest. For hikers, therefore, early summer is the best season, when flowers and snowfields add variety.

Drive to the parking area at the end of Eightmile Creek road (Hike 83, Copper Glance Lake), elevation 4800 feet.

Walk the mining road up Eightmile Creek, staying right at the first junction (unmarked). In about ¼ mile the trail splits. The left goes to Eightmile Pass (Hike 84, Parson Smith Tree—Hidden Lakes); go right and zigzag steeply up 1800 feet in a scant 3 miles through open forest to Billy Goat Pass, 6600 feet, on the border of Pasayten Wilderness.

Hike a few hundred feet over the pass and find Burch Mountain trail No. 538 angling upward on the east (right-hand) side. This well-constructed trail was once used by horses to supply a lookout on top of Burch Mountain. At first the tread is lost in meadows, but as the hill-

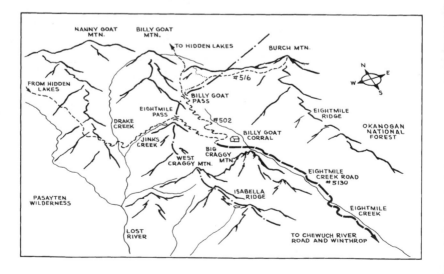

side steepens the trail becomes distinct and, except for dodging an occasional tree growing in the path, following it is no problem. The ascent is abrupt, quickly emerging to views southeast to Isabella Ridge and beyond to a horizon of 8000-foot peaks, the most dramatic being Big Craggy. Gaining some 600 feet in ¾ mile, the trail nearly reaches the ridge top, then contours around a high, rocky knoll to a broad saddle at 7200 feet. From there it switchbacks up to the 7782-foot summit of Burch Mountain, 5 miles from the road-end. The lookout cabin has been gone many years but the views are as good as ever.

Big Craggy Peak from Burch Mountain trail

Foot bridge over marsh on Drake Creek trail

CHEWUCH RIVER
Pasayten Wilderness

86 DOLLAR WATCH MOUNTAIN

Round trip 28 miles
Allow 3–4 days
High point 7679 feet
Elevation gain 4000 feet in,
1100 feet out
Hikable mid-July through
mid-September

Map: Green Trails No. 19 Billy
Goat Mtn.
Current information: Ask at
Methow Valley Ranger District
about trail Nos. 502A, 502,
451, and 462

This is a country for the fanciful. There are fanciful names, fanciful views, and trails to take you anywhere you fancy to go. Dollar Watch

Mountain sits smack in the middle, ideal as a destination in itself or as a sidetrip on a many-day loop. Campsites are plentiful; some even have water all summer.

Drive to the end of Eightmile Creek road (Hike 83, Copper Glance Lake) and the hikers' parking area, elevation 4800 feet.

Hike from the end of Eightmile Creek road 2½ miles to Billy Goat Pass, 6600 feet (Hike 83).

Pause to enjoy the long view out to rolling hills of the Methow Valley, then cross over. In a hundred feet pass the Burch Mountain trail (Hike 85) and plunge on down to Drake Creek, 5500 feet. Good camps here—with water, yet. At 5 miles cross Two Bit Creek and join the Drake Creek trail. The united way ascends an old burn to the broad gap (scoured out by the continental glacier) of Three Fools Pass, 6000 feet, and casually drops through woods and meadow toward Diamond Creek. At 6½ miles, about ½ mile below the pass, pass a well-used campsite and, at 7 miles, Diamond Point trail No. 514. Stay left on trail No. 502, cross the creek, 5500 feet, and begin a long sidehill, keeping nearly constant elevation into the valley of Larch Creek.

At 8½ miles there is a shortcut. Turn left on trail No. 451A (perhaps unsigned) which goes down to the left. However, it is easier to stay on the main trail another ½ mile to a campsite at Larch Creek, 5700 feet, and then go left on trail No. 451 climbing to Dollar Watch Mountain.

The Dollar Watch trail climbs steadily with occasional views south to Three Fools Pass and Nanny Goat Mountain. At 2 miles above Larch Creek it passes through the upper basin of Tony Creek, the last reliable water supply before Dollar Watch Pass and Mountain. At 3 miles above Larch Creek, 12 miles from the road, the faint tread of trail No. 451 branches right (east), crossing Two Point Mountain to reach Larch Pass, the first of several loop possibilities. Shortly beyond here the main trail crosses Dollar Watch Pass, 6950 feet, and drops to a campsite bench, 6870 feet, and a junction with East Fork Pasayten River trail No. 451.

The old lookout trail up Dollar Watch is lost in the bench meadows, so contour the upper slopes, find tread again, and climb to a saddle at 7063 feet. The trail branches; keep right, switchbacking to the old lookout site atop Dollar Watch Mountain, 7679 feet, 14 miles from the road. Presumably the watch was an Ingersoll pocket turnip. (Mickey Mouse watches came later.)

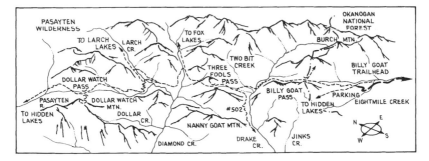

87 FORGOTTEN TRAILS OF THE METHOW VALLEY RANGER DISTRICT

In the 1930s fire lookouts were located at strategic points throughout the forest, and almost all had fantastic views. A few were accessed by roads but most by trail. In the 1950s aerial patrols took over the lookout jobs and the posts were abandoned; for lack of use, the trails were abandoned. Now with hikers crowding existing trails, there is a need to find the abandoned ones. In wilderness areas these are relatively easy to locate and, except for stepping over a few logs, in general the tread is in excellent shape. However, outside wilderness, as in the case of Doe Mountain and Setting Sun Mountain, logging obliterated the lower reaches of the trail and locating the remaining tread is often difficult.

Doe Mountain, elevation 7154 feet

Round trip 6–8 miles
Elevation gain 2600 feet

Map: Old 15-minute USGS Doe
   Mountain

Views overlooking the Chewuch River valley, the rocky summits of Ike Mountain and Farewell Peak, Winthrop farms, Mt. Gardner, Silver Star, and into the North Cascades.

Due to logging, the driving directions are changing, but to start with drive the Chewuch River road (Hike 83, Copper Glance Lake). Drive past the Eightmile Creek road No. 5130, past Falls Creek Campground, and go left uphill on road No. 5140 for 4.3 miles, then left on (5140)145 to the highest point you can drive near Doe Creek.

The trail followed Doe Creek at this point but is lost in the brushed-over clearcut. Follow abandoned spur roads to timber or locate tread. Where the mountain steepens, the trail crossed Doe Creek and contoured upward to the left until it reached the summit ridge. Look carefully here. The tread is faint at this point and if you miss the turn on the way down, you could end up miles away on the wrong road. On the ridge, go right and follow the ridge to the top.

Setting Sun Mountain, elevation 7253 feet

Round trip 4–6 miles
Elevation gain 2500 feet

Map: Trail not shown on any map
   printed after 1950, but see
   USGS McLeod Mountain

A great lookout site in the Methow Valley District on the boundary of the Pasayten Wilderness. Dramatic views into the Lost River gorge, to the peaks of the Pasayten, and across the Methow Valley to Silver Star.

The first time we hiked this trail it started from an old (even then) cabin, still standing, on the Lost River and went several miles up Yellowjacket Creek and then headed up a draw to the lookout. A primitive trail servicing a telephone line ran eastward along the ridge top to who knows where. Logging has obliterated so much of the trail it is almost impossible to find, so the easiest way is up a very steep ridge to intersect the telephone trail.

From near Mazama, follow Goat Creek road No. 52 and then road No. 5225 (Hike 73, Goat Peak). Go by the sideroad to Goat Peak Trail and approximately 11 miles from road No. 52 reach a pass at 5000 feet and park.

Either attempt to find the old trail located in the small valley to the west or scramble up the very steep ridge to the north and intersect the telephone line trail about ¾ mile from the summit.

Mount Silver Star and Snagtooth Ridge from Setting Sun Mountain

Dipper (also known as water ouzel) feeding in stream

 88 BLACK LAKE

Round trip 8½ miles
Hiking time 4 hours
High point 3982 feet
Elevation gain 800 feet
Hikable mid-May through
** October**
One day or backpack

Map: Green Trails No. 20
** Coleman Peak**
Current information: Ask at
** Methow Valley Ranger District**
** about trail No. 500**

A mile-long lake surrounded by forested peaks 7000 feet high. A quick and easy walk from the road, Black Lake may be the most popular spot in the whole Pasayten Wilderness.

Drive from Winthrop to the junction of the East Chewuch and West Chewuch River roads (Hike 83, Copper Glance Lake) and continue 15.5 miles on road No. 51. Turn left on Lakes Creek road No. (5160)100 for 2.4 miles to the road-end and trail No. 500, elevation 3162 feet.

With only minor ups and downs, the trail follows close by Lake Creek in delightful forest; come in early August to feast your way on blueberries and raspberries, usually ripe by then. At about 1½ miles note a boulder, 10 by 20 feet, that rumbled down the ridge in the winter of 1984–85, crashed and smashed through the trees, and came to rest wedged among four trees just a few feet from the trail.

Having entered the Pasayten Wilderness along the way, at a little

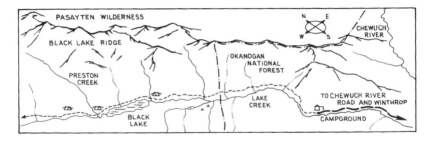

216

over 2 miles the trail reaches the shore of Black Lake, 3982 feet, 4¼ miles. Both ends of the lake have campsites; those at the far end may be horsier.

The crowds stop at the lake. For solitude continue a mile along the shore path and 7 more miles to tiny Fawn Lake, and then just keep on tramping deeper into the heart of wildness.

Black Lake

ANDREWS CREEK— CATHEDRAL LAKES

Round trip 42 miles
Allow 5–7 days
High point 7400 feet
Elevation gain 4900 feet in,
400 feet out
Hikable July through September

Map: Green Trails No. 20 Coleman
Peak
Current information: Ask at
Methow Valley Ranger District
about trail Nos. 504 and 533

The most-photographed scene in the eastern Pasayten Wilderness is Upper Cathedral Lake, sitting in a rock bowl amid ice-polished slabs, beneath the leaping cliffs of 8601-foot Cathedral Peak and 8358-foot Amphitheater Mountain. Cameras infest the place in fall, when the larch trees are bright gold, but also in summer, carried on hands and knees over the miles of lush herbaceous meadows and stony tundra which demand the close-up lens. For all the beauty and the fame, though, crowds are thin, held down by 21 miles of trail.

From the junction of the East and West Chewuch River roads (Hike 83, Copper Glance Lake), drive road No. 51 some 17 miles to Andrews Creek trail No. 504, elevation 3050 feet.

The trail has a fit of steepness at the start but after crossing Little Andrews Creek and a little divide settles down, at about ½ mile dropping a bit into Andrews Creek valley. Alternating between long valley-bottom flats and short, abrupt steps, it proceeds patiently toward its remote destination. At about 1 mile begins the 2-mile swath of a 1984 forest fire. At 3⅓ miles, near Blizzard Creek, pass two small buildings and the cablecar of a stream-gauging station. At about 4 miles the path divides. The main trail goes right, above a bluff, gaining and losing 200 feet. Straight ahead is a narrow "hikers-only," water-level trail that is

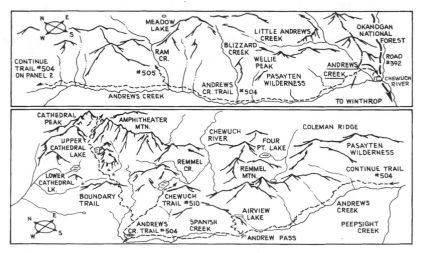

Cathedral Lake

a delight, if the water hasn't washed part of it away.

At 5½ miles pass the Meadow Lake trail. At about 8 miles begins an earnest climb to Andrews Pass, 6700 feet, 13 miles from the road. On one side rises the west face of Remmel Mountain, on the other the rounded dome of Andrews Peak.

The way now loses 400 feet into Spanish Creek valley, at 15 miles passing the Spanish Creek trail. The ever-expanding meadows submerge memories of the long, sweaty, and usually fly-bitten miles. Choose a spot for a basecamp near the junction with the Boundary Trail, close by the tread or off in a secluded nook. But *camp*—the sites at Cathedral Lakes are few and small and probably full and those at Remmel Lake are very horsey.

Boundary trail No. 523 goes right, passing Chewuch River trail No. 510, to Upper Cathedral Lake, 7400 feet, 21 miles from the road. You definitely will want to walk the roller-skate–smooth slabs and examine the gouges made by the glaciers; this area has experienced both local alpine glaciation, from such cirques as that of the Cathedral Lakes, and continental glaciation from accumulation centers in Canada, which sent out ice sheets that rode over and rounded the tops of all the peaks in the eastern Pasayten except a very few, including Cathedral.

You also may wish to drop on a sidetrail to Lower Cathedral Lake. Nor should you forget that the Boundary Trail goes west, ascending to just under the summit of Bald Mountain; spend a night on top and see who comes to the dance. A very large proportion of the Cascades terrain that satisfies the technical definition of "tundra" is located hereabouts; wander it this way and that, to the summit ridge of Amphitheater, should it please you. Sit amid the high-alpine blossoms and the lichen-covered stones and gaze to the Arctic Ocean.

90 CHEWUCH RIVER— REMMEL LAKE

Round trip 34 miles
Allow 3–5 days
High point 6871 feet
Elevation gain 3400 feet
Hikable July through September

Map: Green Trails No. 20 Coleman
  Peak
Current information: Ask at
  Methow Valley Ranger District
  about trail No. 510

Much of what has been said about Cathedral Lakes (Hike 89) also can be said about Remmel Lake—and indeed, they are near enough together that visiting back and forth is easy and quick. There are meadows around the shore, covered in season with blue lupine and deep red paintbrush and yellow "sunflowers." There are higher and drier meadows—true tundra, as in the Arctic, spongy and wet early in the season, buckled into small ridges and mounds by frost heaves, and peppered with innumerable holes of Columbian ground squirrels—"rockchucks" which behave in a most marmotlike manner, diving into their homes to escape the ever-patroling raptors, as well as the fun-loving humans who carry .22 pistols for the amiable all-seasons (illegal) sport of "plinking."

Drive from Winthrop 30 miles on the Chewuch River road (Hike 83, Copper Glance Lake) to its end at Thirtymile Camp and the start of Chewuch River trail No. 510, elevation 3500 feet.

Heavily stomped and tramped by horses, hikers, and cattle (the route is still listed as a stock driveway), the trail starts wide and dusty and pretty much stays that way, except when it's wide and muddy. In 1 mile it enters the Pasayten Wilderness. Just 300 feet are gained in the scant 3 miles to Chewuch Falls. The way passes swampy Pocket Lake to the junction with the Fire Creek–Coleman Ridge trail (Hike 91) at

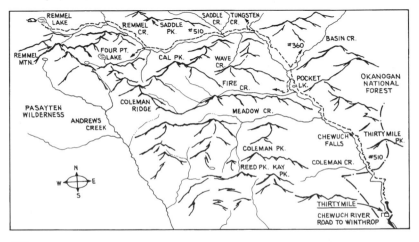

Remmel Lake and Remmel Mountain

about 5 miles, and at 8 miles Tungsten Creek trail, having gained thus far only 1100 feet. At 12 miles is the junction with Four Point Lake—Coleman Ridge trail (Hike 91). The tread now grows tired, worn, and rocky but the angle inclines upward only a little as forest thins to parkland. The rugged north face of Remmel Mountain appears and the path flattens to the shore of Remmel Lake, 6871 feet, 14 miles from the road.

If there were a market for horse apples, this would be a good field to harvest. The lake is ringed with campsites but unless one has grown up in a barnyard and *likes* that smell, finding a spot to eat supper is a problem. One would think that the Forest Service would keep horses at least 500 feet from camps and lakeshores or designate some of the campsites for hikers. For clean camps continue above the lake to a small creek. But watch out for sheep, too. They also have the right-of-way over hikers.

221

91 FOUR POINT LAKE— COLEMAN RIDGE LOOP

Loop trip 41 miles
Allow 3–5 days
High point 7300 feet
Elevation gain 4000 feet
Hikable late June through
  September

Map: Green Trails No. 20 Coleman
  Peak
Current information: Ask at
  Methow Valley Ranger District
  about trail Nos. 510, 561,
  and 505

If Four Point Lake alone is the goal—as it may well be, rimmed as it is by white granite, pines and larch, and a silver forest, in views to the cliffs of 8685-foot Remmel Peak—the easiest approach is to hike the Chewuch River trail (Hike 90) 12 miles and turn left 3 miles on the Four Point Lake trail. However, long and rugged though the loop is, there are compensations.

Four Point Lake and Remmel Mountain

Drive from Winthrop 30 miles on the Chewuch River road (Hike 83, Copper Glance Lake) to its end at Thirtymile Camp and the start of Chewuch River trail No. 510, elevation 3500 feet.

Hike the Chewuch River trail (Hike 90) 5¼ miles and turn left on the Fire Creek trail No. 561. Ford the river (no cinch in early summer), 4400 feet, and strike off up the steep trail, torn to shreds by cows (they graze here in alternate years), gaining 800 feet in switchbacks, then moderating. The way traverses a succession of wet meadows where tread is lost in a maze of cow tracks and pies (when thoroughly dry, these latter make as excellent a fire as buffalo chips). In one of the cow-mushed meadow-marshes, watch for a hiking boot half-buried in muck. What became of the hiker? Somewhere in the muck is an unmarked junction. Go right and search for the Coleman Ridge trail No. 505.

At about 6 miles from the Chewuch River the Coleman Ridge trail tops the divide, 6800 feet, between Fire Creek and Andrews Creek and proceeds steeply up the meadows of Coleman Ridge to 7200 feet. When the tread vanishes, watch for cairns. At the ridge-end the trail plummets some 300 feet, then climbs more meadows to a 7300-foot saddle between Andrews Creek and Four Point Creek. Here is a view to Four Point Lake, followed by a descent over a rockslide of gleaming white granite. At 11 miles from the Chewuch River (16 miles from the road) a little detour leads to the shore of Four Point Lake, 6830 feet.

A horse trail once continued to the top of 8685-foot Remmel Mountain to service the fire lookout located there from 1932 to 1956. The trail was abandoned and expunged from government maps, but hikers report the tread survives the official "disappearing." From the spur to Four Point Lake go back about ½ mile to a series of switchbacks, follow a stream up a few feet, and scout on the hillside for evidence of human and equine presence in the form of a well-preserved trail.

To complete the loop, descend steeply 3 miles (the sign says 2) from Four Point Lake to a ford of the Chewuch River, an easy step when the water is low, and proceed down and out 12 miles to the car.

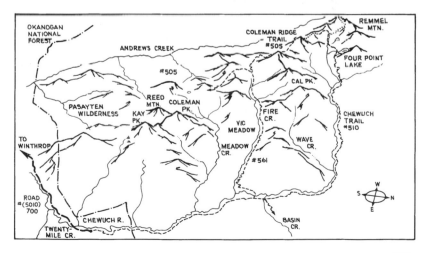

Historic lookout built in late 1920s on North Twentymile Peak

CHEWUCH RIVER
Unprotected area

92 HONEYMOON CREEK— NORTH TWENTYMILE PEAK LOOKOUT

Round trip 13 miles
Hiking time 7 hours
High point 7437 feet
Elevation gain 4200 feet
Hikable June through October

One day or backpack
Map: Green Trails No. 52 Doe Mtn.
Current information: Ask at
 Methow Valley Ranger District
 about trail No. 560

Behold an infinity of forested ridges extending from Silver Star Mountain in the west to Canada north, Tiffany Mountain east, and beyond the Methow Valley south. In all the wild scene only a single road can be seen, along the Chewuch River a vertical mile below. Ah, but the hand of man, if hidden, is everywhere busy, sawing and chopping.

To be sure, a clearcut gives him away but most of the logging is selective, meaning he is selecting the beautiful, big, old ponderosa pine and Douglas fir, leaving the small trees, which never will be allowed to grow old, big, and beautiful unless placed in protected wilderness. Fill the canteens before starting, for this is the *eastern* North Cascades, where the sun shines bright all day, except during thunderstorms. The trail is closed to motorcycles; hopefully, any fat-tired bikers you encounter will not be going 55 miles per hour training for the world championship downhiller at Metabief, France (similar to the World Cup downhill ski races).

Drive North Cascades Scenic Highway 20 to the center of Winthrop, turn west on the Chewuch River, signed "Pearrygin Lake State Park," pass the sideroad to the lake, and at 6.5 miles cross the Chewuch River to a junction. From this point go upstream, enter the national forest, where the road becomes No. 51 (Hike 83, Copper Glance Lake). At 11.3 miles from the junction turn right 0.6 miles on road No. 5010, then left 2 miles on road No. (5010)700 to the trailhead, elevation 3200 feet. A gutsy driver with a gutsy car can continue another 0.3 mile on road No. (5010)740 to the trailhead.

Walk or ride the rough road to the signed start of trail No. 560. With good tread, the trail gains 500–800 feet a mile. At 2 miles is the first and last water at a campsite beside Honeymoon Creek. At about 5 miles the way attains the ridge crest and views that grow steadily in the last 1½ miles to the summit, 7464 feet.

The lookout cabin on the ground was built in 1923 and may be the state's last example of the cupola design; it is on the National Historic Register. The 30-foot tower was built in 1948 and was staffed until the 1980s.

An abandoned trail goes east 10 miles to Thirtymile Meadows and road No. 39. If the proposed Twentymile-Thirtymile Wilderness is not established (as it was *not* by the 1984 Washington Wilderness Act), this trail likely will be reopened—for motorcycles. Barring that catastrophe, the first mile along the ridge from the summit is a marvelous meadow stroll. One would love to camp here if one could find (or carry) water. But one would not love to be here when the lightning bolts are zapping prominently upright organisms.

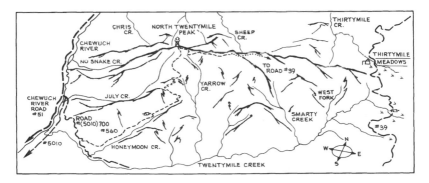

93 TIFFANY MOUNTAIN

**Round trip from Freezeout Pass
to the summit 6 miles
Hiking time 4 hours
High point 8242 feet
Elevation gain 1700 feet**

**One-way trip via Tiffany Lake
8 miles
Hiking time 5 hours
High point 7100 feet
Elevation gain 800 feet**

**Hikable July through September
One day
Map: Green Trails No. 53 Tiffany
Mountain
Current information: Ask at
Tonasket Ranger Station about
trail No. 345 and about one-way
trail No. 373**

A superb ridge walk to an 8242-foot summit, the views west to distant peaks of the North Cascades, north into the Pasayten Wilderness, and east to farmlands of the Okanogan. The hike can be done as a round trip or—by use of two cars or a non-hiking companion to move the car—as a one-way trip.

Drive north from Winthrop on the paved East Chewuch River road (Hike 83, Copper Glance Lake). At 6.6 miles, just before the road crosses the Chewuch River, turn right on road No. 37. In less than 2 miles the road turns uphill and follows Boulder Creek. In 13 miles go

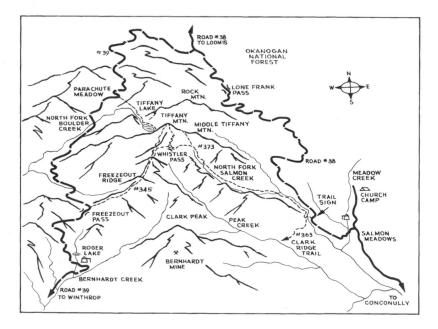

Tiffany Mountain from Tiffany Meadows

left on road No. 39 and continue 3 miles on rough road to Freezeout Pass and the trailhead, elevation 6500 feet.

(To place a car at the alternate trailhead, drive 4 more miles to Tiffany Lake trail, 6240 feet. If making this a one-way hike start here; the section out of Tiffany Lake is difficult and easier to go up than down.)

From Freezeout Pass the trail climbs steadily 1½ miles through trees, then 1 mile above timberline, and begins a contour around the east side of the peak. Be sure to make the ½-mile (each way) sidetrip up grassy slopes (the original trail was obliterated by past grazing) to the unlimited views from the top of Tiffany Mountain, once the site of a fire lookout, elevation 8245 feet.

For the one-way trip, at Tiffany Lake hike upstream, following faint traces of the trail. At about 7100 feet the trail improves; go right to Whistler Pass. The trail again becomes faint but the way is easy to see.

94 SMARTY CREEK—NORTH TWENTYMILE PEAK LOOKOUT

Round trip to lookout 17 miles
Hiking time 9 hours
High point 7437 feet
Elevation gain 1600 feet in,
   300 feet out
Hikable June through October
One day or backpack

Maps: Green Trails No. 21
   Horseshoe Basin, No. 53
   Tiffany Mountain
Current information: Ask at
   Tonasket Ranger Station
   about trail No. 371

A trail open to all users and, except during hunting season, used by virtually no one. Strange, considering the miles of meadows, then miles of ridge-walking, and a sidetrip to the historic fire-lookout cabin atop North Twentymile Peak, and its from-here-to-forever views of forests and valleys and mountains. The flowers, the ridge vistas, the modest elevation gain, and the many good camps (except for the years cattle are present) make this route something special. However, the trail is seldom maintained and easy to lose; the experience is as much an adventure in routefinding as an enjoyable hike. No manufacturer's miracle boots will keep the feet dry through the endless succession of bogs.

The Long John Swamp Roadless Area (a lynx recovery zone) once had a vast system of trails; all but Smarty Creek have been abandoned for many years. The chance of seeing a lynx is almost nonexistent and the chance of seeing other people only slightly better.

Smarty Creek trail No. 371 starts on road No. 39 and finishes 10 miles away, back on road No. 39. Either trailhead is as good as the other. If transportation can be arranged, it could be a one-way trip. The trail is described here from the South Fork Twentymile Creek trailhead to the North Twentymile Peak Lookout.

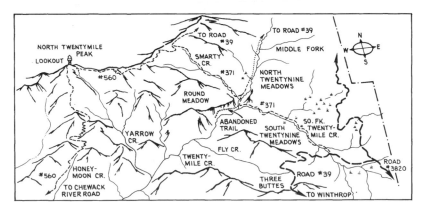

Headwaters of North Twentymile Creek

Drive from Winthrop on the East Chewuch River road (Hike 93, Tiffany Mountain). Just a few feet east of the Chewuch River bridge, turn north on road No. 37. At 13 miles go left on road No. 39 to the 6500-foot saddle in Freezeout Ridge and the Tiffany Mountain trailhead (Hike 93). The road drops and again climbs to a 6900-foot saddle near Tiffany Springs Campground. At 13 miles from the junction of road Nos. 37 and 39, cross South Fork Twentymile Creek and find Smarty Creek trail No. 371 (sign missing in 1994), elevation 5900 feet.

The trail follows the creek downstream, mostly in glorious meadows (and bogs), the tread almost impossible to find but the route obvious. At about 2 miles the meadows end as the valley narrows to a V. Finding the trail, and staying on it, become very important here. At 2½ miles is a junction and an ancient trail sign. Go right, up North Fork Twentymile Creek, a scant ½ mile. Cross the creek and climb steeply to another junction and sign. Go left, downstream a bit, then up along Smarty Creek, skirting one final meadow. (The whole trail is named for this short section.) An earnest climb leads to the ridge top and at 5½ miles another junction. For the lookout go left on trail No. 560, up and down the crest in picture-window views steadily enlarging. The crest rises at last above timberline and the views climax atop North Twentymile Peak, 7437 feet, 8½ miles from the road.

For the one-way trip, back at the Smarty Creek trail junction go right on the ridge crest, then drop a bit and climb to a 6965-foot high point, and then descend West Fork Twentymile Creek to Skull Camp. Turn upstream and follow Twentymile Creek through mile-long, sometimes marshy North Twentymile Meadows, past Lightning Camp and another mile to road No. 39, reached exactly 10 miles by road from the starting point. Not counting the sidetrip to the lookout, the hike totals 12 miles, elevation gain 2100 feet.

95   BERNHARDT TRAIL

**Round trip to North Summit
  6 miles
Hiking time 4 hours
High point 7400 feet
Elevation gain 1700 feet
Hikable July through September**

**One day
Map: Green Trails No. 53 Tiffany
  Mountain
Current information: Ask at
  Tonasket Ranger Station
  about trail No. 367**

Sometimes steep and sometimes very steep, the trail named for Mr. (or Ms.) Bernhardt (we don't know who he or she was, or is) ascends through forest to fields of windswept or sunstruck or rain-flattened grass on the slopes of Clark Peak. At its junction with the North Summit trail a hiker has three options: climb Clark Peak, climb Tiffany Mountain, or take off on an 11-mile loop.

Drive from Winthrop on the East Chewuch River road 6.6 miles, and just before the Chewuch River bridge go right on road No. 37, following the river a short way, then climbing into Boulder Creek valley. In an-

Tiffany Mountain from side of Clark Mountain

other 13 miles (sign says "Winthrop 19 miles") go left on road No. 39 for 1.2 miles and find Bernhardt trail No. 367, elevation 5700 feet.

In a scant ½ mile the trail crosses Bernhardt Creek and then a tributary—twice. In about 1 mile it skirts a boggy meadow and around 1½ miles starts up, seldom bothering with switchbacks. At about 2¼ miles the path goes left of a sturdy log cabin with a leaky roof (attention, Bernhardt family) to an unmarked junction. The right dead-ends in ½ mile at some diggings, presumably Bernhardt's; go left, in the sometimes-steeply gear, taking care not to stray off on the many animal paths. At 3 miles, 7400 feet, are North Summit trail No. 369 and the options.

Option No. 1. Turn around and go home. But first, sidetrip left ¼ mile for a striking view of Freezeout Ridge and Tiffany Mountain.

Old cabin with leaky roof on Bernhardt trail

Option No. 2. Pick your way up open slopes to the top of Clark Peak, 7900 feet.

Option No. 3. Go left (north) on the North Summit trail a very scant 2 miles to Whistler Pass, 7600 feet. Stay on the trail to the summit of Tiffany Mountain, 8242 feet. Descend Freezeout Ridge trail No. 345 to road No. 39 and walk it downhill 2 miles to the Bernhardt trailhead, for a loop total of 11 miles.

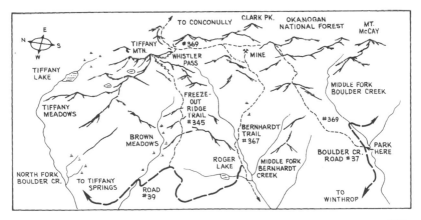

96 NORTH SUMMIT TRAIL

Round trip 11 miles
Hiking time 6 hours
High point 7500 feet
Elevation gain 2300 feet in,
   250 feet out
Hikable June through September

One day
Map: Green Trails No. 53 Tiffany
   Mountain
Current information: Ask at
   Tonasket Ranger Station
   about trail No. 369

Considering the quality of the scenery, it is amazing this trail is not used more. The North Summit trail is an old stock driveway, which might not sound much like fun, but the cows and sheep haven't been around these parts in years, ever since the cowboys and shepherds moved their enterprises to the lower country, where they were less likely to have their animals frozen to death in an August blizzard. So, it's a long and lonesome ridge of pines and meadows, the flora the more interesting because on sunny slopes there is sagebrush, and on wetter slopes, rock gardens of lupine, paintbrush, buckwheat, and stonecrop. The views, too, are distinctive, combining long looks out to the rolling highlands of Eastern Washington and long looks west to distant peaks of the North Cascades. Closer up are the green meadows of Clark Peak and Tiffany Mountain. Bring full canteens; there's no water.

By use of two cars, this trip can be combined with the Bernhardt trail (Hike 95) or Tiffany Mountain (Hike 93).

Drive from Winthrop on the East Chewuch River road 6.5 miles (Hike 86, Dollar Watch Mountain). Just before the Chewuch River bridge go right on road No. 37, following the river a short way, then climbing into Boulder Creek valley. In another 11.4 miles (sign says "Winthrop 19 miles") go right another 2.5 miles to a gravel pit (just east of milepost 18) and North Summit trail No. 369, elevation 5850 feet. Park on shoulder.

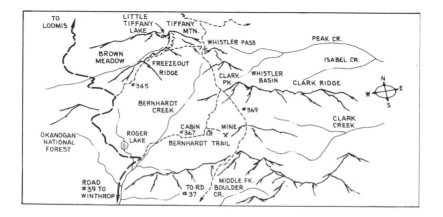

Tiffany Mountain from North Summit trail

There is no sign, only a faint boot-beaten path which starts up the right side of the gravel pit, crosses over the top, and enters forest. In ½ mile the route skirts the top of a large sagebrush meadow, marked by large cairns. The way returns to trees and at about 1¼ miles crosses another sagebrush meadow, the cairns fewer and smaller; if you lose the route, contour and climb, searching for cairns; find tread in the trees on the far side. Woods and meadows alternating, the trail climbs to a 7500-foot saddle and crosses the ridge to a great spot, 2½ miles from the road, to view the world and call it a day.

From the viewspot follow the ups and down, first on the east side, then the west side of North Ridge for a long mile, then steeply drop 250 feet to a low point. The way swings around the east slopes of the next high point of the crest to the next low point at 3½ miles, and here meets the Clark Ridge trail. The North Summit trail now contours the west side of Clark Peak, passing the Bernhardt trail at 4½ miles and at 5½ miles ending at Whistler Pass. At the pass is a four-way inter-section offering a choice of climbing Tiffany Mountain, taking the unmaintained Tiffany Lake trail, descending the Freezeout Ridge trail, or turning around to go back the way you came.

97 HORSESHOE BASIN (PASAYTEN)

Round trip to Sunny Pass 9 miles
Hiking time 6 hours
High point 7200 feet
Elevation gain 1200 feet
Hikable late June through
mid-October

One day or backpack
Map: Green Trails No. 21
Horseshoe Basin
Current information: Ask at
Tonasket Ranger Station about
trail No. 533

At the northeast extremity of the Cascades is a tundra country so unlike the main range a visitor wonders if he/she hasn't somehow missed a turn and ended up in the Arctic. Meadows for miles and miles, rolling from broad basins to rounded summits of peaks above 8000 feet, in views south over forests to Tiffany Mountain, east to Chopaka Mountain and the Okanogan Highlands, north far into Canada, and west across the Pasayten Wilderness to glaciered, dream-hazy giants of the Cascade Crest.

Drive from Tonasket to Loomis and turn north. In 1.5 miles turn left at signs for Toats Coulee, cross the valley of Sinlahekin Creek, and start a long, steep climb up Toats Coulee on road No. 39. At 11 miles from Loomis is North Fork Campground and in another 5 miles is a junction. Go right on a narrow road No. (3900)500 signed "Iron Gate." Turn right and drive 7 rough and steep miles to the road-end and beginning of Boundary Trail No. 533, elevation 6100 feet, at Iron Gate Camp (no water) on the edge of the Pasayten Wilderness.

The first ½ mile is downhill along the abandoned road to the old Iron Gate Camp (no water). The trail from here begins in small lodgepole pine (most of this region was burned off by a series of huge fires in the 1920s) on the old road to Tungsten Mine, which sold stock as recently as the early 1950s. The grade is nearly flat ½ mile to cool waters of a branch of Clutch Creek and then starts a moderate, steady ascent. At 3¼ miles the route opens out into patches of grass and flowers. After a brief steep bit, at 4 miles the way abruptly emerges from trees to the

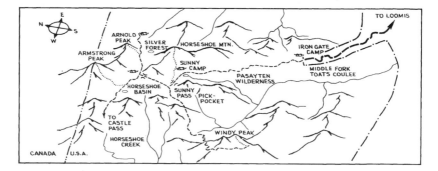

Louden Lake in Horseshoe Basin

flowery, stream-bubbling nook of Sunny Basin and splendid Sunny Camp, 6900 feet.

The trail climbs ½ mile to 7200-foot Sunny Pass; be prepared to gasp and rave. All around spreads the enormous meadowland of Horseshoe Basin, demanding days of exploration. From the pass the Tungsten road drops left and the "pure" trail goes right, contouring gentle slopes of Horseshoe Mountain to grand basecamps in and near the wide flat of Horseshoe Pass, 7000 feet, 5¾ miles, and then contouring more glory to tiny Louden Lake, 6¾ miles (this lake dries up in late summer), and then on and on as described in Hike 98, Boundary Lake.

The roamings are unlimited. All the summits are easy flower walks— 7620-foot Pick Peak, 8000-foot Horseshoe Mountain, and 8090-foot Arnold Peak. The ridge north from 8106-foot Armstrong Peak has the added interest of monuments to mark the U.S.-Canadian boundary. A more ambitious sidetrip is south from Sunny Pass 6 miles on the down-and-up trail to 8334-foot Windy Peak, highest in the area and once the site of a fire lookout. Don't omit a short walk east through Horseshoe Pass to the immense silver forest at the head of Long Draw.

BOUNDARY TRAIL

One-way trip (main route) from Iron Gate via Castle Pass to Harts Pass 94 miles
Allow 10 or more days
High point 7600 feet
Elevation gain 13,000 feet
Hikable July through September

Maps: Green Trails No. 16 Ross Lake, No. 17 Jack Mountain, No. 18 Pasayten Peak, No. 19 Billy Goat Mtn., No. 20 Coleman Peak, No. 21 Horseshoe Basin, No. 50 Washington Pass
Current information: Ask at Methow Valley Ranger District or Tonasket Ranger Station about trail No. 533

As the golden eagle flies, it's 40 miles from the east edge of the Pasayten Wilderness to the Cascade Crest; as the backpacker walks it's twice that far, and some distance still remaining to reach civilization. Though the Pasayten country lacks the glaciers of more famous mountains west, and with few exceptions the peaks are rounded, unchallenging to a climber, there is a magnificent vastness of high ridges, snowfields, flower gardens, parklands, cold lakes, green forests, loud rivers. The weather is better and summer arrives earlier than in windward ranges. The trails are high much of the distance, often above 7000 feet, but are mostly snowfree in early July, an ideal time for the trip.

Length of the route precludes a detailed description in these pages. In any event the journey is for experienced wilderness travelers who have the routefinding skills needed to plan and find their own way. The notes below aim merely to stimulate the imagination.

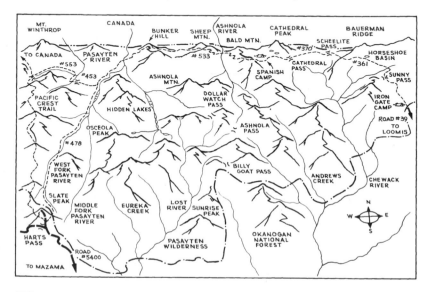

Boundary Trail and Remmel Mountain near Cathedral Pass

Begin from the Iron Gate road-end (Hike 97, Horseshoe Basin) and walk to Horseshoe Basin and Louden Lake (6¾ miles). With ups and downs, always in highlands, the trail goes along Bauerman Ridge to Scheelite Pass (13¾ miles), the old buildings and garbage of Tungsten Mine (17¾ miles), and over Cathedral Pass to Cathedral Lakes (22 miles). The route this far makes a superb 4–7-day round trip from Iron Gate.

Continue west to campsites at the junction of Andrews Creek trail (26 miles) and the first descent to low elevation, at the Ashnola River (31¼ miles). Climb high again, passing Sheep Mountain (34½ miles), Quartz Mountain (38 miles), and Bunker Hill (43 miles), then dropping to low forests of the Pasayten River (50½ miles).

Follow the Pasayten River upstream past the abandoned and impassable Harrison Creek trail No. 453, and turn up Soda Creek to Dead Lake (60 miles), 5100 feet. Ascend Frosty Creek past Frosty Lake to Frosty Pass (66 miles) and on to Castle Pass (67 miles). From here take the Pacific Crest Trail 27 miles south (Hike 100) to Harts Pass, ending a trip of some 94 miles.

(For a shorter alternate, hike up the Pasayten River to Three Forks and ascend the West Fork Pasayten to Harts Pass. Trails branch west from this valley route to reach the Cascade Crest at Woody Pass and Holman Pass.)

However, for the true and complete Boundary Trail, go west from Castle Pass on the Three Fools Trail (Hike 80), hike south to Ross Dam and cross Ross Reservoir to the Little Beaver, and traverse the North Cascades National Park via Whatcom and Hannegan Passes (Hike 12), concluding the epic at the Ruth Creek road.

99 MOUNT BONAPARTE

Round trip 9 miles
Hiking time 6 hours
High point 7258 feet
Elevation gain 2752 feet
Hikable mid-June through October

One day
Map: USGS Mt. Bonaparte
Current information: Ask at
  Tonasket Ranger Station
  about trail No. 306

No, campers, we're not in the North Cascades here, but well to the east across the Okanogan Valley, in highlands that may be considered a suburb of the Selkirk Range. Two unique features of the mountain are the highest fire lookout in Eastern Washington and the original lookout building, constructed in 1914 of hand-hewn logs (see the ax marks) and now on the National Register of Historic Buildings.

Lookout cabin built in 1914 on top of Mount Bonaparte. Originally the corner posts were taller and supported a small observation platform.

Among the 20 miles of trail in the roadless area (proposed for wilderness status, but omitted from the 1984 Washington Wilderness Act, leaving the job still to be done) around Mt. Bonaparte are three routes to the top, each with its own attractions. The South Side trail, 5½ miles long, starts at 4400 feet on road No. (3300)100 and gives views of Bonaparte Lake. Antoine trail, 6 miles, is a favorite with horse-riders. The Myers Creek trail described here is the shortest and starts highest, but the way is dry and has no views until the summit.

Drive east from the north end of Tonasket on county road No. 9467, signed "Havillah." In 15.7 miles, just short of Havillah Church, turn right on a road signed "Lost Lake." Pavement ends in 0.9 mile; turn right on road No. 33. At 4.2 miles from the county road turn right on road No. (3300)300 (abbreviated on the sign to 300). Follow it 1.2 miles to the trailhead, elevation 4500 feet. (Logging may change the exact starting point.)

Mt. Bonaparte trail No. 306 starts on a logging road, crosses a creek, and climbs ¼ mile to a permanent roadblock (some cars drive this far). The trail itself is, or was, a road, now abandoned, through a replanted clearcut. Dodge several motorcycle runways; follow horse- and footprints straight ahead. At 1¼ miles is the end of logging and the start of virgin forest of lodgepole pine. The trail steepens to a junction at 2½ miles with the South Side trail. At 3¾ miles is a junction with the Antoine trail. Lodgepole pines yield to subalpine fir, which at 4½ miles yields to open meadows and all-around-the-compass views over forested hills to valley ranches. The summit of the Okanogan Highlands has been attained, 7258 feet.

Below the modern lookout tower is the 1914 lookout building, slightly bent out of shape by the weight of winter snow. The tower atop the cabin had to be removed years ago. In early days the lookout communicated by heliograph, an instrument that aimed a beam of sunlight and by means of a shutter transmitted Morse code to a receiver as far away as 20–30 miles. On cloudy days and at night the lookout did not communicate, not until telephone lines were installed in the 1930s. When the lines were broken by falling trees or limbs the lookout did not communicate, not until the 1960s and the proliferation of radios.

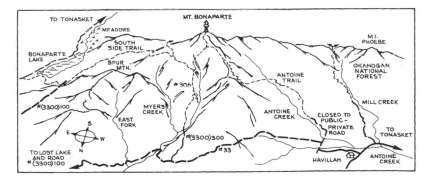

100 PACIFIC CREST TRAIL

One-way trip Allison Pass to
  Stehekin River 87 miles
Allow 10–12 days
Elevation gain 12,400 feet
Hikable August through
  September

Maps: Green Trails No. 82
  Stehekin, No. 50 Early Winters,
  No. 18 Pasayten Peak, No. 17
  Jack Mountain
Current information: Ask at
  Methow Valley Ranger District
  about trail No. 2000

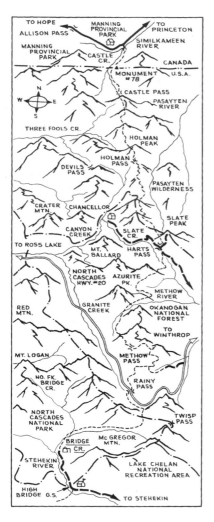

For rugged mountain scenery, the portion of the Pacific Crest National Scenic Trail between the Canadian border and Stevens Pass is the most spectacular long walking route in the nation. Undependable weather, late-melting snow, and many ups and downs make it also one of the most difficult and strenuous.

Few hikers have time to complete the trip in one season; most spread their efforts over a period of years, doing the trail in short sections. Those taking the whole trip at once generally prefer to start from the north, since pickup transportation at journey's end is easier to arrange at the south terminus. Though higher, the northern part of the trail lies in the rainshadow of great peaks to the west and thus gets less snow than the southern part; the north country and south country therefore open to travel simultaneously.

There is no legal way for a hiker to cross the Canadian–U.S. border on the Pacific Crest Trail. However, U.S. Forest Service wilderness permits for hiking in the Pasayten Wilderness on the U.S. side of the border were available until 1985, when they were no longer needed, at the visitors' center in Manning Provincial

Pacific Crest Trail contouring around Slate Peak

Park, Canada. Hikers must draw their own conclusion and decide whether or not to join the hundreds of folks who cross the border on this and the Monument 83 Trail (Hike 82).

Drive Trans-Canada Highway 3 to Manning Provincial Park and find the trailhead on an unmarked sideroad 0.5 mile east of the hotel-motel complex at Allison Pass.

Allison Pass to Harts Pass

One way 40 miles   **Elevation gain about 8000 feet**
Allow 4 days

Hike 7½ miles up Castle Creek to the international boundary at Monument 78. Look east and west from the monument along the corridor cleared by boundary survey crews for what reason nobody knows,

Pacific Crest Trail above Swamp Creek valley

but they keep on doing it. Ascend Route Creek to Castle Pass, from which point south to Harts Pass the trail is almost continuously in meadowland, touching Hopkins Pass, climbing to Lakeview Ridge, crossing Woody Pass into Conie Basin and Rock Pass into Goat Lakes Basin, dropping to Holman Pass, swinging around Jim Peak to Jim Pass, Foggy Pass, and Oregon Basin, crossing a shoulder of Tamarack Peak into Windy Basin, and from there continuing to Harts Pass as described in Hike 79 (Windy Pass).

Harts Pass to Rainy Pass

One way 31 miles   **Elevation gain about 4400 feet**
Allow 4 days

From Harts Pass the next road junction is at Rainy Pass. The trail contours around Tatie Peak to Grasshopper Pass (Hike 78), drops to Glacier Pass, drops more into the West Fork Methow River, climbs over Methow Pass, and contours high around Tower Mountain to Granite Pass and on to Cutthroat Pass and down to Rainy Pass (Hikes 72 and 70).

Rainy Pass to High Bridge

One way 16 miles   **Elevation gain none**
Allow 2 days

The next segment is all downhill along Bridge Creek to the Stehekin River road. Walk east to the Bridge Creek trail and descend forest to the road at Bridge Creek Campground (Hike 49, Park Creek Pass). Hike 5 miles down the Stehekin River road to High Bridge Campground. To continue south, see *100 Hikes in Washington's North Cascades: Glacier Peak Region* (I. Spring and H. Manning).

Coleman Glacier from Bastille Ridge

STILL MORE HIKES IN THE NORTH CASCADES

This book covers the 180 miles west–east from slopes of Mt. Baker to the Okanogan Highland and the 40 miles from Cascade Pass to Canada. Companion volumes—*100 Hikes in Washington's North Cascades: Glacier Peak Region* (I. Spring and H. Manning), *100 Hikes in Washington's Alpine Lakes,* 2d ed. (V. Spring, I. Spring, and H. Manning), *50 Hikes in Mount Rainier National Park,* 3d ed. (I. Spring and H. Manning), and *100 Hikes in Washington's South Cascades & Olympics,* 2d ed. (I. Spring and H. Manning)—reach south. Another—*103 Hikes in Southwestern British Columbia,* 4th ed. (Macaree)—follows the North Cascades over the border to their end. Shorter walks than those herein are described in *Best Short Hikes in Washington's North Cascades & San Juan Islands* (E. M. Sterling). The interface of Western Washington lowlands and front ridges of the Cascades is treated in *Footsore 3: Walks and Hikes Around Puget Sound: Everett to Bellingham* (H. Manning), that of Central Washington sagebrush steppe and the eastern slope of the Cascades in *55 Hikes in Central Washington* (I. Spring and H. Manning). Approaches to and routes up peaks are the subject of *Cascade Alpine Guide: Climbing and High Routes* (F. Beckey), a series of three volumes.

The 100 hikes have been selected to be representative of all the varied provinces of the (far) North Cascades and neighboring ranges to the east. However, it's a big country with many other comparable trips. The aforementioned books describe many. Following is a sampling— some covered by the books, some not—that can be particularly recommended. The lack of detailed recipes may be compensated for by greater solitude.

NOOKSACK RIVER

Silesia Creek: Reached from Twin Lakes.

Bastille Ridge: Spectacular view of Coleman Glacier reached after a difficult river crossing.

Chilliwack River from Canada: Excellent forest walk from Chilliwack Lake.

Price Lake: Climbers' path to rock-milky lake under Price Glacier.

BAKER RIVER

Baker Lake Shore: 9-mile trail on east side of lake. Find trail 1 mile north of dam or hike the Baker River trail 1 mile, cross the river on a horse bridge, then walk back to the lake and grand views.

Anderson Lakes, Watson Lakes, and Anderson Butte: See *Best Short Hikes.*

Dock Butte: See *Best Short Hikes.*

Blue Lake: ¾-mile walk. See *Best Short Hikes.*

SKAGIT RIVER–ROSS LAKE

Slide Lake: A long drive on road No. 16, then an easy 1 mile. See the massive rockslide that dammed the lake. See *Best Short Hikes.*

Sauk Mountain: Aerial views of Skagit and Sauk Valleys. See *Best Short Hikes.*

Diablo Lake trail: From Diablo Dam above cliffs to powerhouse below Ross Dam.

Ruby Creek: River walk from Panther Creek to Canyon Creek across from the North Cascades Highway.

Ruby Mountain: Abandoned trail, long climb, but spectacular views for the experienced hiker.

Perry Creek: Sidetrip on virtually vanished trail from Little Beaver into a hanging valley.

Silver Creek: Unmaintained dead-end trail on the west side of Ross Lake. Reached by boat.

McAllister Creek: Dead-end trail from Thunder Creek.

CASCADE RIVER

Marble Creek: See *Best Short Hikes.*

Trapper Lake: Rough trail to a deep cirque east of Cascade Pass.

LAKE CHELAN-STEHEKIN RIVER

Flat Creek: Dead-end, 3⅓-mile trail into a scenic valley under the LeConte Glacier.

Rainbow Lake: Popular trail to alpine lake.

Junction Mountain: Dead-end trail with views of Agnes and Stehekin valleys.

Prince, Canoe, and Fish Creeks: Long, steep access trails from Lake Chelan to the Chelan Summit.

Boulder Creek: To War Creek Pass and Chelan Summit.

TWISP RIVER

Hoodoo Pass: 6½ miles into the heart of the Chelan Summit.

Fish Creek Pass: Long, easy 9½-mile hike up Buttermilk Creek to Chelan Summit.

War Creek: A 10-mile but much easier trail to War Creek Pass than the grueling approach from Stehekin.

Reynolds Creek: Joins the Boulder Creek trail in 7 miles.

North Creek: Steep, dry, 5-mile trail to a tiny mountain lake or down Cedar Creek to Early Winters.

METHOW RIVER

Baron Creek: From Chancellor.

Beaver Creek: This trail near Winthrop has been drastically shortened by logging roads.

Foggy Dew Ridge: A forest walk to viewpoint.

Gardner Mountain: A high ridge walk.

Lookout Mountain: Trail to lookout above Twisp. See *Best Short Hikes.*

Pearrygin Creek: Drastically shortened by logging roads.

EARLY WINTERS CREEK

Early Winters: Remnants of trail not obliterated by Highway 20 along Early Winters Creek and Washington Pass.

Willow Creek: Climbers' route to camp on Silver Star Mountain.

GRANITE CREEK

East Creek–Mebee Pass: Steep climb on old Indian and miners' route.

Mill Creek–Azurite Pass: Stiff climb beginning on an old mining road.

Cabinet Creek: Abandoned from Highway 20 to Gabriel Pass.

CHEWUCH RIVER

Mt. Barney: Trail to alpine meadows.

Meadow Lake: Steep sidetrail from Andrews Creek to lake and Coleman Peak.

Crystal Lake: 9 miles to small alpine lake.

OKANOGAN RIVER

Mt. Bonaparte: South Side trail to lookout from road No. (3300)100.

Pipsissewa Point: 2 miles to viewpoint of Bonaparte Lake. Also reached by road No. (3300)100.

KETTLE RANGE

Thirteen Mountain: Difficult to follow to Thirteenmile Mountain and Thirteenmile Basin.

South Kettle Range: A ridge walk south of Sherman Pass.

Kettle Crest Trail North: 13 miles, much of the way in meadows.

Columbia Mountain: 2¼ miles from Sherman Pass to historic lookout built in 1914.

White Mountain: 7 miles south from Sherman Pass to lookout site.

APPENDIX

The Green Trails maps listed for each trail are all most hikers need. For the benefit of those who love poring over maps, the following 7.5-minute USGS maps are listed below for each trail.

1 Heliotrope Ridge—USGS Goat Mountain, Mt. Baker (trail not shown on map)
2 Skyline Divide—USGS Mt. Baker, Bearpaw Mountain
3 Canyon Ridge—Point 5658—USGS Glacier, Bearpaw Mountain
4 Excelsior Mountain—USGS Bearpaw Mountain
5 Church Mountain—USGS Bearpaw Mountain
6 Welcome Pass—Excelsior Ridge—USGS Mt. Larrabee
7 Yellow Aster Butte—USGS Mt. Larrabee
8 Gold Run Pass—Tomyhoi Lake—USGS Mt. Larrabee
9 Twin Lakes—Winchester Mountain—USGS Mt. Larrabee
10 Nooksack Cirque—USGS Mt. Larrabee, Mt. Sefrit, Mt. Shuksan
11 Goat Mountain Lookout Site—USGS Mt. Larrabee
12 Hannegan Pass and Peak—USGS Mt. Sefrit
13 Copper Mountain— USGS Mt. Sefrit, Copper Mountain
14 Easy Ridge—USGS Mt. Sefrit, Copper Mountain, Mt. Blum
15 Whatcom Pass—USGS Mt. Sefrit, Copper Mountain, Mt. Redoubt
16 Lake Ann—USGS Shuksan Arm
17 Chain Lakes Loop—USGS Shuksan Arm
18 Ptarmigan Ridge—USGS Shuksan Arm
19 Elbow Lake—USGS Twin Sisters Mountain
20 Cathedral Pass—USGS Twin Sisters Mountain, Baker Pass
21 Park Butte—Railroad Grade—USGS Baker Pass
22 Scott Paul Trail—USGS Baker Pass
23 Boulder Ridge—USGS Mt. Baker, Shuksan Arm, Baker Pass (not shown on map)
24 Rainbow Ridge—USGS Shuksan Arm (trail not shown on map)
25 Swift Creek— USGS Shuksan Arm
26 Shannon Ridge—USGS Mt. Shuksan
27 Little Shuksan Lake—USGS Mt. Shuksan
28 Baker River—USGS Lake Shannon, Mt. Shuksan
29 Cow Heaven—USGS Marblemount (trail not shown on map)
30 Lookout Mountain—Monogram Lake—USGS Big Devil Peak
31 Hidden Lake Peaks—USGS Eldorado Peak, Sonny Boy Lakes
32 Boston Basin—USGS Cascade Pass
33 Cascade Pass—Sahale Arm—USGS Cascade Pass
34 Thornton Lakes—Trappers Peak—USGS Mt. Triumph

69 Silver Star—USGS Silver Star Mtn., Mazama (trail not shown on maps)

70 Cutthroat Pass—USGS Washington Pass

71 Maple Pass—USGS Mt. Arriva, McGregor Mountain, Washington Pass, McAlester Mountain

72 Golden Horn—USGS Washington Pass

73 Goat Peak—USGS Mazama

74 Lost River—USGS Mazama, Robinson Mountain

75 Robinson Pass—USGS Slate Peak, Robinson Mountain, Pasayten Peak, Mt. Lago, Mazama, Lost Peak

76 West Fork Methow River—USGS Robinson Mountain and Slate Peak

77 Trout Creek—USGS Slate Peak

78 Grasshopper Pass—USGS Slate Peak

79 Windy Pass—USGS Slate Peak, Pasayten Peak

80 Three Fools Trail—USGS Slate Peak, Pasayten Peak, Shull Mountain, Castle Peak, Skagit Peak, Hozomeen Mountain

81 Silver Lake—USGS Slate Peak, Pasayten Peak (trail not shown on maps)

82 Cascade Loop Trail and Monument 81—USGS Frosty Creek, Castle Peak

83 Copper Glance Lake—USGS Sweetgrass Butte, Billy Goat Mountain

84 Parson Smith Tree—Hidden Lakes—USGS Billy Goat Mountain, Lost Peak, Ashnola Mountain, Tatoosh Buttes

85 Billy Goat Pass—Burch Mountain—USGS Billy Goat Mountain (trail not shown on map)

86 Dollar Watch Mountain—USGS Billy Goat Mountain, Lost Peak, Ashnola Mountain

87 Forgotten Trails of Winthrop Ranger District—Doe Mountain, USGS Doe Mountain. Setting Sun Mountain, USGS McLeod Mountain (trails not shown on maps)

88 Black Lake—USGS Mt. Barney

89 Andrews Creek—Cathedral Lakes—USGS Remmel Mountain, Mt. Barney, Coleman Peak

90 Chewuch River—Remmel Lake—USGS Remmel Mountain, Coleman Peak, Bauerman Ridge

91 Four Point Lake—Coleman Ridge Loop—USGS Remmel Mountain, Bauerman Ridge, Coleman Peak

92 Honeymoon Creek—North Twentymile Peak Lookout—USGS Doe Mountain, Coleman Peak

93 Tiffany Mountain—USGS Tiffany Mountain

94 Smarty Creek—North Twentymile Peak Lookout—USGS Tiffany Mountain, Coleman Peak, Horseshoe Basin

95 Bernhardt Trail—USGS Tiffany Mountain

96 North Summit Trail—USGS Tiffany Mountain, Old Baldy (trail not shown ony map)

97 Horseshoe Basin (Pasayten)—USGS Horseshoe Basin

98 Boundary Trail—USGS Horseshoe Basin, Bauerman Ridge, Remmel Mountain, Ashnola Pass, Ashnola Mountain, Tatoosh Buttes, Frosty Creek, Castle Peak

99 Mount Bonaparte—USGS Mt. Bonaparte

100 Pacific Crest Trail—USGS McGregor, McAlester, Washington Pass (not shown), Mt. Arriva (not shown), Slate Peak, Pasayten Peak, Shull Mtn., Castle Peak

INDEX

THE MOUNTAINEERS, founded in 1906, is a nonprofit outdoor activity and conservation club, whose mission is "to explore, study, preserve, and enjoy the natural beauty of the outdoors...." Based in Seattle, Washington, the club is now the third-largest such organization in the United States, with 15,000 members and five branches throughout Washington State.

The Mountaineers sponsors both classes and year-round outdoor activities in the Pacific Northwest, which include hiking, mountain climbing, ski-touring, snowshoeing, bicycling, camping, kayaking and canoeing, nature study, sailing, and adventure travel. The club's conservation division supports environmental causes through educational activities, sponsoring legislation, and presenting informational programs. All club activities are led by skilled, experienced volunteers, who are dedicated to promoting safe and responsible enjoyment and preservation of the outdoors.

If you would like to participate in these organized outdoor activities or the club's programs, consider a membership in The Mountaineers. For information and an application, write or call The Mountaineers, Club Headquarters, 300 Third Avenue West, Seattle, Washington 98119; (206) 284-6310.

The Mountaineers Books, an active, nonprofit publishing program of the club, produces guidebooks, instructional texts, historical works, natural history guides, and works on environmental conservation. All books produced by The Mountaineers are aimed at fulfilling the club's mission.

Send or call for our catalog of more than 300 outdoor titles:

The Mountaineers Books
1001 SW Klickitat Way, Suite 201
Seattle, WA 98134
1-800-553-4453